101 WAYS TO PROMOTE YOUR WEB SITE

Third Edition

Filled with Proven Internet Marketing Tips, Tools, Techniques, and Resources to Increase Your Web Site Traffic

Susan Sweeney

MAXIMUM PRESS
605 Silverthorn Road
Gulf Breeze, FL 32561
(850) 934-0819
www.maxpress.com

Publisher: Jim Hoskins

Manager of Finance/Administration: Donna Tryon

Production Manager: ReNae Grant

Cover Designer: Lauren Smith Designs

Compositor: PageCrafters Inc.

Copyeditor: Ellen Faulk

Proofreader: Jacquie Wallace

Indexer: Susan Olason

Printer: P.A. Hutchison

Library of Congress Cataloging-in-Publication Data

Sweeney, Susan, 1956-
101 ways to promote your web site: filled with proven Internet
marketing tips, tools, techniques, and resources to increase your web
site traffic / Susan Sweeney.— 3rd ed.
p. cm.
ISBN 1-885068-57-3
1. Internet marketing. 2. Web sites—Marketing. I. Title: One
hundred one ways to promote your web site. II. Title: One hundred and
one ways to promote your web site. III. Title.
HF5415.1265 .S93 2001
658.8'4—dc21

2001002404

Acknowledgements

Wow, the third edition. It seems like yesterday I was writing the first edition. Time flies when you're having fun.

As always, I'd like to thank my dynamite team at Connex Network for their help and support: Ed Dorey and Andy MacLellan have worked tirelessly this year to make sure everything on the consulting side ran smoothly. Thanks so much for your help with the consulting and with the books. Our eldest daughter Kaitlyn joined the Connex team in the edit process making sure all the URLs were accurate and accessible. Great job Kaitlyn! Anne Edwards did her best to make sure I was busy speaking and didn't get to see much of Bedford at all. To that end, I'd also like to express my appreciation to the folks at CAIS, the company that provides such great high-speed Internet access to hotels all over the world. Much of my work was done on the road this year, and hotels with CAIS Internet connectivity sure made this possible.

Thanks to Jim Hoskins and Donna Tryon at Maximum Press. This is our sixth book together. It's always a pleasure to work with you. One of these days we're going to have to meet face to face!

Many, many thanks to ReNae Grant of PageCrafters, who is absolutely wonderful to work with. ReNae manages the process of taking my files through the copy editing, typesetting, and printing process and makes sure we have a great-looking finished product.

The Internet is a fascinating and vast, publicly accessible resource from which we can learn a great deal. I'd like to thank all those people who share their information so freely on the Net with sites like WilsonWeb *(www.wilsonweb.com)* by Dr. Ralph Wilson and newsletters like The Internet Home Business Marketing Newsletter by Robert Smith, Jayde Search Smart, Chronicles, Internet Gazette, and I-Sales by John Audette.

Special thanks to my absolutely wonderful husband, Miles, who makes all things possible. I wouldn't be able to do what I do if not for you. Also thanks to our three amazing children—Kaitlyn, Kara, and Andrew—for their love, encouragement, and support. Love you more than the last number!

Special thanks to my mom and dad, Olga and Leonard Dooley, for always being there and for instilling in me the confidence to know that I can do anything I set my mind to. It's amazing what can be done when you "know you can."

Disclaimer

The purchase of computer software or hardware is an important and costly business decision. While the author and publisher of this book have made reasonable efforts to ensure the accuracy and timeliness of the information contained herein, the author and publisher assume no liability with respect to loss or damage caused or alleged to be caused by reliance on any information contained herein and disclaim any and all warranties, expressed or implied, as to the accuracy or reliability of said information.

This book is not intended to replace the manufacturer's product documentation or personnel in determining the specifications and capabilities of the products mentioned in this book. The manufacturer's product documentation should always be consulted, as the specifications and capabilities of computer hardware and software products are subject to frequent modification. The reader is solely responsible for the choice of computer hardware and software. All configurations and applications of computer hardware and software should be reviewed with the manufacturer's representatives prior to choosing or using any computer hardware and software.

Trademarks

The words contained in this text which are believed to be trademarked, service marked, or otherwise to hold proprietary rights have been designated as such by use of initial capitalization. No attempt has been made to designate as trademarked or service marked any personal computer words or terms in which proprietary rights might exist. Inclusion, exclusion, or definition of a word or term is not intended to affect, or to express judgment upon, the validity of legal status of any proprietary right which may be claimed for a specific word or term.

Table of Contents

Chapter 3:
Web Site Elements That Keep 'Em Coming Back   42

Chapter 7:
Search Engine and Directory Submissions   106

Chapter 8:
Utilizing Signature Files to Increase Web Site Traffic   142

Chapter 9:
The E-mail Advantage   152

Chapter 10:
Effective Promotional Use of Newsgroups   174

Chapter 11:
Effective Promotion Through
Publicly Accessible Mailing Lists   191

Chapter 12:
Establishing Your Private Mailing List   205

Chapter 13:
Developing a Dynamite Link Strategy   215

Chapter 14:
Affiliate Programs   231

Chapter 18:
The Cybermall Advantage   308

Chapter 19:
Maximizing Media Relations   324

Chapter 20:
Increasing Traffic Through Online Publications   346

Chapter 21:
Web Rings as a Promotion Tool   360

Chapter 22:
Webcasting   370

Chapter 23:
Grand Opening Tips for Your
Web Site Virtual Launch   388

Chapter 24:
Effective Offline Promotion   391

Chapter 25:
Web Traffic Analysis   399

Introduction

"We are crossing a technology threshold that will forever change the way we learn, work, socialize and shop. It will affect all of us, and businesses of every type, in ways far more pervasive than most people realize."

Bill Gates
Comdex 1994

Over the last few years there has been literally a tidal wave of companies building Web sites. This phenomenal boom in Web site creation and online traffic has intensified the battle for the consumer's time and attention. The secondary component or required follow-on to Web site design involves developing comprehensive online marketing strategies to capture online market share. The need for information and advice on developing Internet marketing strategies is tremendous.

Building a Web site, however, is just the first step. Driving business to your site takes knowledge, planning, time and effort. If you are intent on maintaining a competitive advantage, then you need to build the traffic to your site by implementing an effective Internet marketing strategy.

Whether you are an experienced marketing professional, or just dreaming of starting your own Internet business you will benefit from the information contained in this timely book. *101 Ways to Promote Your Web Site* offers comprehensive, hands-on, step-by-step advice for building Web site traffic using hundreds of proven tips, tools and techniques to achieve optimal results. You will find out how to:

- Make your site unique, attract new visitors and keep them coming back

- Prepare and submit to hundreds of search engines and directories to be listed in the top search results

- Maximize your Web site promotion using meta-indexes

- Pull traffic to your site by implementing a personalized, targeted e-mail campaign

- Develop an effective banner ad campaign to draw the right customer to your site

- Use Newsgroups and mailing lists to communicate with your target market and build your reputation

- Hype your company in the media for increased exposure through interactive press releases

- Increase company and brand awareness with webcasting and rich media

- Use one of the most effective Internet marketing tools – *Links*

- Find and use free promotion tools available on the Internet

- Keep visitors coming back to your site

- How to develop your own Affiliate or Associate Program

- How to use Permission and Viral Marketing effectively

You will be provided with a wealth of information on how to use specific promotion, marketing, and advertising strategies to increase the traffic to your site. Entrepreneurs, corporate marketing managers, small business owners and consultants, will be given a proven method to turn their commercial Web site into an online success.

Your "Members Only" Web Site

The Internet world changes every day. That's why there is a companion Web site associated with this book. On this site you will find updates to the book and other Web site promotion resources of interest. However, you have to be a member of the "101 Ways Insiders Club" to gain access to this site.

When you purchased this book, you automatically became a member (in fact, that's the only way to join), so you now have full privileges.

To get into the "Members Only" section of the companion Web site, go to the Maximum Press Web site located at *http://www.maxpress.com* and follow the links to the *"101 Ways"* area. From there you will see a link to the *"101 Ways Insiders Club"* section. When you try to enter, you will be asked for a user ID and password. Type in the following:

- For your user ID enter: 101 Ways 3e

- For your password enter: lulu

You will then be granted full access to the "Members Only" area. Visit the site often and enjoy the updates and resources with our compliments—and thanks again for buying the book. We ask that you not share the user ID and password for this site with anyone else.

Susan Sweeney's Internet Marketing Mail List

You are also invited to join Susan Sweeney's Internet Marketing Mail List at *http://www.connexnetwork.com* to receive a bi-weekly e-mail with Internet Marketing tips, tools, techniques and resources.

1

Defining Your Objectives

With millions of Web sites competing for viewers, how do you get the results you're looking for? When asked if they are marketing on the Internet, many people say, "Yes, we have a Web site." However, having a Web site and Internet marketing are very different things. Yes, usually you need a Web site to market on the Internet. However, a Web site is simply a collection of documents, images, and other electronic files that are publicly accessible across the Internet. Your site should be designed to meet your online objectives and should be developed with your target market in mind. Meanwhile, Internet marketing encompasses all the steps you take to reach your target market online, attract visitors to your Web site, encourage them to buy your products or services, and make them want to come back for more.

Having a Web site is great, but it is meaningless if nobody knows about it. Likewise, having a brilliantly designed product brochure does you little good if it sits in your sales manager's desk drawer. It is the goal of this book to help you take your Web site out of the desk drawer, into the spotlight, and into the hands of your target market. You will learn how to formulate an Internet marketing strategy and match it with your objectives, your product or service, and your target market. This chapter provides you with an overview of this book and introduces the importance of

- Defining your online objectives

- Developing the Internet marketing strategy that is appropriate for your product or service

- Defining your target market and developing your Web site and online marketing strategy with them in mind

Commom Objectives

Before you even start to create your Web site, you must clearly define your online objectives. What is the purpose of your Web site? Brainstorm. Generate a list of primary and secondary objectives. Every element of your site should relate back to your objectives. When you decide to update, add, or change any elements on your Web site, examine how these changes relate to the primary and secondary objectives you have identified. If there is not a clear match between your objectives and your intended changes, you might want to reconsider the changes. It's amazing how many Web sites have been developed without adequate planning or tie-in with the corporate objectives.

Some of the most common primary objectives include

- Advertising your product or service

- Selling your product or service

- Providing customer service and product support

- Providing product or corporate information

- Creating and establishing company identity or brand awareness

Advertising Your Products or Services Online

The objective of some sites is simply to advertise but not directly sell an event, product, or service. A prime example of this is a movie studio that develops a Web site to promote a "soon-to-be-released" movie.

The objective is to create awareness or a "buzz" about the movie, generate interest in the film, and, ultimately, have a large number of people attend the movie when it is released. This type of site might include multimedia clips of the movie, pictures and stories of the actors in the movie, viral marketing ("Tell a friend about this movie") elements to encourage word-of-mouth marketing, an intriguing story about the film, press releases for entertainment writers, and other elements to help them achieve their objective with their target market in mind.

Selling Your Products or Services Online

Selling products or services online is a common objective. The Internet provides a broad geographic reach and a huge demographic reach. Often businesses combine the objectives of advertising their products or services with trying to sell them through their Web site. This works well because not only are visitors given information about your products and services, but they are given the option of easily ordering and purchasing online. The easier you make it for people to make a purchase from your company, the more likely they will be to buy. You will also have to provide detailed information on your products and services, your return policies, guarantees and warranties, and shipping options. If you are planning to sell directly from the site, you will also need to address security issues.

Providing Online Customer Service or Support

You may decide that the main reason for your business to have an online presence is to provide more comprehensive customer service and support. A great benefit of a Web site is that you can provide customer assistance 24 hours a day, 7 days a week, 365 days a year. If your company develops software, it would be a good idea to include downloadable upgrades as well as an FAQ (Frequently Asked Questions) section where you can provide solutions to common problems. By providing an easy way for your customers to solve their problems, you will increase customer loyalty. You will also increase the likelihood that they will return to your company when they need to improve their system. You should also include the appropriate contact information if customers have more complicated problems to be solved and need to talk to a human.

Providing Product or Corporate Information

Some organizations simply wish to provide information on their products or services to a particular target market. Others may want to provide corporate information to potential investors. Information-driven Web sites tend to be text-oriented, with graphics used only to accentuate the points being made and to provide visual examples. These types of sites usually have an FAQ section where they provide useful and pertinent information on their company, products, or services. If the organization courts the media, it might include a Media Center, which could include all its press releases, a corporate backgrounder, information on key company officials, articles that have been written about the company, and a gallery of relevant pictures that the media can use, as well as a direct link to the company's media person.

Creating and Establishing Company Identity or Brand Awareness

Another objective might be to create and establish company identity or brand awareness. To "brand" your product, a memorable name and an eye-appealing product logo are necessities. Also, the graphics developed for your Web site must be top-notch and reflect the colors associated with the product logo. A catchy slogan will further promote brand identity. The same branding techniques are also applicable to establishing corporate identity. If building and reinforcing corporate and brand identity are important to you, your Web site must have a consistent look and feel. Likewise, all offline promotional campaigns and materials must be consistent with your online presence.

Based on the success of companies such as America Online, Yahoo!, Netscape Communications, Amazon.com, and eBay, it is apparent that branding a company or product on the Web can occur swiftly. It is amazing how quickly these relative newcomers to the business world have achieved megabrand status. Although they all had significant financial resources, each company used a combination of online and offline advertising to meet their objectives. Their Web sites reflect the branding idea. Each of their sites features a prominent logo, consistent imagery, and a consistent color scheme. Check out the sites of these upstarts that have become big online players if branding is your goal. There is a lot we can learn from them.

Other Things to Consider Up Front

Although setting your primary objectives is vital, it is just as important to identify your secondary objectives. By setting appropriate secondary objectives, you will be more prepared to achieve all your online goals. Many companies identify only primary objectives for their Web site and completely neglect secondary objectives that will help them to succeed online. Following are some common secondary objectives for online businesses to consider:

- The site should be designed to be search engine friendly.

- The site should be designed to encourage repeat traffic.

- The site should encourage visitors to recommend the site to others.

- The site should include elements to leverage its sales force.

- The site should be designed to encourage visitors to give permission to send them e-mail on a regular basis to build an online community.

- The site should be designed to encourage customer loyalty.

- The site should encourage visitors to stay a while and visit many areas of the site.

Designing Your Site to Be Search Engine Friendly

Creating a search engine friendly site should be an objective of every company that wants to do business on the Internet. Search engines are the most common way for Internet surfers to search for something on the Net. In fact, 85% of all people who use the Internet use search engines as their primary way to look for information. By using keywords relating to your company in appropriate places on your site, you can improve how search engines rank you. You want these chosen keywords in the "keyword meta-tags" as well as in each page's "description meta-tag." Some of the other places where you want to have these keywords are your domain name if possible, your page titles and page text, your alt tags for graphics, and your page headers. Recently, many search engines have begun to put emphasis on the number of links to your site to determine your ranking. This means that the more Web sites you can get to link to your site, the higher your Web site will be shown in search engine results. (See Chapter 6 for more information on designing your site for the search engines.)

Including Repeat Traffic Generators on Your Site

Every Web site should be designed to entice its site visitors to return again and again. No matter if the primary objective of your Web site is to sell your products and services or create brand awareness, generating repeat traffic to your Web site will help you achieve these goals. Generating repeat traffic to your site is a key element of your online success and can be accomplished in numerous different ways. Using contests and competitions, as well as games, advice columns, and many more techniques, will increase your Web traffic. Chapter 3 describes many of these repeat traffic generators in much more detail.

Getting Visitors to Recommend Your Site

The best exposure your Web site can get is to be recommended by a friend or "unbiased" third party. It is critical that you try to have your Web site recommended as often as possible; therefore, you should have a way for people to easily tell someone about your site. The best way to encourage people to recommend your site is to have a "Tell a Friend" button on your site. You may want to include some variations on this as well. Under articles or press releases, you can have an "E-mail this article to a friend" to try to have people refer their friends and associates to your site. Virtual postcards are also a good way to get people to send more people to your Web site. Using virtual postcards on your Web site is discussed in detail in Chapter 4.

Leveraging Your Sales Force

If your objectives include trying to sell your products, you may want to leverage your sales force by making use of an affiliate or associate program. Affiliate programs once again use the advantage of having your site recommended to create traffic to your site. The difference is that an affiliate program is more formal than just having your site recommended by site visitors and usually involves a contractual agreement. Most affiliate programs involve having an affiliate program agreement, having specific links placed on the affiliate's site to yours, and having software to track where your traffic is coming from so that you can compute and send referral fees to your affiliates as they are earned. The contract will usually state the compensation you will pay to your affiliates for the sales they produce. This is one more way to have other people working to build traffic to your Web site. (See Chapter 14 for details on affiliate or associate programs.)

Using Permission Marketing

You always want your company to be seen as upholding the highest ethical standards, so it is important not to send out unsolicited email, or "spam," promoting your company or its products. This is why it's important to develop a mailing list of people who have given you permission to send them messages, including company news and promotions. When you're developing your Web site, an objective should be to get as many visitors to your site as possible to give you their e-mail address and ask to be included in your mailings. You can do this by having numerous things for your visitors to sign up to receive such as newsletters, notices of changes to your Web site, coupons, or new giveaways. Chapter 3 has many examples of ways to encourage visitors to request to be added to your e-mail list.

Creating Loyalty Among Visitors

The way to create loyalty among visitors is to provide them with some incentives for joining your online community and provide them with proof that you really appreciate their business. You can do this by having a "Members-only" section of your Web site that has special offers for them as well as discounts or freebies. When people sign up to join your "Members-only" section, you can ask for their permission and their e-mail address to send them e-mails regarding company or product promotions and news.

Including "Stickiness" Elements

To get your visitors to visit your site often and have them visit a number of pages every time they visit, you need to provide interesting and relevant content. You want to have your site visitors feel as if they are part of your online community and to make your site one of the sites they visit every day. You create "stickiness" by including many elements that keep your visitors' attention. Your site could have an advice column for people to read that changes daily, descriptions of your many products, a discussion forum with constantly changing interesting conversations relative to your products, a news section that is updated daily, as well as a weekly contest they can enter. The combination of these elements would create stickiness for the visitors on your site.

A Final Word on Objectives

Setting your Web site's objectives before you begin building your site is essential so that you can convey to your Web master what you want your Web site to achieve. You will obviously want to create a number of different objectives for your site, but many of the objectives you set will work together to make your Web site complete.

Whatever your objectives may be, you must carefully consider how best to incorporate elements in your Web site and your Internet marketing strategy to help you achieve them. Successful marketing on the Web is not a simple undertaking. Before you begin to brainstorm over the objectives of your Web site, be certain you have read and studied all the information that is pertinent to the market you are attempting to enter. Read everything you can get your hands on, and examine the findings of industry experts.

After you have designed, created, and presented your Web site for the world to see, test your site on a small group of individuals in your target market. Then, after analyzing their feedback, you can tweak your site before engaging a larger audience. For instance, let's say you are a software developer and you provide an evaluation copy of your software on your Web site for potential customers to download. The people testing your software may be very interested in your product, but perhaps they commented that the download form requires too much information and takes too long to complete. You might want to tweak the form before you promote your software site to a larger audience. Reducing the amount of information people must submit in order to test your software might be the key to obtaining more downloads. Greater distribution of your software would then likely correlate to higher sales.

Another example would be if your home page utilized a lot of Flash and other multimedia effects, and the majority of visitors to your site did not have the latest technology installed on their systems. Given this situation, you might consider simplifying your home page by removing some of the multimedia effects or creating a second version of your home page for people who are not able to use the latest Internet technologies. Thus, everyone who comes to your Web site will then have the opportunity to enjoy your site, read your message, gather information about your product or service, and so on.

Once you have tested your site and your marketing strategy, do not stop there. Continue testing and tweaking your online marketing strategy until you find the methods, tools, and techniques that work best. Also, whenever you add something to your Web site or your online strategy, ask yourself, "Is it consistent with my online objectives, my product or service, and my target market?"

In Chapter 2, Web site essentials are discussed in detail to assist you when the time comes to develop your site. You will learn which elements to include on your Web site and how to implement these elements properly in conjunction with your objectives.

Product or Service

Web sites and Internet marketing strategies will differ depending on the product or service you are selling. A company that markets toys will have to develop a fun and interactive Web site that is attractive to children. The Web site will then have to give children a way to tell their friends about the site as well as a reason to return to the site. The toy company might wish to offer an electronic postcard service whereby children can send a colorful and musical message to their friends and tell them about the site.

Another idea would be to provide a "wish list" service. Children could make a list of the toys they want, and this list would be sent to the parents via e-mail. The parents could then make more targeted purchasing decisions and may become loyal to the toy company's site. Likewise, some toy companies offer reminder services that send an e-mail message to visitors who have registered and completed the appropriate questionnaire to remind them of a child's birthday and to offer suggestions for gift ideas. Once again, this promotes sales and repeat traffic, and increases customer loyalty.

In another example, a software development company may want to provide downloadable demo versions of its software products and allow people to review its products for a specified period of time before they must make a purchasing decision. When consumers decide to buy the software, a robust e-commerce system will need to be in place to handle the orders.

A travel agency's Web site might include features such as an opt-in mailing list to send people information on weekly vacation specials or a page on the site detailing the latest specials. They might also want to include downloadable or streaming video tours of vacation resorts to entice visitors to buy resort vacation packages. Another idea would be to have a system in place to help customers book vacations, rent cars, and check for available flights. The travel agency might also want to store customer profiles so that they can track where particular customers like to sit on the plane, the type of hotel room they usually book, and their credit card information, to make bookings more efficient for the customer and the agency.

If you are marketing a service online, it is difficult to visually depict what your service is all about. Visitors to your site need some reassurance that the service you are selling them is legitimate and valuable. Therefore, you might wish to include a page on your site that lists testimonials from well-known customers. This will give prospective customers more confidence about purchasing your service.

The bottom line is that the product or service you are selling will determine the direction of your Web site development process and the features that will be included. Remember to think of your online objectives first, then storyboard the site on a sheet (or several sheets) of paper. Once you are satisfied that you have included elements in your site to meet your online objectives, your product or service, and your target market (which we will speak of next), you can proceed with the coding of your site.

Target Market

This is your target audience—the people to whom you are trying to market your product or service. Determine why people decide to buy your product or service and then focus the development of your Web site to emphasize these elements. What is the most important factor in your potential customers' buying decision? Is it price? Product quality? Availability? Your company's reputation? Post-sale service and guarantees? These factors will directly determine the tone and content of your site.

You have to consider all of your target markets and make sure you have addressed each of their needs from your site. Your main target market may be your potential customer, but other target markets might include existing customers, the media, those who influence the buying decision for your potential customers, associates, or affiliates.

If you intend to market children's products, your Web site will be colorful and the text simple and easy to understand in keeping with what appeals to your target market. Chances are, fun-looking graphics will be used extensively on your site to draw children further into it (see Figure 1.1). If you market financial services, your Web site will require a more professional approach. The graphics will convey a clean appearance, and the text will be informative and written in a businesslike fashion (see Figure 1.2). As this example demonstrates, the content and tone of your site must be tailored to your target market. After all, this is the best way to attract the attention of the people who are interested in purchasing your product or service.

Another aspect of the design of your Web site to consider with regard to your target market is their propensity to utilize the latest technologies and the configuration they are likely to be using. An online business that markets custom-made, streaming multimedia presentations would expect its clientele to be technically inclined. These clients are more likely to have the latest software, Web browser technologies, and faster machines.

On the other hand, clients of a vendor who sells gardening supplies online might be less likely to have fully embraced the latest technologies. Most people looking for these products will be connecting from home rather than from their workplace. They may have a slow dialup connection to the Internet, slower machines, and outdated software. They might still be using the Web browser that was originally installed

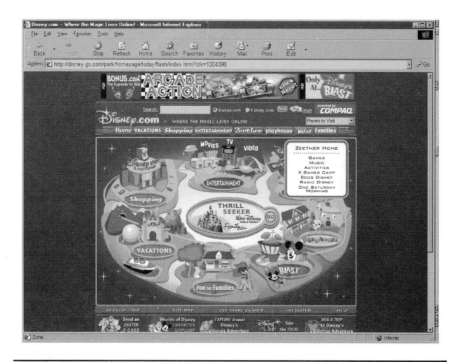

Figure 1.1. Web sites designed to appeal to children include fun, colorful images.

on their system simply because they are uncomfortable downloading the latest version of the browser, are unaware of the more recent version, or are uninterested in downloading a large file. If your target market includes this demographic, you will have to be careful with your use of Java, Flash, and large graphic files.

What does this mean for developing and designing your Web site? Well, streaming multimedia developers could design their Web sites with more graphics and dynamic multimedia effects because their clients expect to be impressed when they visit the developer's site. If gardening supplies vendors designed their site similarly, many of their clients could be alienated because the site would be too slow to load. They might take their business elsewhere. The gardening supplies vendor's site will require a more basic design: less concentration on large graphics and multimedia effects and more focus on presenting information.

Figure 1.2. A business-oriented site incorporates informative text and a clean, magazine style layout.

You must know the profile of the people who are interested in your product, service, or information, and develop your Web site to appeal to this target market. This book describes how you can use a variety of Internet tools and resources to promote your Web site. You will learn how to design your site to achieve higher search engine rankings and how to submit your Web site to major search engines, Web directories, and meta-indexes. E-mail is also an important communication method. Chapter 9 steps you through proper e-mail "netiquette" and explains the concept of conducting an e-mail marketing campaign to help you reach your target market.

You will also learn about using newsgroups, mailing lists, interactive press releases, affiliate programs, banner ads, online and offline publications, and webcasting (rich media) to promote your Web site to thousands of potential customers. Once you have absorbed the content of this book and developed an Internet marketing strategy that is focused on your objectives, product or service, and your target market, you will begin to reap the benefits of Internet marketing.

Marketing your Web site can be a full-time occupation. Some organizations have a team of Internet marketing specialists to build, maintain, and promote their site. For others, the online business is a part-time endeavor and they have only an hour or two each week to spend promoting and developing their Web site. Whatever your situation, the better informed you are about Internet marketing, the better chance your online business will have to succeed. Ensure that your site is user-friendly and is designed with your target market, product or service, and objectives in mind. The more you put into the development and implementation of your Internet marketing strategy, the greater the return will be to your online business.

Internet Resources for Chapter 1

Bplans.com
http://www.bplans.com
A business planning resource center.

ConsultHQ
http://www.consulthq.com
Free marketing resources for professionals.

Business Planning Center
http://www.businessplans.org
Business and marketing planning, and business strategy information, advice, and software.

Tilburg University
http://marketing.kub.nl/links.htm
An exhaustive list of marketing-related links.

Marketing Resources, Ltd.
http://www.mrlWeb.com
Business-to-business marketing solutions, marketing tips, and a newsletter.

2

Essentials of Web Site Design

Site design, appearance, functionality, and features are all important aspects to consider before you think about promoting your site. If the site is designed to achieve your marketing objectives, looks good, and has a layout that is easy to follow, you are ready to open your doors. There are many key factors to consider that may be overlooked in the initial design stages. A great domain name should be chosen, and whenever possible the company's name should be used. Appropriate titles should be located on each page to identify your company and the page content.

In this chapter, we cover

- Planning your site before a line of code is ever written

- Checking out the competition

- How and why meta-tags should be prepared for each page of your site

- The importance of each page's title, description, and keywords

- Web site features and design guidelines

- The use of graphics

- Top-rated sites

- Encouraging repeat visits

- Incentives for increasing hits

- Corporate identity and your Web site

- Guiding the search engines to you

- Ensuring that your site works with different Web browsers

Getting Started

The phrase "If you build it, they will come" worked in the movies, but it does not work with your Web site. Building a Web site is just the first step. Driving traffic to your site takes knowledge, planning, time, and effort. This book's focus is on increasing traffic to your Web site. To help you achieve the maximum marketing potential of your site, we cover several topics that relate to your Web site content and design. We recommend that the following Internet marketing tips, tools, and techniques be used in conjunction with your overall Web site design.

Before moving on to the promotion of your Web site, it is important to consider the development of the site itself. There are many key factors to consider that may be overlooked in the initial design stages. Remember, designing and developing your site right the first time is easier than backtracking to make edits in the future! In order to build the right Web site, you must design for your target market with your objectives in mind. You must also ensure that your site is search engine friendly.

During the Web site design and development process, we take a number of steps prior to ever writing a line of code, and we recommend that you do the same. The first step is to understand your primary and secondary objectives. It is important that you write them down so that they are easily accessible to you for your own reference and, more importantly, when you are talking to your Web developer about building your site. It will be impossible for your Web developer to build a site to achieve your objectives if you haven't told the developer what those objectives are! The next step is to research your competition and find out what they're doing—meeting and beating the competition online is key!

For every Web site developed through our office, we always take the time to identify every element the competitors are using and how they are using them to enhance the site experience for their users. This process of identifying and analyzing competing sites often unveils key elements that can be included on the Web site being designed for you. Once the online competitive analysis has been performed and you know what elements they're using on their sites and you know what elements you want to include on your site to meet and beat them, you're ready to move on to the storyboard development.

The storyboard is a visual representation of the layout of your site. It clearly identifies, on paper, the content and layout of each page on your site, which can then be reviewed with your Web development team, marketing department, associates, and so on, prior to actually building the Web site. Once the storyboard has been approved, it is time to give consideration to the content on your site. What exactly do you want to say on each page laid out in the storyboard? Preparing content ahead of time will save you significant money in Web development costs, and you also have the assurance of knowing that the content used portrays the exact message you want to get across to your target market. Be sure to review the content for search engine friendliness! Search engine friendliness is discussed in an upcoming chapter. Taking the necessary planning steps prior to developing your site saves time and money, and ensures that the site is developed right the first time. We cover these steps in greater depth in the next few sections of this chapter.

Defining Your Web Site Objectives

Before you plan your online strategy, and certainly before you start construction of your site, it is imperative to determine your online objectives. What do you want your Web site to accomplish? Whom are you trying to appeal to? Do you want to sell directly to your customers? Do you want your site to provide information on your products or services? Do you want to provide customer support and service?

Determine the objectives of your Web site or online presence before you begin to build the site. The most common objectives include

- Advertising products or services

- Selling products or services

- Providing customer service or support

- Providing useful information

- Reinforcing brand image

- Providing product information cost-effectively

When compiling your Web site objectives, you must consider your secondary objectives as well as your primary objectives. Secondary objectives would encompass issues such as wanting your site design to be search engine friendly, wanting to implement elements to encourage repeat visits, designing your site to encourage viral marketing, encouraging visitors to give you permission to send them e-mail on a regular basis, and perhaps including loyalty-building programs to encourage the development of extended customers and positive word of mouth exposure. Spending time defining your primary and secondary objectives is invaluable. If you haven't defined your objectives, it will be very difficult for someone else to successfully build the Web site to achieve them! Know your objectives and build your site around them.

Remember when defining your objectives to consider all potential target markets you want to appeal to. It is important to define all your target markets. Attracting new users to venture onto your site and make the most use of it in an engaging manner is always a goal, but what about repeat visitors or customers? It is much more cost-effective to keep a current customer happy or to generate repeat visitors to your site than it is to focus solely on acquiring new customers or visitors. As such, you are going to want to ensure that appropriate elements for building consumer loyalty and generating repeat traffic are included on your site.

Not only are repeat customers and visitors important, but your target market may also include the media. They can play a significant factor in a company's success online as well. Positive exposure from the media is seen as a third-party, unbiased opinion in the eyes of most consumers and can work in your favor to generate increased business. So if you want to attract the media, then be sure to include elements on your site to appeal to them. This will ensure satisfaction at the end of the process.

Once you have defined your objectives and have clearly defined and addressed your target markets, you're ready to move on to the next step of planning your Web site—researching your competitors.

Using Competitor Sites to Your Advantage

One of your Web site's objectives will always be to meet and beat the competition in terms of search engine rankings and Web site content. In order to do so, you have to understand exactly what it is your competition is doing. Take the time to research competitors and compare them on an element-by-element basis.

There are a number of ways you can identify your competitors online. You probably have some marketing materials from your competitors that include their Web sites that you can review. You can also find competition by conducting searches with the appropriate keywords and seeing which competing Web sites rank highly in the major search engines and directories. Similarly, there are many other resources online you can use to research your competition, including the Yellow Pages (e.g., *www.yellowpages.com, www.canada411.com, etc.)*, Hoovers Online *(www.hoovers.com)*, and Business.com *(www.business.com)*, as well as industry-specific Web portals and directories.

Once you have gathered competing Web sites, you can analyze them element by element to determine which Web elements your competitors include on their site and how their sites compare to one another. Other components you should analyze include the visual appeal of your competitors' sites, content, ease of navigation, search engine friendliness, interactivity, and Web site "stickiness," or what they do to keep people on their site. This information will provide you with details on what you need to incorporate into your site to "meet and beat" the competition.

Storyboarding Your Web Site

Next you are ready to visualize and plan your Web site—integrate your objectives, your target market information, the findings of the competitive analysis, and your own ideas as well as those of others. This is done through the process of storyboarding. The storyboard is the foundation of your Web site. It shows you, on paper, the recommended content and layout for your site. It gives you the chance to review the layout and make changes before development begins.

A Web site storyboard can be thought of much like a hierarchical organizational chart in a business. In a typical hierarchical business structure, the executives sit on top, followed by their subordinates, and so on. Think of your Web site storyboard like this. You begin with your main page at the top. Under the main page you have your central navigation bar. Each of the navigation options should be available on each page, regardless of where the user is on your site. Within each of the sections listed on your main navigation bar, you're going to have subsections, and so on. Figures 2.1a and 2.1b are examples of two modified sections of a storyboard layout developed by our office for a client prior to building their Web site.

When developing your storyboard, remember to keep the layout of your site simple and logical in flow as this is how it will be laid out for the users once the site is completed. Do not move forward with the Web development process until you have finalized the layout of the storyboard, ensuring that it is easy for your target audience to use and provides all the elements you need to achieve your objectives. Review your storyboard to ensure that all of your target markets have been addressed. If you want to address the media, be sure to include a Media Center. If you want to attract potential investors, be sure to include a comprehensive

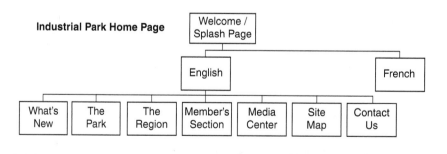

Figure 2.1a. A sample layout of a home page and the main site components.

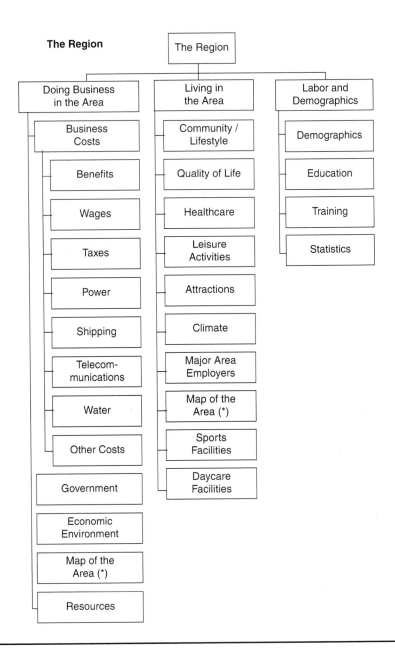

Figure 2.1b. A sample layout of a subsection and the details included within.

Investor Relations section. Give consideration to viral and permission marketing elements that can be included on your site and where they can be included. We discuss these elements in depth in later chapters.

Once you have completed and approved the storyboard, it becomes the blueprint for construction of your site. You are now ready to move onto the actual construction of your site. The remainder of this chapter discusses the content and design elements for your Web site.

Presenting Your Web Site Message Clearly

Visitors to your Web site need to know and understand your message instantly from the very first page of your Web site. If not, visitors can leave your site just as quickly as they could press a button on their TV remote control. Your site must load quickly and immediately direct your visitors toward your message. Do you want them to buy? Browse? Provide feedback? Order? In traditional advertisements, you need to attract the attention of your audience immediately; this is also the case with your Internet audience. However, unlike traditional advertising, you can deliver more information over the Internet than you can in a 30-second commercial or a half-page print ad. However, you must avoid overloading visitors with information. Too much information on the opening page of your site can appear cluttered and unorganized. As a general rule, keep your message simple and to the point.

Realizing the Potential of Your Domain Name

One of the most important decisions you need to make from the start is selecting the right **domain name** (Figure 2.2). Your domain name has a fundamental effect on everything you do online, from credibility to how you market your site. Having your own domain name provides you with many benefits

Domain name
The unique name that identifies an Internet site—
www.sitename.com

- The name itself can increase traffic to your site.

- Having your own domain name builds credibility for your organization.

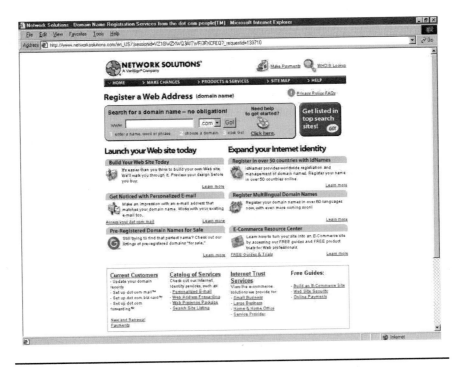

Figure 2.2. Network Solutions is a leading domain name registrar.

- Your presence is mobile when you own your domain name.

- Internet marketing efforts travel with the domain name.

Your domain name should be easy to remember and relate to your online presence. Your company name is usually the best choice and should be used whenever possible. People will generally try *www.yourcompanyname.com* first when searching for a commercial Web site. If customers or potential customers know your company exists, they will find your Web site quickly and easily if your domain name is your company name. If your company name is not well known, you may choose to use a catchy descriptive phrase or the subject of your Web site as its domain name. For example, imagine that you were searching for information on buying a timeshare and one of your search engine results is a site with a **URL** named *www.howtobuyatimeshare.com* with accompany-

URL
Uniform Resource Locator: an address on the Web.

ing text of "Free expert advice on buying a timeshare." What are the chances that you would click through to that site? Pretty good. Keep your domain name simple, easy to remember, and related to the subject of your site.

You can register multiple domain names as well. You might choose this option if there are several business-related keywords you believe potential customers would be inclined to search for. For instance, you might register a domain name for your company's name and a separate domain name for each of the products you are selling. You can have several domain names all pointing to the same Web site. One of the reasons you might consider doing this is that some of the search engines will give your site a higher ranking if the keyword being searched is found in your domain name.

Having your own domain name projects a professional image for your company. One of the benefits of the Internet is that it creates a level playing field for small and medium-sized companies. Having your own domain name projects the image of an established business operating online in a professional manner.

Businesses that develop an online presence without registering their own domain name generally use the domain name of the **ISP** or company that is hosting their site. Your site address would generally have the following:

http://www.yourISP.com/yoursitename

ISP
Internet Service
Provider: the
Internet company
that services your
Web site.

This type of address is not mobile, meaning you can't take it with you should you ever want to move your Web site to another host. If you own your own domain name, it is yours as long as you keep your registration fees current. You then have the option of moving your site to another host without losing your Web address. If you allow your ISP or any other party to take care of the domain name registration process, make sure that you are listed as the actual owner of the domain so that you don't run into problems if you decide to move your site. You want to be listed as both the administrative and the technical contact. This way, the invoice will be sent directly to you so you will never have to worry about making sure your annual fee has been paid. In the long run, listing yourself as the administrative contact will help you skirt any potential complications.

It takes a great deal of time and effort to promote your site online. Getting listed in all the search engines and directories, developing links to your site, and getting listed in meta-indexes all are time-consuming tasks. These listings and links all automatically link viewers to your site address. If you don't own your address, you can't take it with you if you want to move your site to another ISP or host. If you move you will lose most, if not all, of the momentum gained by your previous online marketing activities. Having your own domain name gives you the option to move your site at any time without having a negative impact on your previous marketing efforts.

When conducting business in an international environment, you need the most common top-level domain name, ending in *.com*, which is used around the world. (Canadian sites can use *.ca*. However, to be globally recognized you should use the *.com* designation.) As mentioned earlier, when a person knows of your company and wants to visit your Web site, the first inclination is to check www.yourcompanyname.com.

Your domain name must be registered with a domain name registrar such as Network Solutions. Network Solutions provides domain name registration services for top-level domains including *.com*, *.cc*, *.net*, *.org*, and *.tv*. You can purchase domain names directly from their Web site, or you can have your ISP handle this for you. Verio (*www.verio.com*) is another recognized company that offers domain name registration. These are just two of the many domain name registrars available. Domain Notes (*www.domainnotes.com*) has an extensive directory of domain name registrars and brokers/auctions. It doesn't hurt to check out the different domain name registration sites, as pricing strategies vary. I have seen per-domain name registration fees ranging from $13 to $50. If you are buying multiple domain names, you may be able to achieve discounted prices lower than $13, depending on the number of domains you're purchasing.

Other top-level domains that will soon be available are

- *.aero*—Air-transport industry

- *.biz*—Businesses

- *.coop*—Cooperatives

- *.info*—Unrestricted usage

- *.museum*—Museums

- *.name*—Persons /Individuals

- *.pro*—Professionals, such as lawyers and physicians

Regardless, *.com* looks to hold its place as the dominant and most recognized top-level domain name for some time to come. For updates on the these domain names, upcoming availability of other top-level domains, or policy information on domain names in general, visit ICANN's (Internet Corporation for Assigned Names and Numbers) Web site at *www.icann.org*.

The Essentials of Your Web Site Design

These are design tips that are relevant to all Web sites

- Your online and offline corporate image should be consistent.

- Your site should be easy to read.

- Your site should be easy to navigate. A navigation bar should be consistently located on every page of your site.

- Your Web pages should have a consistent layout.

- Your Web pages should be no larger than 50k.

- Have a "What's New" section to let visitors know what has changed on the site.

- Do not overuse **image maps.**

- Avoid "Under Construction" pages on your site; they are of no value to the visitor. When you have information, post it. Until then, don't mention it.

- Your Web site should steer clear of scrolling marquee text. Scrolling marquees are difficult to read and are not compatible with all browsers. Simply post text directly on your pages if you have something important to say.

Image maps
Large, single images with clickable "hot spots." They are commonly used for site navigation.

- Design for various screen widths. Try to accommodate visitors regardless of the screen resolution they use. Some Web users still run their systems at 640 pixels wide by 480 pixels high, so keep this in mind when designing your site.

- Use thumbnail graphics where applicable. When you have a page with a lot of large images (i.e., an online photo collection), create small "thumbnail" versions of each image and give visitors the option of clicking through to the larger versions. This is far superior to making your visitors wait for a series of large images to load.

- Make your contact information readily available. Perhaps even consider including contact information on every page. This includes your address, phone and fax numbers, and especially your e-mail address. Make it easy for people to get in touch with you.

- Security information. Explain to your customers when transactions or exchanges of information on your Web site are secure. This is important if your site will be accepting credit card orders.

- Privacy policy. Tell people how their personal information (i.e., their name, e-mail address, etc.) will and will not be used. This will make visitors more comfortable submitting inquiries to your site or joining your mail list.

- Minimize use of background sounds and autoplay sounds. Some people surf the Web from their office at work and wish to discretely go from one site to the next. Background sounds and sounds that load automatically can compromise their discreteness. Give your visitors the option of listening to a sound, but do not force it upon them. If you do, you could lose visitors forever.

The tone of your text and the design of your graphics will convey your intended image. For example, if your target audience is business-minded, you will want to keep things simple. Minimize the graphics and use just enough text to get your point across and heighten the interest of your audience. On the other hand, a graphic designer will prefer a more graphic-oriented site with some multimedia effects such as Macromedia Flash. Keep your online image consistent with your offline image. Be consistent with the use of logos, corporate colors, and any other marketing collateral associated with your company.

When determining the text content of your site, be mindful of the fact that your own biases may preclude you from placing information on your site that is second nature to you but important data for your visitors. Review all text content on your site to ensure that you have not omitted anything crucial.

Also, keep text brief. Almost 80% of Web users scan text online as opposed to actually reading it. Therefore, make your key points quickly and succinctly, and use lots of bulleted lists, headers, and horizontal rules to create visual "breaks" in the content. This will keep visitors interested enough to read the information on your site. If they are faced with huge blocks of text, most visitors will be overwhelmed by the quantity of the information and be too intimidated to read your message.

Choose your background and font colors carefully. Using backgrounds that are too busy will obscure your text and will not provide a pleasant viewing experience for your visitor. Only some colors will show up properly on certain backgrounds. A light background with dark text is easiest on the eyes.

White text displays best on black backgrounds, and black text is most readable on white backgrounds. Of course, you can use other color schemes, but choose your scheme carefully, as mentioned. There is nothing worse than a Web site that is unreadable. Also, be mindful that some people might wish to print pages from your site. If you incorporate a lot of your text into the actual graphics on your site, the text might be difficult to read when printed. Also, graphic-intensive sites load more slowly. If you have to incorporate text content into your graphics, be sure that it is sensible to do so.

Don't set your text size too small as this is too hard to read. But don't set it too large as this looks like you are shouting. Also, avoid using ALL CAPS, WHICH ALSO COMES ACROSS AS SHOUTING.

Use the default colors for links whenever possible. Blue text usually indicates an unvisited link. Purple, maroon, or darker blue usually represents a link you have visited, and red is the color of an active link. It should not be difficult for visitors to identify your links. If you decide not to use the default colors, your links should be emphasized in a consistent manner through font size, font style, or underlines.

Ease of navigation is very important to your site. Provide a navigation bar at a consistent location on every page that links to all of the major pages of your site. Make it easy to get from one page to any other. Search engines can index any page from your site, so your home page might not be the first page visitors come to. Never have dead-ends where viewers scroll down a page or two of information only to find that they must scroll all the way back up to the top to move on (because you have no links at the bottom of the page). A consistent-looking and well-positioned navigation bar with functioning links is the key to efficient site navigation.

Also avoid dead links. These are links that don't go anywhere and the viewer usually receives a "404—File not Found" error message from the Web server after clicking on a dead link. Verify periodically that all your links are still active.

Your visitors should be able to get anywhere they want to go on your site in three clicks or less. Develop an effective navigation bar as previously described. If your site is large, you should have an up-to-date site map (explained later in this chapter), which allows visitors to quickly find the information they are seeking on your site. An additional feature you may wish to include is an internal search tool. This allows users to enter their query and have all relevant matches returned, based on their query. This is a particularly useful feature if you sell many products directly on your Web site or if your site contains many pages of content. It allows the user to quickly search for the desired item or information using the product's name or a relevant keyword. Intel operates multiple sites and offers many products and services. To help users locate the information they're looking for, they have integrated a useful search tool, as can be viewed in Figure 2.3. Keep the design of your site consistent. Font types, headers, footers, navigational bars, buttons, bullets, colors, and so on, should be consistent throughout the site to maintain a polished professional look.

Your **home page** should be 50K or less, and your home page should be displayed on no more than one or two screens. Studies have shown that visitors will rarely wait beyond 15 seconds to download a site. Test the download time of your site using different connection speeds to ensure that it is reasonable for all users.

Home page
The main page of a Web site.

Keeping Web Site Graphics in Perspective

Graphics can be pleasant to look at, but be discriminating as you add them to your site. Graphics that are too time-consuming to download may cause visitors to leave your site before they get a chance to see it.

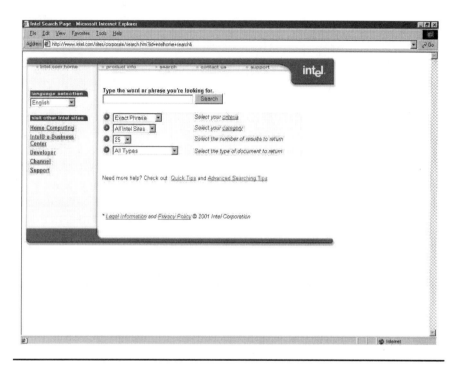

Figure 2.3.   Intel integrates a search tool on its site.

Most of the Internet population uses a dial-up connection of 56K or less. The combined size of your text and graphics on any Web page should not exceed 50K.

Alt attributes
Descriptive text associated with respective images on a Web site.

Some people turn graphics off in their browsers to save time, so you should provide all of your information in text as well as graphics. Use descriptive **Alt attributes** in your image tags. The Alt text will load in place of the images when the graphic does not display for any reason. Visitors who choose not to browse with graphics turned on will have an easier time navigating your site. Also, Alt text is spidered and indexed by a lot of the major search engines. Using keywords in your Alt text in your image tags will improve your ranking in search engines and will provide a description of the images in the event that they are not loaded. If you use any large files for graphics, audio, or video, warn your visitors by providing some text stating the size of the files.

You should curb your use of image maps as well. Image maps are large graphics with clickable "hot spots." Image maps are typically used for navigation. They are useful if your Web site contains five or more major sections. If you do use an image map, make it obvious what portions of the image are clickable and where each link will lead.

Very often, when a large graphic is used for an image map, visitors must wait for the entire image to load before it is apparent where they must click to begin navigating a site. Instead of using a large image map, break the image into smaller images so that visitors will receive faster feedback from your site without having to wait for a huge graphic to load. Also, always provide an alternate text link navigation system to assist people who surf with their graphics turned off.

Providing Ease of Navigation with User-Friendly Site Maps

For very large sites (i.e., sites consisting of 8 to 10 major sections), it is a good idea to include a site map that users can access from any page in your site. Site maps, as shown in Figures 2.4 and 2.5, are usually text-based lists that name all of the site's pages and their content. Site maps make it easy for users to access the information they are looking for without causing them much frustration. Include a link from your main navigation bar to the site map for the easiest possible reference.

Identifying Your Site with Page Titles

Each of the pages in your Web site should be given a title. The title is inserted between the title tags in the header of an **HTML** document. Title tag information identifies and describes your pages. Titles can tell readers where the information contained on a page originated. Most Web **browsers,** such as Netscape, display a document's title in the top line of the screen. When users print a page from your Web site, the title usually appears at the top of the page at the left. When people bookmark your site,

HTML
Hypertext Markup Language:
The coding language that tells a Web browser how to display a Web page's words and images.

Browsers
Software programs that let you "surf" the Internet.

Figure 2.4. Montreal International Airport's site map.

the title appears as the description in their bookmark file. These are all reasons why it is important that a page's title reflect an accurate description of the page.

Go through each and every page of your Internet site, bookmark each one, and check that your titles represent each page clearly without being lengthy. Longer page titles can dilute the relevancy of your keywords. Keeping your page titles brief (5 to 10 words or fewer) will increase the potency of your keywords and earn your pages higher search engine rankings. The titles should always identify your company.

Examples of appropriate titles are

- "Progeny Software—Genealogy Software Specialists"

- "Progeny Software—Free Trial Version"

Figure 2.5. Disney's site map.

And some inappropriate titles are

- "The Best Software Page on the Web"

- "The Software Home Page"

- "Order Form"

Match the keywords you use in your meta-tags with the words you use in your page titles. Search engines check page titles, meta-tags, and page content for keywords. Your pages will be more relevant, and therefore will place higher in the search engines, for certain keywords if these keywords appear in each of these three sections. Position your keywords near the beginning of your page titles to increase your keyword relevancy.

Viewing Your Site Through Browser Eyes

Check your site using different browsers. What viewers see when your site is downloaded depends on what browser they are using. Different browsers will display the same Web site differently. Before you post your site online, check your site with the most popular browsers:

- Netscape Navigator 6.x

- Netscape Navigator 4.x

- Netscape Navigator 3.x

- Microsoft Internet Explorer 5.x

- Microsoft Internet Explorer 4.x

- Microsoft Internet Explorer 3.x

- America Online 6.x

- America Online 5.x

It is obvious that there are a lot of browsers to consider when designing your Web site. Some people may also be using Netscape 2.0, Mosaic, or a text-only browser. When designing your site, consider your target audience. What browsers will your visitors most likely use? If your intended target audience is everyone and anyone, design for the lowest common denominator. Design for Netscape 3.0 and Internet Explorer 3.0 browsers or higher. Very few people continue to use really old browsers, so unless you know your target audience will be using Netscape 2.0 or Mosaic, the 3.0 browser versions are the most appropriate to design for.

If your audience is more likely to be technically inclined and using a fast connection, you can safely design for the latest browser editions and use the latest technologies. In this case, you might wish to use HTML 4.0, Java applets, Active X, or Flash Media to make your Web site more attractive to your visitors.

Generally speaking, design your pages using HTML 3.2 and minimize the number of slow-loading multimedia elements. This will allow everyone to enjoy your site without having to wait several minutes for each page to load. An alternative option is to give the user a choice of using either a high-speed version of your site or a standard HTML version that loads quickly.

Choosing Web Site Features to Meet Marketing Objectives

Many features can be incorporated into your Web site. It is important to look at each feature from both marketing and administrative views before deciding to incorporate it into your site. A **chat room** might seem like a nifty feature to have at first blush, but you have to ask yourself, "What is the marketing value to our company in having this on our Web site? Will it increase targeted traffic to our site? Will it encourage repeat visits from our customers and potential customers? Will it build loyalty? Will it build brand equity? Will it result in increased sales?"

Chat room
A site where you can chat, in real time, with others.

Assuming that you can justify a chat room on your site from a marketing perspective, you must look at the feature from a financial perspective. What will this feature cost to develop? What will be the ongoing costs of operating this feature in technical resources as well as in human resources? What is your budget? Can these resources provide a better return on investment if spent elsewhere? Would you achieve your objectives more effectively if you put these financial resources into banner advertising or other online marketing activities?

Customer-Enticing Traffic Builders

The following "traffic builders" are used to attract and invite visitors to your site.

Free Offers
People love to get something for nothing. Offering something for free is a good way to get lots of traffic to your site. This is great if your objectives include generating lots of general user traffic to your site. Free offers also

---

Meta-indexes
A collection of URLs for
related Internet resources.

---

provide you the opportunity to be linked from the many **Meta-indexes** related to freebies and giveaways. If you are giving something away, you might consider tying it into a registration for your newsletter or mailing list. Some of the things commonly given away include screen savers, icons, software, and games. You should relate giveaways to your company, your products, or your services.

Online Seminars

Online seminars are generally conducted through live chat sessions. Seminars allow current and potential customers to interact in a real-time setting with industry experts and celebrities. This can be a great traffic builder.

Live chat sessions will attract people who are genuinely interested in what your business is selling and all topics related to it. Conducting a seminar will create a more intimate bond between your company and your customers. This encourages repeat business and generates new business as word of mouth spreads and draws more people to your seminars. Eventually, you will have a captive audience to which you can introduce your latest product or service.

Advice Columns

Advice columns are a great way to increase traffic and to gain the respect of your customers. Many companies answer questions that pertain to their products and industry. They also help their customers solve common problems with expert advice. For example, customers on the Tide Web site can ask questions about how to get certain stains out of their clothes.

Coupons

Coupons are an effective way to increase traffic to your site. If your coupons are valuable and you change them daily or weekly, you will encourage visitors to return frequently. Customers can print the coupons off the Web site and redeem them at the physical store location or, if the store is online, the customer can use the coupons on the online storefront.

Contests

Contests are very popular online, particularly when prizes are involved. To encourage repeat visits, you should change the contest regularly or design it in such a way that your visitors can enter often. To get some information about the people who are visiting your site and to help you with your marketing efforts, include a few pertinent questions on the entry form, one of them being "At which e-mail address would you like to be notified of the winner?"

Once the winning candidate is selected, you can send a message to all contest participants to announce the winner. Thank them for their participation and invite them to return to your site. Enticing them with a special offer or a discount on all purchases might be good way to increase traffic to your site. By sending the contestants a message like this, you may generate sales from people who otherwise might not have purchased from you.

Surveys

Surveys are a popular feature for specific industries. Here, you should make sure the information you are gathering is of value to the industry and promise to provide a copy of the final report to all that participate.

Interactive Tours

Interactive tours take your visitors on a virtual tour of your offices, your factory, or your Web site. Visitors can find out how a product is made or how your company operates. This is a great way to provide information on the quality of your materials and workmanship.

You can make your interactive tour more interesting by incorporating a contest with the tour. For the purpose of the contest, ask your visitors detailed questions about the tour. They will be more attentive, and they will absorb your message and the information on your site more clearly. If you can make them understand your message, this can lead to sales.

These are just a few of the many repeat traffic and loyalty-building techniques you can employ on your site. Repeat traffic generators are discussed in detail in Chapter 3. Other critical features to address include viral marketing and permission marketing techniques.

A popular viral marketing technique used is "Tell a friend." Encourage your target market to let others know about your site. The inclusion of a "Let a friend know about this site" or related option would be effective in increasing traffic to your site. You could allow the current visitor on your site to submit a friend's e-mail address so that you can then send them information about visiting your site. In doing so, allow the current visitor to insert a customized message to the recipient so that the e-mail is not viewed as spam. See Chapter 4 for a discussion on viral marketing techniques.

Permission marketing techniques can be used in conjunction with other marketing techniques. If you allow visitors to sign up for a user account on your site, you can ask them at the time of registration if it is okay to send them an e-mail from time to time to let them know of any product promotions that may be of interest to them. Likewise, you could include a message on your What's New page to encourage users to sign up for and receive notification of Web site updates. This gives you permission to contact your users and communicate with them. Repeat traffic, permission marketing, and viral marketing are covered more in depth in their respective chapters. See Chapter 5 for a discussion on permission marketing.

Guiding the Search Engines with Meta-Information

A common problem faced by Internet marketers is how to influence search engines to index their site appropriately and how to ensure that their site appears when people use relevant search criteria. Many of the interesting and creative sites on the Internet are impossible to find because they are not indexed with the major search engines. The majority (85%) of Internet users employ search engines or directories to find Web sites, which they do by typing in a keyword or phrase that represents what they are looking for. A full discussion on meta-tags is included in Chapter 6.

Internet Resources for Chapter 2

DOMAIN NAMES

Network Solutions
http://www.networksolutions.com
The most prominent domain name registrar company.

Verio
http://www.verio.com
Offers domain name registration, hosting, dedicated servers, and so forth.

DomainNotes.com
http://www.domainnotes.com
A great place to find domain name registrars, brokers, and articles pertaining to domain names.

ICANN
http://www.icann.org
The Internet Corporation for Assigned Names and Numbers.

REVIEW YOUR SITE

NetMechanic
http://www.netmechanic.com
A number of tools to improve your site's mechanics, including HTML code validation and GIF optimization.

Web Site Garage
http://websitegarage.netscape.com
Provides services for maintaining and improving your Web site.

Northern Webs
http://www.northernwebs.com
Northern Webs' Engine Tutorial is one of the most recognized leaders in exposing the nuances of the various search engines and explaining what makes them tick. See if your site can stand the test of their exclusive Meta-Medic!

Webmaster's Tools
http://www.arrowweb.com/graphics/tools.html
This site includes interactive tools for Web masters and site designers. Use these tools to submit and promote your Web site or to find problems. They have included site offerings such as utilities site tune-ups, link checking, meta-writing, site submission, and search tools.

How to Build Lame Web Sites
http://www.webdevelopersjournal.com/columns/perpend1.html
A tongue-in-cheek article describing the methods you can utilize to achieve a poorly designed Web site. Don't follow these methods and your site will be fine. A bit old, but still a good read.

KEYWORDS AND META-TAG DEVELOPMENT

Meta-Tags & Search Engines
http://www.webdigger.com/meta_tags.htm
Need to improve your search engine standings? Here are a few ideas to get you started: meta-tags as well as search engine and Web site design tips.

Meta-Tag Analyzer
http://www.scrubtheweb.com/abs/meta-check.html
This will check your meta-tags and your HTML code to help you achieve better placement in search engine results. Let their free Meta-Tag Analyzer program check your meta-tags and help analyze your HTML syntax online.

WordTracker
http://www.wordtracker.com
An online tool for compiling the right combination of keywords. You can run a free trial, but this is a pay service for keyword generation and suggestions.

META-Tag Generator
http://www.submitcorner.com/Tools/Meta
A free meta-tag generator tool to create meta-tags for your Web pages.

How to Use Meta-Tags Tutorial
http://searchenginewatch.com/webmasters/meta.html

World of Design
http://www.globalserve.net/~iwb/search_engine/killer.html
A tutorial for writing meta-tags for higher search engine placement and good descriptions.

A Dictionary of HTML Meta-Tags
http://vancouver-webpages.com/META

REFERENCES

Web Developers Virtual Library (WDVL)
http://www.stars.com
A comprehensive illustrated encyclopedia of Web technology, the WDVL is for Web masters and Internet developers. It's a well-organized goldmine of tutorials, demos, and links to great resources.

The World Wide Web Consortium
http://www.w3c.org
"The World Wide Web Consortium (W3C) develops interoperable technologies (specifications, guidelines, software, and tools) to lead the Web to its full potential as a forum for information, commerce, communication, and collective understanding"—description quoted from site.

CNET Builder.com
http://www.builder.com
An outstanding resource and how-to site for all things related to Web site design.

Whatis.com
http://www.whatis.com
Whatis.com is "definition" paradise. It defines any computer-related word you ever wondered about.

GRAPHICS

The Gif Wizard
http://www.gifwizard.com
You can reduce the size of all your graphics using the Gif Wizard Site Scan Monitor, a free service from Raspberry Hill Publishing.

gif.com
http://www.gif.com
An extensive resource for Web graphic design.

3

Web Site Elements That Keep 'Em Coming Back

There are many little things that will spice up your Web site to "keep 'em coming back." Learn the tips, tools, and techniques to get visitors to return to your site again and again. In this chapter we cover

- Attractive Web site content

- How to have your own What's New page, Tip of the Day, and Awards page

- Hosting online seminars

- Ensuring that you are bookmarked

- Cartoons, contests, jokes, and trivia

- Calendar of events and reminder services

- Interesting bulletin boards

- Online chat sessions, workshops, and discussion groups

- Special guests or celebrity appearances

- Giveaways, awards, and surveys

- Offline tactics for promotion

Encourage Repeat Visits

Just as you would want customers to visit your place of business frequently, so too in cyberspace do you want customers and potential customers to visit often. The more often people visit your site, the more likely they are to purchase something. You want to ensure that the techniques you use to get repeat traffic are appropriate for your target market. For example, if you were having a contest on your site targeted toward children, you would not want to give away a breadmaker as the prize. That would be okay, however, if your target market is families or homemakers. You would want to offer something of interest to the market you are targeting. If your target is business professionals, then something like a Palm Pilot that they could use in their everyday business would be appropriate. If your target market is skiers, then a weekend in Vail might be appropriate. You should always remember your objectives when doing any form of online marketing, because you don't want to do something inappropriate that might drive your target audience away from your site.

Use a What's New Page for Repeat Hits

A What's New page can mean different things to different sites. For some, this page updates users with the summaries of the most recent features and additions to a particular site, as in Figure 3.1. Your What's New page should be accessible from your home page so that when people visit your site they will not have to search through your entire site to find out what is new. If visitors repeatedly find interesting additions in the What's New section, in whatever context you use it, they will come back to your site on a regular basis to check out what's new. Without this, they may visit and search through your site and find that nothing

Figure 3.1. You can use a What's New page to tell users about updates to your site and about what's going on in your company.

was new and they just wasted 20 minutes looking for anything new. Here, too, you can ask if visitors would like to be notified via e-mail when you've added something to the What's New section. It's all about getting their permission to send them e-mail and therefore include them in your community.

For others, What's New may cover What's New in their industry or What's New in their product line. Whatever it is, you should always make sure that it is of interest to your target market. Again, you can ask your visitors if they would like to be notified when updates are made to your Web site. This once again gives you permission to e-mail them and present them with new information that will make them want to come back to your site again.

Free Stuff—Everyone Loves It

Giving items away for free is a great way to increase traffic—everybody likes a freebie. If you give something away each week, you are sure to have a steady stream of repeat traffic. When you have freebies or give-aways on your site, your pages can also be listed and linked from the many sites on the Internet that list places where people can receive free stuff. To find these listings of free stuff, simply go to a search engine and do a search on "Free Stuff Index" or "Free Stuff Links." You will be amazed at how many people are giving things away online.

You don't have to give something away to everyone. You could simply have a drawing every week. You could then ask entrants if they would like you to notify them of the winner, which again gives you permission to e-mail them. An example of a site that has a monthly draw is Lobster Direct (*http://www.lobsterdirect.com*). Lobster Direct is a site that ships live Nova Scotia lobsters anywhere in North America the next day via an overnight delivery service. They have a drawing for a lobster dinner for four every month (see Figure 3.2). So, every month many people enter this drawing for their chance to win the free lobster. When the drawing is done, Lobster Direct e-mails everyone to inform them of the winner, at the same time taking the opportunity to remind them of the monthly specials. This certainly can't hurt sales.

If you want to bring only people from your target market to your site, then don't give away mainstream things like screen savers, shareware games, utilities, and so on. Try to give away something that only people interested in your industry would want. If you don't care what traffic comes your way, and any traffic is good traffic, then give away useful things that everybody needs. Try to have your logo and URL displayed on the item. For example, a neat screen saver can be made that displays your logo and URL. When this is made available as a download, there are no handling or shipping charges associated with it. If your freebie is something that has your URL on it and is something that is generally kept around a computer, it reminds and encourages people to visit your site. A mouse pad with your URL would be a good example.

You should change your freebie often and tell people from your site how often you do this. Something like "We change our free offer every single week! Keep checking back or **Click Here** to be notified by e-mail when we update" will work well.

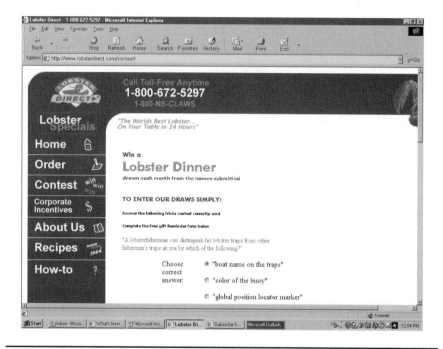

Figure 3.2. Lobster Direct has a monthly drawing for a free lobster dinner for four delivered to your door overnight.

Give a Taste of Your Product with Sample Giveaways

Use a traditional marketing approach and give away free samples of your product from your Web site. After giving away the samples, follow up with an e-mail. Ask the people who received a sample what they thought of it, if they had any problems, and if they have any questions. Direct the samplers back to your Web site for more information and discounts on purchasing the regular version of the product. If you have a number of products, you might consider alternating your free samples. Ask if visitors would like to be notified by e-mail when you change your free sample. This gives you permission to e-mail the visitors on a regular basis to remind them about the sample. You also get to update them with new information regarding your Web site, your products, or your company. This will entice them to visit your site again. Make sure you include your signature file in your e-mail message.

Resisting a Deal with Coupons and Discounts is Hard

Offer coupons and discount vouchers that can be printed from your site. You can change the coupon daily or weekly to encourage repeat visits. People will come back to your site again and again if they know they will find good deals there. This is a great strategy to use in conjunction with a free sample giveaway. If people liked the sample, give them a coupon to purchase the regular version at a discount. If they like the regular version, they may purchase it again at full price or recommend the product to a friend. You can also ask people if they would like to be notified by e-mail when you update the coupons on your Web site. This once again gives you the opportunity to present them with new information about your business. Offering coupons is a great idea if you have a physical location as well as a Web site. These can be your loss leader to get customers to come into your store.

You can develop a coupon banner ad that links to your site, where the coupon can be printed. The banner ads should be placed on sites frequented by your target market. You can trade coupons with noncompeting sites that target the same market that you do. Your coupon on their site links to your site, and their coupon on your site links to their site.

By offering coupons from your Web site, you also cut down your overhead cost because people are printing the coupons on their own printers, thus not using your paper. Remember that you should have terms and conditions on the coupons that are available for printing. For example, you should have an expiration date. Someone could print a coupon, then visit your store in a year and try to use it. You should try to have the expiration date close to the release of the coupon. This will entice the visitor to use the coupon more quickly and then come back for more coupons.

Today we are seeing an increase in the amount of coupon-related sites that are appearing on the Internet. CoolSavings.com *(http://www.coolsavings.com)* is an online coupon network where businesses can advertise and place coupons for their products and services, as seen in Figure 3.3. The site has been operating since 1997 and provides the service to businesses in the United States only. Sites like this are a good way to promote your business, for they receive a high amount of traffic. CoolSavings.com has been a household name since it launched its national advertising campaign during 1999. If you offer coupons from your

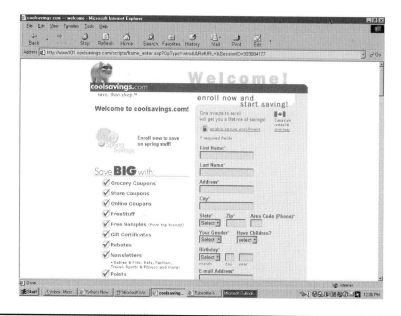

Figure 3.3. CoolSavings.com offers coupons from businesses to people all over the USA.

site, it would benefit you to be listed on these sites. If you are not aiming for a national appeal, you should search to find out if there are coupon networks in the geographic location that you are targeting (see Figure 3.4). Other coupon sites are listed in the Internet Resources section at the end of this chapter. There are meta-indexes to sites with coupons or discounts from which you can be linked for greater exposure.

A Calendar of Events Keeps Visitors Informed

A comprehensive, current calendar of events related to your company or your industry will encourage repeat visits. A sample calendar is shown in Figure 3.5. Your calendar should always be kept up-to-date and be of value to your readers. A calendar of events for a band might show their scheduled appearances. A calendar of events of what is going on in your business community is very appropriate for a Chamber of Commerce or Board of Trade site. This will encourage a lot of

Figure 3.4. The Coupon Network targets people in the province of Nova Scotia by offering coupons for that geographic region.

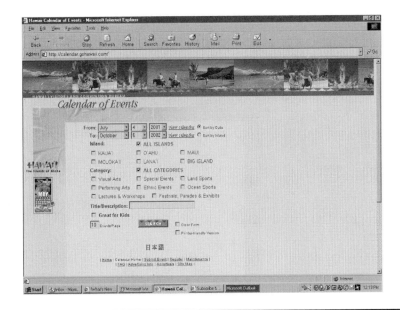

Figure 3.5. You can use a Calendar of Events to keep your audience informed of what's coming up in the future.

repeat traffic as long as it is current and complete. Calendars of events are also appropriate on community sites, because residents access these calendars often in order to stay current with what is going on. Again, you can ask people if they'd like to be notified via e-mail when you update your calendar of events.

Luring Customers with Contests and Competitions

Contests and competitions are great traffic builders. According to Jupiter Communications, a New York-based market research firm, online contests are among the fastest growing online activities. They report that 49% of all American Internet users have entered online contests.

Some sites hold regular contests on a weekly or monthly basis to generate repeat visitors. Holding contests is also a great way to find out about your target market by requesting information on the entry form.

What type of contest you hold depends upon your Internet marketing objectives. If you want to attract as many people as possible to your site regardless of who they are, then offer items such as money, trips, cars, computers, and so on, as in Figures 3.6 and 3.7. If you would like to attract potential customers from your target market, then give away something that relates to your products and industry.

You could simply request that people fill out an electronic ballot including their name, address, phone number, and e-mail address to enter the contest. If you want to find out something about the people entering, ask them to answer a question about your products. If the prize is one of your products, consider asking entrants to write a short essay outlining why they would like to have the product you are giving away. You can award the winner(s) with the product and follow up with the other entrants. These people may be in a position to buy your products, and you will have gained some valuable knowledge from the essays submitted.

If your product is appropriate for a prize that would be of interest to many different types of people, you might consider finding contest sites that would be willing to offer your product as the prize on their site. This will generate brand awareness for your product. You could have the site show a picture of your product with a link to your site.

Figure 3.6. Contests are a great way to encourage repeat traffic.

Figure 3.7. Pizza Hut offers visitors a chance to win free pizza for a year.

The contest site should be more than happy to do this because you are offering to give something for free that adds value to that site.

You can turn a contest into a competition. If your Web site relates to cooking or baking, ask entrants to submit their best recipe using your food product. People will visit your site to see the winning recipes, and you may get some ideas for future marketing efforts. Other competitions may include things like best photo with product X, best short story about product X, best drawing of product X, and so on. This creates better brand awareness and reinforces sales of your product. The closer the contest relates to your product, the better. Instead of offering just one prize, offer a number of smaller prizes as well. This makes the odds look better and people feel they have a better chance of winning.

Before you go ahead with holding any kind of contest, check out all of the legal issues. There may be restrictions that you don't know about (e.g., you may be required to purchase a legal permit to hold lotteries). You should also remember to ask the entrants the e-mail address at which they would like to be notified of the winner. This, again, grants you permission to e-mail them to tell them who the winner was, and also to inform them of the specials that you may have at your site that month.

You might want to allow people to enter your contest every day rather than holding a monthly or weekly contest. This will encourage them to come back to your site daily.

You will want to promote your contest through public and private mail list postings, newsgroup postings, your e-mail signature file, press releases, and links from contest sites. Some popular contest sites you might want to be listed from include:

- Contest Guide *(http://www.contestguide.com)*

- Contest Hound *(http://www.contesthound.com)*

- Free Mania *(http://www.freemania.net/contest.html)*

- 100 Top Contest Sites *(http://www.100topcontest.com)*

- Red Hot Sweeps Sites *(http://www.redhotsweeps.com)*

Using Employment Opportunities to Increase Visitors

People involved in a job search or interested in new job opportunities will revisit your site occasionally to see your list of available positions. See Figure 3.8 for a sample employment page.

Creating Useful Links From Your Site

Provide visitors with links to other sites similar to yours or a meta-index of links that would be of interest to your target market (see Figure 3.9). Do not put outbound links on your home page. Place them down a level or two after the visitors have seen all the information you want them to see before you provide the links away from

Figure 3.8. Lycos provides information on employment opportunities from its Web site.

Figure 3.9. The Travel Industry Association of America provides useful links for travel industry professionals from its site.

your site. Try exchanging links with others so you receive a link from their site to your site. As long as the links are of value to your visitors, people will come back to see if you have found any new and interesting sites for them to visit.

You might consider asking if visitors would be interested in being notified when you update your list of links, or just updates to your site in general. By offering this, if they choose to do so, you have the opportunity to send people an e-mail message and remind them about your site while presenting them with new information about what might be going on with your site. Remember to use your signature file containing your URL. This way, viewers can link through to your Web site directly from the e-mail.

Investing in Online Chat Sessions

Chat rooms are very popular and, to some, even addictive. If you have a chat forum on your site, make sure that the topic relates to your business and that participants are likely to be your target market. To encourage repeat visitors, you could change the topic from day to day or week to week. You could also have celebrity appearances in your chat sessions. These sessions should be regularly scheduled, and the upcoming events should be posted on your site so that your visitors will know what is going on when, and will not miss the session if it is of importance to them. They could be on Sunday from 3 to 5 p.m., or on Tuesday from 7 to 9 p.m. Also remember to have the information in your signature file and do some postings through your appropriate mail lists and newsgroups to promote the event.

You should try to post the topics of the discussions at least a week in advance so that your visitors will remember to come for the entire session if they are interested in the topic. You would be surprised how many people would schedule time so that they could chat with someone special or knowledgeable in an area that interests them. You might also think of asking your visitors if they would be interested in being notified of upcoming chat sessions or celebrities who may be visiting your site to chat. This again gives you the opportunity to e-mail people, at their request, and present them with information that will entice them to visit your site again. You can also ask your community whom they'd like to see as a guest or what topics they would like to have discussed.

Providing a Tip of the Day to Encourage Repeat Visits

Have a section that offers cool tips that relate to your business, your products or services, or your target market, as in Figure 3.10. These tips can be from one sentence to one paragraph long. If visitors find your advice helpful, they will return repeatedly to see what interesting piece of information you have displayed that day. Ask your visitors if they would be interested in receiving the tip via e-mail or if they would like notification when the tip has been updated so they could then visit your Web site.

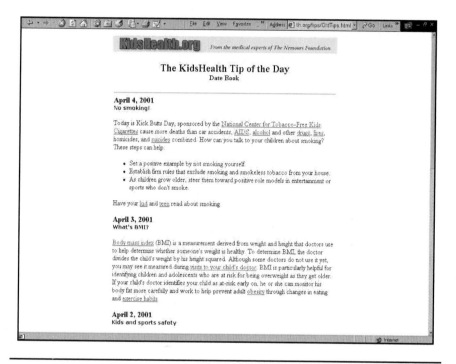

Figure 3.10.   Health Tip of the Day. Tips of the Day can encourage repeat visitors.

Ensuring That Your Site Gets Bookmarked

Encourage visitors to add you to their bookmark list. Somewhere on your site, display the call to action "Bookmark me now!" (see Figure 3.11). A call to action is often effective. Make sure the title of the page that has the "Bookmark me now!" clearly identifies your site and its contents in an enticing way, because the title is what will appear in the bookmark file as a description. Whenever I see "Bookmark this site now!" I always consider it. Sometimes I do and sometimes I don't, but I always consider it. Often, when the call to action is not presented, I don't think about it and don't bookmark it. Then, days later when I want to go back there, I wish I had remembered to bookmark.

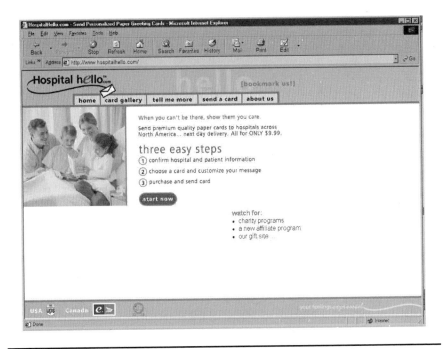

Figure 3.11. When you see a "Bookmark this site now!" or "Bookmark Us!" call to action, nine times out of ten you will at least consider it.

World Interaction with Bulletin Boards

It can be very satisfying to see people join in from all over the world just to interact with each other about a topic that relates to your Web site, as shown in Figure 3.12. Beware, you will have to keep an eye on the messages and may even have to play referee occasionally.

Inviting Visitors to Contribute with Surveys

Performing surveys is a way to increase the traffic to your site. For people to want to fill out the survey and see the results, the survey topic must be interesting. To encourage input, the survey results might

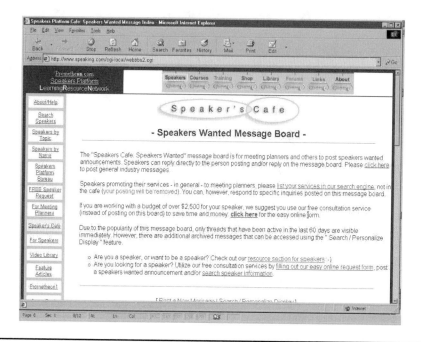

Figure 3.12. The Speaker Café is a great bulletin board where people can request information about professional speakers for conferences and trade shows.

be available to participants only. Your survey could be on a topic concerning current events or something pertaining to your industry. The more controversial or debatable the topic of the survey, the more people will visit to contribute or see the results. If you want to draw a very targeted audience, pick a topic that would be interesting to that market alone.

In performing these surveys, you are building repeat traffic and you are gathering valuable information on your market. If you hold an interesting survey every week or every month, then you will be sure to retain a loyal audience of repeat visitors. If your surveys are newsworthy, then you can send out press releases to publicize the results and gain publicity for your site.

Your surveys should be short and to the point. Let people know why you are asking them to do the survey and when the deadline is. Make your questions clear and concise. The responses should be Yes/No or multiple choice. When reporting the results, don't just put them on your Web page; post the results to newsgroups and mailing lists that would be interested. Don't forget to add your sig.file. If you are holding weekly or monthly surveys, let people know via your sig.file what the next survey topic will be and that there is more information on your Web site.

Again, you should ask people if they'd like to be notified of survey results, either via e-mail or by prior notification as to when the results will be posted on the site so they will be able to visit your site and find out. You might also ask if they'd like to be notified when you are conducting a new survey.

Encourage Repeat Visits with Your "Site of the Day"

Having your own "Site of the Day" (see Figure 3.13) or "Site of the Week" (see Figure 3.14) listing will mean a lot of work, searching the Internet for a cool site to add or looking through all the submissions. However, if your picks are interesting to your audience, you may find that avid Internet users come back every day to see what great new site is listed. Remember that this must be updated on schedule; displaying a week-old Site of the Day will reflect poorly on your site and your company. For more information, see Chapter 16 about hosting your own award site.

Keep Them Happy with Cartoons

Displaying relevant cartoons keeps your site dynamic and fun. You do not necessarily have to create all of the content and features yourself. If you update this weekly, ask if visitors would like to be notified via e-mail when you update your Web site. A good example of a site that uses cartoons is the Myke Ashley-Cooper Cartoons4Fun site *(http://*

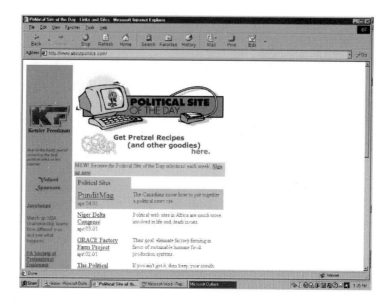

Figure 3.13. The Political Site of the Day focuses on different politically related Web sites and offers an e-mail notification service to inform its visitors of the new Site of the Day.

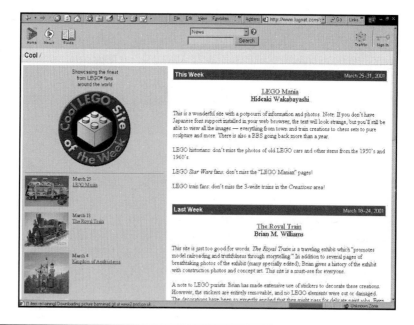

Figure 3.14. Cool Lego Site of the Week showcases Lego fans around the world and their works of art.

www.cartoons4fun.com/c4f.shtml), which continuously provides humor to its viewers (see Figure 3.15).

Benefiting From Humor with Jokes and Trivia

"Laughter is the best medicine" and could prove to be a popular feature of your Web page (see Figure 3.16). People enjoy trivia, or a "Thought of the Day" (see Figure 3.17), and there are many sources for you to draw from. Be sure to update regularly. Again, this gives you the opportunity to ask if your visitors would like to be notified when you update your Web site.

Who Doesn't Love Games?

More and more sites are featuring fun activities and games. (A sample game site is shown in Figure 3.18.) Just about anything goes here. You

Figure 3.15. The Cartoons4fun site offers amusing cartoons to its viewers and has an e-mail list that informs visitors when a new cartoon is placed on the site.

Figure 3.16.   About.com has a Joke of the Day that you can view online or can sign up to receive in your e-mail box in the form of a newsletter.

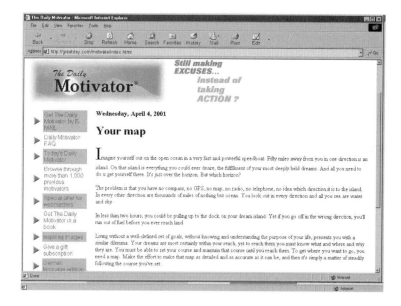

Figure 3.17.   The Daily Motivator (greatday.com) allows you to sign up to receive your daily motivation via e-mail and also encourages others to put the Daily Motivator on their sites.

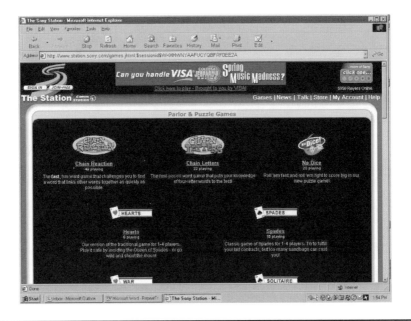

Figure 3.18. Sony Online has many games for its users to enjoy.

can host anything from a Star Wars trivia contest to having guests play an interactive game with other visitors.

Keep Customers in Touch with Update Reminders

Ask visitors to your site if they would like to be notified when there are updates or content changes to your pages. This is similar to a mailing list except that you only write to the "list" when changes have been made. This is effective when you have a newsletter or a frequently visited calendar of events on your site.

Special Events Reminder Services

People can sign up to be reminded of something via e-mail on specified dates (see Figure 3.19). This feature was originally thought of by

Figure 3.19.   FindGift.com has a reminder service where you can register to receive e-mail reminders for special dates.

a florist to remind people about important dates. You can remind people about any number of things relating to your business. If you own a site that sells fishing and hunting gear, you could get people to sign up to be reminded when certain fishing or hunting seasons start. You should try to develop a reminder service that relates to something that you sell from your site. In your reminder you can include suggestions about what fishing fly works best at this time of the year.

Reminder services are becoming very popular with e-commerce sites. Their services are very much appreciated by busy people who are not good with remembering dates. This has saved me on more than one occasion and made it very easy to purchase from the site that provided the reminder. I have five nieces and nephews across the country. I have registered their birthdays with a site that also asked for some details about the reminder—things like what the date is, the relationship that I have with the person, their ages, things they enjoy, and how far ahead of time that I want to be notified. Like clockwork, 10 days prior to Kyle's birthday, I got this e-mail: "Susan, your nephew Kyle's birthday is in 10 days. He will be 12 years old. Kyle likes Gameboy video games. We happen to have several that may be appropriate as a gift for Kyle. Click here for more details."

I am then able to choose the gift that I want to purchase, the paper I want it wrapped with, and the text that I want on the card that will be attached to the gift. Then I simply provide the address I want it sent to and give them my credit card number, and they send it off. Everyone is happy, especially me.

Adding Image with Advice Columns

Some Web sites are incorporating advice columns, as in Figure 3.20. People will return again and again to read the e-mails asking for advice and to see the responses that are given. This also helps perpetuate an image of your company as an expert in your given field.

Internet Resources for Chapter 3

More Hits for Your WWW Site
http://www.adze.com/zine/morehits.html
Instruction on how to get people to keep coming back to your site.

Web Developers Virtual Library (WDVL)
http://www.stars.com
A comprehensive illustrated encyclopedia of Web technology, the WDVL is for Web masters and Internet developers. It's a well-organized goldmine of tutorials, demos, and links to great resources.

10 Secrets of the Web Masters
http://www.i-strategies.com/10secret.html
A guide to Web design and strategy to attract visitors and make them return.

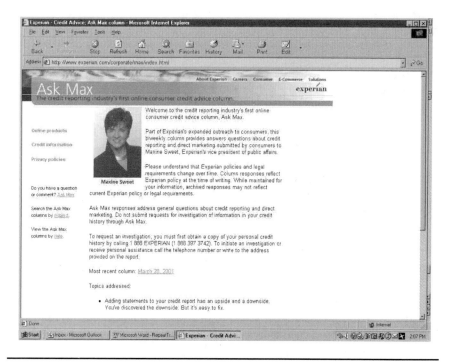

Figure 3.20.   A column that gives consumer credit advice.

Design Tips

Web Page Design—Introduction
http://www.wpdfd.com
Web design from the perspective of typography and graphics to keep visitors happy; no HTML.

Yale Style Manual—Table of Contents
http://info.med.yale.edu/caim/manual/contents.html
A good example of a detailed Web design manual to keep visitors coming back.

Pulling the Plug-Ins
http://www.cio.com/archive/webbusiness/060198_main_content.html

Web plug-ins are finally on the outs with Web designers. So how should you cram all that interactivity in your Web pages without alienating your visitors? Go here and find out.

Conservatism of Web Users
http://www.useit.com/alertbox/980322.html
Statistics show that Web users are adopting new Web technologies at slower rates, affecting how you should design your site.

4

Spreading the Word with Viral Marketing

Viral marketing, which is often referred to as "word of mouse" marketing, enables you to capitalize on referrals from an unbiased third party—the consumer! The power that peers and reference groups have over the purchasing decision is phenomenal. Similar to how a positive testimonial from a reliable source can add credibility to a product or service, the opinions of friends, business associates, and family can also help influence a consumer's purchasing decision. By implementing various viral marketing techniques on your Web site, you are provided with a dynamite opportunity to leverage the opinions of the consumer's reference groups.

Capitalizing on Viral Marketing Opportunities

You can use viral marketing techniques in a number of different ways throughout your Web site. By placing a "Tell a Friend About This Product" or "Share This Page with a Friend" button on your site, you enable users to quickly and easily spread the word about your site and your products. Visitors can click on the button, provide appropriate information in the "To" and "From" fields (including name and e-mail address of both the recipient and the sender), and a brief message. The important fact to remember is that the message is being sent through the business's site and not the sender's personal account. Although the message is personalized, your business can include additional information about the product, including features, benefits, the price, and a link directly to the page where the recipient can purchase the item. Since the message is personalized from a friend, the recipient will be more apt to visit the site to find out more about the product than he or she would be if the e-mail came from a traditional corporate e-mail campaign.

Amazon.com (see Figure 4.1) is a prime example of a company that has implemented viral marketing features throughout the site. When visitors browse through Amazon.com's 3 million-plus product listings, they are always presented with the opportunity to "Tell a Friend About This Product." Providing this feature leverages the effectiveness of the

Figure 4.1. Amazon.com leverages the opinions of its customers by incorporating a "Tell a Friend About This Product" option for all of the products on the Web site.

Amazon.com Web site and ultimately results in increased sales for the company. Virtual Crafts (see figure 4.2) also provides Web site visitors the opportunity to "Tell a Friend" about their site and their products.

In addition to the aforementioned techniques, there are many different ways that you can implement viral marketing techniques on your Web site. If you have a newsletter on your site, you can add a "Tell a Friend About This Newsletter" button on the site. You can also incorporate a message in the body of your e-mail newsletter encouraging readers to forward a copy to friends they think would benefit from the information included in the newsletter. You should also include information in the message on how to subscribe to the newsletter. The recipients will then be able to send a copy of the newsletter to their friends, who will in turn be presented with the opportunity to subscribe and regularly receive the newsletter. The opportunities for viral marketing are endless.

Figure 4.2. VirtualCrafts.com has a "Tell a Friend" option on its site to help spread the word about its craft products.

The Hotmail Example

MSN.com *(http://www.msn.com)* has capitalized on viral marketing to the fullest extent with its Hotmail service. Hotmail is a free e-mail service that is provided by MSN.com and is used by millions of people around the world. Why is a free e-mail account a viral marketing technique? Because whenever a message is sent from a Hotmail account, a tagline is automatically inserted into the body of the e-mail message that tells the user about Hotmail's e-mail service. The message reads as follows:

> *Get Your Private, Free E-mail from MSN Hotmail at http://www.hotmail.com.*

This small message results in hundreds of new e-mail accounts being opened daily on the Hotmail Web site. Although Hotmail doesn't provide any commercial services (i.e., they don't sell anything), this viral marketing technique creates mass exposure for the MSN.com Web site. Visitors typically login to their Hotmail account on the MSN.com Web site, which creates exposure for the other product and service offerings available on MSN.com (see Figure 4.3).

Blue Mountain—Taking Viral Marketing to the Next Level

Blue Mountain (see Figure 4.4), the site that is synonymous with free electronic greeting cards or e-cards, is a business that is truly taking viral marketing to the next level. Initially Blue Mountain received thousands of visitors daily who all sent electronic greeting cards to friends all over the world. Today Blue Mountain still offers this free service to the public, but it also provides a wide range of gift-purchasing opportunities as well. The following step-by-step guide illustrates how Blue Mountain is attempting to capitalize on its viral marketing strategy.

Initally when you visit the Blue Mountain Web site, you are presented with an array of different options such as e-cards, gifts, paper greeting cards, and downloadable screensavers. When you decide to send a friend an electronic greeting card and finally select a greeting card from the thousands of cards available on the site, you are asked to fill out the contact information for the individual who will be receiving the card. This process is illustrated in Figure 4.5.

Figure 4.3. Thousands of people access their Hotmail account through the MSN.com Web site every day, thus creating exposure for MSN.com's other product and service offerings.

Figure 4.4. Blue Mountain has one of the largest collections of electronic greeting cards on the Internet.

In an attempt to capitalize on the traffic their free electronic greeting card service brings, Blue Mountain asks visitors if they would be interested in attaching a gift to this message (as can be seen in Figure 4.6). Blue Mountain has partnered with various online retailers to offer a wide variety of gift products including flowers, chocolates, gift certificates, paper greeting cards, and prepaid calling cards. At the visitor's expense, he or she can easily attach a gift to the electronic greeting card. When recipients receive an electronic greeting card, they will also be notified of the gift that they will be receiving via traditional mail. It is at this point that Blue Mountain continues to leverage its viral marketing strategy. The following message appears at the bottom of all Blue Mountain cards that arrive in a recipient's e-mail box:

Send FREE Blue Mountain cards to friends and family (and attach gifts too!)

http://www.bluemountain.com

By including this message, Blue Mountain encourages the recipient to visit the Blue Mountain Web site to reply to the sender with

Figure 4.5. Visitors can send electronic greeting cards to multiple recipients on the Blue Mountain site.

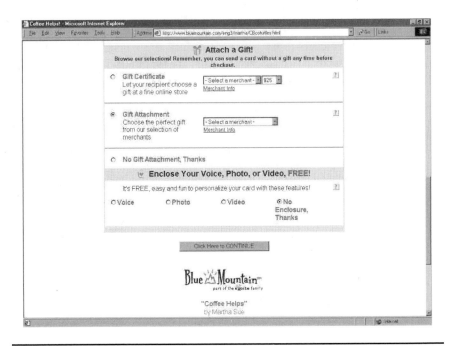

Figure 4.6. Visitors can then purchase and attach real gifts to their electronic greeting card, which are sent to that individual via traditional mail.

another electronic greeting card. Blue Mountain doesn't miss an opportunity! When a card recipient views the e-card, he or she is provided with a "Reply with an eNote card!" call to action and also a "Send this card to someone else" call to action. This again provides Blue Mountain with the opportunity to sell the individual gift products attached to any e-card that is sent. Through viral marketing, Blue Mountain is able to spread the word about its business quickly and in a cost-efficient manner.

Virtual Postcards

Today a large number of businesses, especially those that are tourism-oriented, are increasing traffic to their sites by offering virtual postcards on their Web site, which enables them to capitalize on viral marketing opportunities. Visitors can send virtual postcards to their family and friends. The postcard should not actually be sent as an attachment, but rather, an e-mail notice is sent saying that a postcard is waiting for them at a particular Web address. By clicking on the Web address, the recipient is sent to the Web site to view the personalized postcard.

An example of this would be Carlson Wagonlit Travel *(http:// www.carlsontravel.ca)*, a site that gives visitors the opportunity to send their friends colorful postcards via e-mail from different locations around the world (see Figure 4.7). When you send a postcard to your friend, he or she receives an e-mail containing a link to the page where the postcard can be viewed. When your friend clicks through to view the postcard, there is also a Carlson Wagonlit Travel logo and links to other sections of the Web site. Offering electronic postcards is a great way to generate repeat visitors to your site and to spread the word about your site through the use of viral marketing.

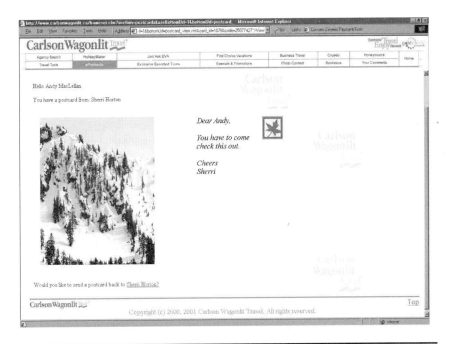

Figure 4.7. Carlson Wagonlit Travel *(http://www.carlsontravel.ca)* offers free virtual postcards to generate exposure for its Web site.

Internet Resources for Chapter 4

Viral Marketing Tips
http://www.emage-emarketing.com/viral-marketing.htm
Dr. Ralph Wilson provides some valuable information and tips on how to leverage viral marketing on your Web site in this dynamite article on viral marketing.

Viral Marketing Case Studies
http://www.viralmarketer.com/vmcases.html
This extensive list of viral marketing case studies provides an in-depth look at many successful online businesses that are leveraging viral marketing opportunities on their Web site.

Word of Mouse Marketing
http://www.brw.com.au/newsadmin/stories/brw/20000428/5426.htm
This is a terrific article about viral marketing, or "word of mouse" marketing.

5

Permission Marketing

Permission marketing is an important, yet often overlooked, aspect of Internet marketing. When you put forth the additional effort in proactively asking your target market to do something, you will receive a much better response than if you just sit back and "hope they do it." Similarly, if you ask people for their permission to send them materials on a specific topic, and they accept, you do not risk intruding on their privacy. Companies that force content on individuals through the Net hold little credibility in the eyes of their target market—and bad news spreads fast. When you play your cards right, permission marketing can be a valuable asset to any marketing campaign. In this chapter we discuss permission marketing and its uses to provide you with a greater understanding of this topic.

Permission Marketing Explained

Permission boils down to asking your target market and Web site visitors for the authority to perform a specific action—for their permission to do, or send them, something. Many businesses and advertisers compete for the attention of their target market on a daily basis, but it is very difficult to break through all of the advertising clutter. The key to permission marketing is to get your target market to willingly volunteer to participate in the process. In order to do this, whatever it is you are proposing must be of value to your target market—you have to make it clear to the user by answering the question "What's in it for me?" If your target market sees no benefit in participating, then they simply will not participate—it's that simple.

Chapter 3 discusses many ways to encourage people to give you permission to add them to your online community. These will be most effective if you leverage the permission marketing with a call to action and a repeat traffic generator. Examples would include

- "We change our coupons every week! <u>Click here</u> to join our mail list to be notified as soon as we update."

- "<u>Click here</u> to join our mail list and receive our bi-weekly Internet marketing tips, tools, techniques, and resources newsletter."

- "We have new specials on a regular basis. <u>Click here</u> to be notified by e-mail when we post our new specials."

- "We have a new contest every three weeks. Keep checking back or <u>Click here</u> if you'd like to be notified by e-mail every time we begin a new contest."

- "We constantly update our Calendar of Events. Keep checking back or <u>Click here</u> if you'd like to be notified by e-mail every time we update."

What makes permission marketing so effective? Permission marketing is not intrusive. Your target market volunteered to receive the information you're sending because it is of interest to them, and as a result they expect to receive it. This significantly increases the likelihood of your target market's viewing the material that has been sent to them and their being receptive of it. When implemented correctly, permission marketing can be a valuable asset in acquiring new customers and maintaining relationships with existing ones. We discuss some of the ways in which you can use permission marketing to increase your online marketing success in the next section.

Uses of Permission Marketing

Permission marketing techniques can be integrated with many Internet marketing tools, including newsletters, surveys, contests, and so on. Chapter 3 covers many repeat traffic and customer loyalty-building tools that you can use on your Web site. Permission marketing is an excellent way to enhance the use of those tools—a few of which are covered in depth in this chapter.

Newsletters are one of the most popular uses for permission marketing. You can ask visitors if they would like to receive notification of new products, updates to your site, relevant tips, advice, industry news, and so on—whatever might be of interest to your target market. People who sign up to receive your newsletter do so because they have a clear interest in what it is you have to say. In your newsletter you can integrate strategic promotional opportunities to encourage the user to come back to your site or to take some other course of action. If your newsletter is about recent happenings in your business or new product updates, encourage the user to "click here" to see the updates and then, when they do, transport them to your Web site. A newsletter keeps you in front of your target market and constantly reminds them of your presence. Permission marketing opens the door for communication with your target market; this is an important step in building a long-lasting and profitable relationship with them.

Warranty registrations offer you an opportunity to capitalize on permission marketing. On the warranty registration card or online registration form for your product, you can include a section encouraging the consumer to sign up to receive additional information on your products and services. Many software vendors integrate the warranty or user registration process into their software and allow the user to submit it via the Internet once complete. On the registration form the software vendor will usually ask consumers if they would like to be notified of upgrades to their product or if they would like to receive additional information on new products being released. The consumer would then click "yes" to receive additional information or "no" to not receive any additional information. Users usually will click "yes" because they want to be notified when updates become available. Along with the information they requested, you can include relevant promotional opportunities. The simple act of posing the question increases your chances of capturing your consumers because you have put the idea into their head—something that may not even have crossed their mind beforehand.

Contests and sweepstakes represent another ideal opportunity to put permission marketing to work. In this case, the contest is the primary motivator to encourage people to sign up. The e-mail notification sent out to notify each contestant of the winner can also include promotional material and can encourage people to visit your Web site. In order for people to sign up for your contest, it must be of significant interest to them.

800.com is an online electronics retailer. When consumers visit this site, they are immediately presented with the opportunity to enter a daily contest to win electronic-related merchandise. One recent prize was a Rio MP3 Player (see Figure 5.1). There is a direct correlation with the prize being given, the target market, and the purpose of the site, and as a result of the strategic fit, 800.com receives many entrants into its contests.

Figure 5.1.   800.com's contest for a Rio MP3 Player.

Once users enter the contest, they are sent an e-mail confirmation (see Figure 5.2) stating that the entry was received. Also included in the e-mail is a viral marketing call to action to tell others about the contest as well as a call to action for the user to visit the site and shop around. Referring back to the contest window, directly under the e-mail address entry field is the option for the visitor to sign up to receive details on the latest hot deals at 800.com. This is an excellent example of how to combine contests, newsletters, and permission marketing and maximize the opportunity. Not only is the target market encouraged to enter the contest, but they are also encouraged to sign up for the hot deals newsletter while their interest is piqued.

Subject: You've been entered to win!

You've been entered to win!

We've received your entry information for the "800.com Win Everyday Giveaway" at 800.com. You may be the next big winner, so stay tuned. A winner will be selected every weekday starting on or about April 6, 2001 and notified via email at that time.

Feel free to forward this email, or link below, to friends and family so they too have a chance to win a FREE Rio MP3 Player (model # RIO800, retail value $269.95) and a Case Logic Bag (model # MP3BLUE, retail value $9.95). Simply tell them to enter here:
http://www.800.com/bannerad.asp?keycode=151550

At 800.com, you'll find a complete selection of products in addition to information and customer service that go beyond your expectations. Click here to see for yourself: http://www.800.com/bannerad.asp?keycode=151551

Thanks again for entering.

Sincerely,

800.com

****
This message was sent to you because this email address was entered in our "Win Everyday Giveaway." You will not be receiving further email information from us unless you request it.

Figure 5.2. 800.com confirms contest entry with an e-mail.

A Point to Remember

When used correctly, permission marketing can be a very rewarding and cost-effective means of promotion; however, if you make ill use of this technique, you can do more harm than good. In order to avoid this pitfall, remember that you should never send your target market anything that they did not ask to receive, and you should never use their personal information for anything other than what they were told they were signing up for.

If you send your target market information they did not ask for, they will consider it spam. If you use their personal information for anything other than what your visitors expect, you could find yourself in bad public light as well as in significant legal trouble. Misuse of permission marketing also damages your relationship with your target market because you have violated their trust. This can also lead to bad publicity as the target market will be very likely to turn around and tell many of their friends and associates about their bad experience with your company, ultimately resulting in lost business for you.

Companies that are successful in their permission marketing endeavors tend to leverage their campaign by prominently displaying their privacy and security policies. People like to know how their personal information will be handled and are very reluctant to hand over their details to a company or organization that does not explain how their information will be used. Privacy and security policies help in building trust and confidence with your target market.

A Closing Comment on Permission Marketing

Permission marketing adds leverage to online marketing campaigns. Once you are in front of your target market, you want to take every opportunity to stay there and continue to communicate with them time and time again. Permission marketing helps you achieve this, but it is a game of give and take. You give them a reason to give you permission to send them e-mail, they provide you with the permission and their personal information, you provide them with valuable content; there is a trade-off and the cycle continues. Over time, you will gain more knowledge about your target market which will empower you to provide them with a better overall experience in dealing with your company through more targeted promotions and better fulfillment of customer needs. Why should you use permission marketing? To summarize, permission marketing can return a much higher response rate over intrusive advertising; it can increase sales, build your brand, and help develop relationships with your target market; and it is cost-effective.

Internet Resources for Chapter 5

DM Review: Customer Relationship Report: Interruption versus Permission Marketing
http://www.dmreview.com/master.cfm?NavID=55&EdID=2812
An interesting article on the benefits of permission marketing.

MessageMedia: Ten Rules for Permission-based E-mail Marketing
http://www.messagemedia.com/rc/ten_guides.shtml
MessageMedia primarily delivers e-mail marketing, online customer intelligence, and online customer care services. This is an article from the resource center on its site pertaining to the guidelines companies should follow when developing permission-based e-mail marketing campaigns.

ClickZ: Permission Marketing
http://www.clickz.com/column/perm.html
You should look at ClickZ's section on permission marketing, updated weekly by Nick Usborne.

The Direct Marketing Association
http://www.the-dma.org
Web site of The Direct Marketing Association, the leading direct-marketing organization.

Canadian Marketing Association
http://www.cdma.org
The Canadian Marketing Association represents information-based marketers—those who reach consumers through media such as the Internet, television, telephone, radio, and addressed advertising mail. CMA provides a voice for responsible marketers and has earned a reputation for leadership in the area of self-regulation with respect to consumer protection, privacy, electronic commerce, and marketing to children.

6

Designing Your Site to be Search Engine Friendly

Let's assume your site is built and you feel that you are now ready to submit to the search engines and directories where your customers and prospective clients must easily find your site. You need to be listed in as many search engines as possible. Who knows which is the preferred directory or search engine of potential clients? When people conduct Internet searches, they rarely go beyond the first few pages of results. If you want to be noticed, you will need to appear in the top 20 search results. But before you submit to the search engines, you have to be sure your site is search engine friendly. In this chapter, we cover

- The key elements of Web site design to accommodate search engines

- Using your competition and industry leaders as guidance

- The all-important content

- The importance of keywords in all aspects of your Web site

- Meta-tags and how to optimize them for search engine placement

When Internet users are looking for a particular product, service, subject, or information pertaining to an area of interest to them, how do they do it? The most common search tool used is the search engine. Because search engines can bring significant volumes of traffic to your site, you must understand how the major search engines work and how the design of your site can influence the indexing of your site by the search engines. This chapter will help you do just that.

Search engines are becoming increasingly complex in their scope of offerings, with the line between search engine, directory, portal, and content site becoming ever more blurred. No longer do search engines just offer their search service. More often than not, you will find a wealth of headline news, rich media entertainment, online shopping, a variety of complimentary directories such as an online version of the Yellow Pages, and the integration of other search engines' and directories' indexed information into their own. Personalization features such as the ability to customize how a page is displayed are also becoming prominent with some of the major search engines. Some search engines even offer users a free e-mail service! They do this because to maintain or grow their market share, they have to—people expect it, and it is a part of keeping up with the times as well as the highly competitive environment. Although search engines continue to change, there is one thing that remains constant, and that is that people use them to find what they're looking for. You need to ensure that your site is designed to meet the criteria set forth by the search engines so that your site can be properly indexed and listed.

Understanding Search Engines

Search engines use programs or intelligent agents, called **bots**, to actually search the Internet for pages, which they index using specific parameters as they read the content. The agent will read the information on every page of your site and then follow the links. For example, AltaVista's spider continually crawls the Web looking for sites to index and, of course, indexes sites upon their submission. Inktomi also uses a spider; however, a user cannot search Inktomi's information directly. Instead, the user will submit its site to other search

Bots
Programs used by search engines to search the Internet for pages to index.

engines and directories that use Inktomi's search engine technology. Inktomi is very important in the search engine community, so be sure your site is easily accessible to its spider. A detailed discussion on submissions to search engines and directories can be found in Chapter 7.

Registering with search engines is fairly simple. In most cases, you simply have to submit your URL or Internet address on their submission form. Even if your URL is not registered with search engines, a number of the major search engines will eventually find you since their bots are continually roaming the Internet looking for new sites to index. There are millions of sites out there, so I suggest that you be proactive and register your site to ensure a speedier listing. Once you are registered, some of the bots will periodically visit your site looking for changes and updates.

A common problem faced by Internet marketers is how to influence search engines to index their site appropriately and how to ensure that their site appears when people use relevant search criteria. Many of the interesting and creative sites on the Internet are impossible to find because they are not indexed with the major search engines. The majority (85%) of Internet users employ search engines or directories to find what they are looking for on the Web. They do this by typing in a keyword or phrase that represents what they are looking for. The following sections explore how to make your Web site more search engine friendly.

Many search engines and directories either partner with or license the use of another search engine or directory's search technology. If you submit your site to a search engine that uses Inktomi's index, then the design of your site influences how you're indexed in all search engines that rely on Inktomi for their search results. In a similar fashion, you will find other search engine and directory data intermixed or included in some form with another search engine's or directory's data.

When designing your site, you must always keep the search engines in mind. Something as simple as a drop-down menu on your site can cause problems with the search engines and the indexing of your site if implemented incorrectly. You want to do everything you can to ensure that your site is designed to meet the needs of your target audience while remaining completely search engine friendly. Search engines can produce a significant amount of traffic to your site if you can manage to be placed in the top search results. The following sections discuss some of the most common issues experienced by individuals and companies with respect to the search engines and Web site design.

To keep up-to-date with the latest in search engine happenings and trends, I recommend that you join the I-Search Discussion List, published by *(http://www.adventive.com)* and moderated by Detlev Johnson, a leading search engine expert. Search Engine Watch *(http://www.searchenginewatch.com)* is a great site for up-to-the-minute details on search engine ranking criteria and news.

Frames

From a marketing perspective, you should avoid **frames** when developing your Web site. Frames may result in some search engines' being unable to index pages within your site, or they can result in improper pages being indexed. Also, many people simply prefer sites that do not use frames. Frames also cause problems when someone wants to bookmark or add to their favorites a particular page within a framed site. Usually only the home page address is shown.

> **Frames**
> The division of a browser's display area into two or more independent areas.

What I mean by "improper pages being indexed" is that content pages will be indexed, and when the search engines direct users to these content pages, they will likely not be able to navigate your site because the navigation frame probably will not be visible. To prevent this, one technique you can use is a Robots meta-tag in the head section of your HTML that does not allow bots to proceed beyond your home page. As a result, though, you can really submit only your home page, which means you have less of a chance of receiving the high rankings you need on the major search engines. Alternatively, you should include textual links to all major sections within your site to accommodate those users who enter your site on a page other than a home page, and to assist the search engines with indexing your site.

Some search engines can only read information between the <NOFRAMES> tags within your master frame. The master frame identifies the other frames. All too often the individuals who apply frames ignore the <NOFRAMES> tags, which is a BIG no-no. If you do not have any text between the <NOFRAMES> tags, then the search engines that reference your site for information will have nothing to look at.

This will result in your site being listed with little or no information in the indexes, or you will be listed so far down in the rankings that no one will ever find you anyway. To remedy this situation, insert textual information that contains your most important descriptive keywords between the <NOFRAMES> tags. This will give the search engines something they can see, and it also helps those users who are browsing with non–frame-compatible browsers.

Now that the search engines have found you, you still have a problem. They can't go anywhere. Create a link within your <NOFRAMES> tags to allow search engines and users with non–frame-compatible browsers to get into your site. Frames are a headache when designing your site to be search engine friendly. To make your life easier and from a marketing perspective, it's better to avoid them altogether.

Image Maps

I recommend that you also stay away from **image maps** when designing your Web site. An image map is a single graphic or image that has multiple links to different pages or resources. Image maps can prevent some search engines from getting inside your site—you're basically locking the door on many of the search engines. This may result in some of the pages on your site not being indexed, or none of your site being indexed at all. If you do use image maps, make sure that your site is easy to navigate with **hyperlinks**. This will ensure that search engines will find all of your pages and index them. Another tip is to create a **site map** that has text links to all relevant pages within your Web site. Once you have created your site map, submit it to all the search engines. This will help the search engines to index all the pages within your site.

Image map
A graphical image where a user can click on different areas of the image and be linked to different destinations.

Hyperlink
An automatic link that connects a word, phrase, or picture on one Web page to another Web page.

Site map
A Web page that provides links to all major sections of a Web site.

Dynamic Pages and Special Characters

Don't bother submitting to the search engines those pages that consist of CGI content or have question marks (?) in the URL. Search engines simply won't index them. In addition, some search engines such as Lycos will not index sites with the ampersand (&) or percent sign (%) character.

CGI (Common Gateway Interface)
Programs used to enable Web servers to interact with users.

Meta-refresh

Have you ever visited a site and then been automatically transported to another page within the site? This is the result of a **meta-refresh tag.** This tag is an HTML document that is designed to automatically replace itself with another HTML document after a certain specified period of time, as defined by the document author. Now that I've mentioned this, don't use them. Search engines generally do not like meta-refresh tags. Infoseek will not add sites that use a fast meta-refresh. If you do use a meta-refresh tag to redirect users, then it is suggested that you set a delay of at least seven seconds and provide a link on the new page back to the page they were taken from. Some businesses use meta-refresh tags to redirect users from a page that is obsolete or no longer there. Meta-refresh tags also may be used to give an automated slideshow.

Meta-refresh
A tag used to automatically reload or load a new page.

Splash Pages and the Use of Rich Media

A splash page is basically an opening page that leads into a site. Often splash pages consist of a Java or a Macromedia Flash intro that can be slow to load for some users.

Some Web sites use splash screens that consist of an eye-pleasing image and an invitation to enter the site. Many splash pages implement techniques that automatically send you to the home page once you've seen the splash page, and others will invite you to "Click to enter" in some form or another. Why do people use splash pages on their sites? For one, they usually look beautiful. Another reason is to provide the user with something to look at while images or content for the home page loads in the background. Individuals also use splash pages as a means of advertising. Splash pages are usually very attractive in appearance, but they often lack content relevant to search engines.

If you do use a splash page on your site, be sure you include the proper meta-tags within your HTML header. This is important so that search engines that use meta-tags can access this information. This ultimately affects your ranking and how your site is displayed to users in the search results. If possible, include a paragraph or statement on your splash page that pertains to your site's content. This can help boost your rankings on some of the major search engines that both do and do not use meta-tags. Some search engines will review your opening paragraph and use this information when developing a description for your site that is presented in their search results.

Use of Tables

> **Tables**
> Information arranged in columns and rows.

Tables can pose indexing issues with some of the search engines. Tables are a common feature found on many Web sites to display information and position content, but if implemented incorrectly, they can cause the search engines some confusion. Also, by using tables close to the top of a page, you are potentially forcing the content you want search engines to see farther down on your page. Because some search engines look only so far, you might be hurting your chances of receiving a high ranking. If you are using tables, place any important information pertaining to the page content above the table if possible to help prevent any potential problems.

Here's an interesting problem some search engines suffer from: Assume you have a Web site, the main color of the background is white, and you have a table on the page with a dark background. If you were to use white in the table, some of the major search engines would pick this up as using same-color text on the same color background and would ignore your site's submission because it will be considered spam to them. Using tables is okay; many people do it—just be careful with your choice of colors.

Spamming

Some Internet marketers try various techniques to trick the search engines into positioning their sites higher in search results. These tricks do not work with every search engine, and if it is discovered that you are trying to dupe the search engines, some may not list you at all. They have been programmed to detect some of these techniques, and you will be penalized in some way if you are discovered. A few of the search engine tricks pertaining to Web site design are as follows:

- Repeating keywords over and over again hidden in your HTML and Meta-tags. For example, <!games, games, games, games, games, . . .>.

- Repeating keywords over and over again by displaying them at the bottom of your document after a number of line breaks.

- Hiding keywords by displaying them in your document using a very small font.

- Repeating keywords in your document by making the text color the same as the background color.

- Making frequent and regular title changes so that the bots think your site is a new site and they list you again and again.

- Changing the name of your site to have a space, exclamation mark (!), or A as the first character so that you come up first in alphabetical lists.

Any time you make significant changes to your site, you should resubmit your site to the search engines. Search engines normally revisit on a regular schedule. However, these search engines are growing smarter every day—some monitor how often the site is updated and adjust their "revisit" schedule accordingly.

Keywords Are Critical

Keywords are an important aspect of every Web page because the search engines use keywords in determining your site's ranking, and these are the words people are most likely to use when they're searching for your site. Selecting the right combination of keywords for each page on your site is critical to your success. When creating your keyword list, don't use just nouns. Think of descriptive words that may be associated with benefits of your products or services. For example, if your site offers information on weight loss, then some of your keywords may be "weight," "weight loss," "diet," "exercise," "nutrition," and so on. You can also add some keywords that describe advantages a person may receive from visiting your site, such as "thin," "slim," "healthy," "in shape," and so forth.

When determining what your keywords will be, always keep the customers or your target visitors in mind. Try to think as they would if they were to do a search for information on your topic. Don't just think about what people would do to find your site, but what they would do if they didn't know your company existed and were looking for the types of products and services you provide. If you find this a difficult exercise, then ask around. Talk to both people that know about your business and people that don't. Ask what keywords they would use to find a site like yours.

Start by taking your corporate materials, brochures, and other marketing materials and indiscriminately highlighting any words that individuals might search on if they are looking for products or services the company has to offer. Record these words in a text document in your word-processing program.

Next, edit the list by deleting words that either are too generic (for example, "business") or are not appropriate for keyword purposes. Review each word and ask yourself if people would search using that word if they were looking for your products or services.

Always use the plural when forming your keywords. (Adding an "s" forms the plural.) If you list "game" as your keyword and someone uses "games" to do a search, then your site will not be found. If you include the word "games" in your keywords and someone requests information on the word "game," then your site will be found because "game" is part of the word "games." Don't use both versions because you're then running the risk of spamming the search engines, and you want to be able to use other keywords to increase your chances of achieving high rankings. The only time it is appropriate to use both the singular and the plural is if the plural does not include the singular in its entirety; for example, "dairy" and "dairies"—in that case, you should list both the singular and the plural as part of your keyword list. It is also important to note that when most people perform their searches, they will use the plural version. You're more likely to search for "computers" than you are to search for "computer."

Now, reorganize the words in order of importance. By having the most important words first, no matter how many keywords the particular directory will allow, you are ready to submit—simply copy and paste the keywords onto the directory's form.

Now you have a good master keyword list. Different directories allow different numbers of keywords to be submitted. Because you have organized your list with the most important words first, you simply include as many of your keywords as the directory will allow. When a directory will allow multiple submissions for the same URL, you might consider submitting as many times as it takes to include all your keywords. You won't have to change your description or other information every time, just the keywords.

If you plan to submit every page of your site, your master list provides a valuable document. For each page that you are indexing, take a copy of the comprehensive list and delete words that are not appropriate for that particular page. Then reprioritize the remaining keywords based on the content of the page you are indexing. This is then the keyword list for that particular page. Repeat this procedure for every page you will be indexing. This is also a great procedure when you are developing the keyword meta-tag for each page of your site.

There is often the question as to whether to include your competitor's name in your keywords. This follows the premise that if someone searches for them, they will find you as well. My position on this is NO. Due to the fact that several of the search engines read only the first 200 characters for keywords, you would be losing vital space to include keywords that describe or even name a competitor's products or services. In addition, there have been recent legal battles regarding the use of competitors' names within one's keywords.

Your keywords list should always be included in your submissions to directories and in your keywords meta-tags. However, there is much more you can do to be listed in a higher position in search results. You should include your most important keywords in other places, such as

- Your page title

- Your description

- The first 200 to 250 characters of your page

- the beginning, middle, and end of your page text

- Between the <NOFRAMES> tags if frames are used on your site

- In "alt" attributes

- In the keywords meta-tag

- In the description meta-tag

- In the comments tag

- In any page <H1>headers</H1> used.

Some search engines rank sites by how early the keyword appears on the site. The earlier a keyword is mentioned on your site, the higher your site may be positioned in search results. And remember the points made earlier . . . though you don't want to repeat a keyword hundreds of times (some search engines are on to this), you do want to repeat keywords a number of times on each page of your site.

You can check the effectiveness of your keyword placement and utilization by using Web traffic analysis reports. This is discussed fully in Chapter 25. You can use Web traffic analysis reports to determine what sites are referring people to you. You can strip down this information further to view only search engine referrals. By looking at this information, you can see exactly what keywords people are using to find you and you can alter the keywords used based on this information. Refining your keywords is one of the key elements to success—you're letting the search engines tell you what you're doing right and what you could be doing better.

Know Your Competition

Check out your competition. I use the term "competition" very loosely. I mean your industry's leaders (whether or not you compete directly)—people who are selling noncompeting products to your target market, as well as your direct competitors. Search their names and see what they are using for descriptions and keywords. Next, search using some of your keywords and see what sites receive top rankings. This research will illustrate why they have received such a high ranking—and you can incorporate what you've learned into your Web site or doorway page for that search engine or directory.

What does this mean? No one knows exactly how each search engine works, but by searching for your most important keywords and observing what the top-ranking sites are using with respect to their page content, title tags, description meta-tags, keywords meta-tags, and so on, you can formulate a good plan of attack. Remember that if you don't appear in the first two or three pages of search results, it is unlikely that prospective visitors will access your site through the search engine.

Check to see what meta-tags your competitors have. Not only can you learn from the sites that catch your eye, you can also learn from your competitors' mistakes. After you have done a thorough job of this market research, you will be in a good position to develop a description that is catchy and adequately describes your site.

To check your competition's meta-tags in Microsoft Internet Explorer, you simply go to their site, then click on "View" from your menu bar and select "Source" from the drop-down menu. This will bring up the source code for that respective page in whatever your default text browser is. For most people this will be Notepad. Looking for the same information in Netscape is just as easy. From the menu bar, select "View" and then select "Page Source" from the drop-down menu.

Keep in Touch with the Trends

There are a number of services available that can help you with selecting the most appropriate keywords for your site. These services base their suggestions on results from actual search queries. WordSpot *(http://www.wordspot.com/)* and Wordtracker *(http://www.wordtracker.com/)*

are two such examples. Wordtracker references a number of sources including Infoseek, Google, Lycos, Yahoo!, and AltaVista for its suggestions and comparisons.

Guiding the Search Engines with Meta-Information

As we noted earlier in this chapter, a common problem faced by Internet marketers is how to influence search engines to index their site appropriately and how to ensure that their site appears when people use relevant search criteria. The majority of Internet users employ search engines or directories to find Web sites, which they do by typing in a keyword or phrase that represents what they are looking for.

Retaining a certain measure of control over how search engines deal with your Web site is a major concern. Often Web sites do not take advantage of the techniques available to them to influence search engine listings. Most search engines evaluate the "Meta-HTML" tags in conjunction with other variables to decide where to index Web pages based on particular keyword queries.

The Web Developer's Virtual Library defines a Meta-HTML tag as follows:

> *"The META element is used within the <u>HEAD</u> element to embed document meta-information not defined by other HTML elements. The META element can be used to identify properties of a document (e.g., author, expiration date, a list of key words, etc.) and assign values to those properties."*

> *An HTML tag is used in the Head area of a document to specify further information about the document, either for the local server or for a remote browser. The Meta-element is used within the Head element to embed document Meta-information not defined by other HTML elements. Such information can be extracted by servers/clients for use in identifying, indexing, and cataloging specialized document Meta-information. In addition, HTTP servers can read the contents of the document Head to generate response headers corresponding to any elements defining a value for the attribute HTTP-EQUIV. This provides document authors with a mechanism for identifying information that should be included in the response headers of an HTTP request.*

To summarize this lengthy definition, meta-information can be used in identifying, indexing, and cataloging. This means you can use these tags to guide the search engines in displaying your site as the result of a query.

Meta and Header Elements

A header without meta-information will look like this:

- <url1><html>

- <url1><head>

- <title>Game Nation—Gaming Software Specialists</title>

- </head>

If you want your site to be displayed properly in search engines, you should create a header as follows:

- <url1><HTML>

- <url1><HEAD>

- <TITLE>Document Title Here</TITLE>

- <url1><META-NAME="keywords" CONTENT="keyword1, keyword2, keyword3">

- <url1><META-NAME="description" CONTENT="200-character site description goes here">

- <url1><META-NAME="robots" CONTENT="index, follow">

- <url1><!—Comments Tag, repeat description here?>

- <url1><HEAD> indicates the beginning of the header, and the ending of the header is marked by </HEAD>.

- <url2><TITLE> indicates the title of the page. The end of the title is marked by </TITLE> which is called the closing tag.

<META-NAME="keywords" CONTENT="... "> tells search engines under which keywords to index your site. When a user types one of the words you listed here, your site should be displayed as a result. A space must be used to separate the words. Do not repeat any of the words more than five times. (Many of the bots will not recognize repeated words). And you should list the most important words first because some bots read only the first 200 characters. You should create a keywords tag for each page of your site listing appropriate keywords for each separate page.

<META-NAME="description" CONTENT="..."> should be added to every page of your site. It is used to provide an accurate description of the page to which it is attached. Keep the description under 200 characters or it may be cut off when displayed by the search engines.

<META-NAME="robots" CONTENT=" "> tells certain bots to follow or not follow hypertext links. The W3 Consortium white paper on spidering (spiders are defined below) offers the following definition and discussion:

- <url1><META-NAME="ROBOTS" CONTENT="ALL | NONE | NOINDEX | NOFOLLOW">

- <url1>default = empty = "ALL" "NONE" = "NOINDEX, NOFOLLOW"

- <url1>The filler is a comma-separated list of terms:

- <url1>ALL, NONE, INDEX, NOINDEX, FOLLOW, NOFOLLOW.

Note: This tag is meant to provide users who cannot control the robots.txt file at their sites. It provides a last chance to keep their content out of search services. It was decided not to add syntax to allow robot-specific permissions within the META-tag. INDEX means that robots are welcome to include this page in search services.

FOLLOW means that robots are welcome to follow links from this page to find other pages. A value of NOFOLLOW allows the page to be indexed, but no links from the page are explored. (This may be useful if the page is a free entry point into pay-per-view content, for example. A value of NONE tells the robot to ignore the page.)

The values of INDEX and FOLLOW should be added to every page unless there is a specific reason that you do not want your page to be indexed. This may be the case if the page is only temporary.

<!—Comments Tag, repeat description here?—!> is a tag that is read by the Excite and Magellan spiders. A spider is an artificial intelligence agent that reads all of the information on a page and develops a "page description." The comments tag can be used to trick a spider into displaying an accurate description of your pages. The description that a spider creates without this tag often may not be pleasing, and usually doesn't depict what your pages are actually about.

Use Descriptive Page Titles

Each of the pages in your Web site should be given a title. The title is inserted between the title tags in the header of an HTML document. Title tag information identifies and describes your pages. Titles can tell readers where the information contained on a page originated. Most Web browsers, such as Netscape, display a document's title in the top line of the screen. When users print a page from your Web site, the title usually appears at the top of the page at the left. When someone bookmarks your site, the title appears as the description in his or her bookmark file. These are all reasons that it is important that a page's title reflects an accurate description of the page.

Go through every page of your Internet site, bookmark each one, and check that your titles represent each page clearly without being lengthy. Longer page titles can dilute the relevancy of your keywords. Keeping your page titles brief (5 to 10 words or fewer) will increase the potency of your keywords and earn your pages higher search engine rankings. Also, keep in mind that Internet Explorer will bookmark approximately 50 characters, whereas Netscape bookmarks around 40. Your page titles should always identify your company.

Match the keywords you use in your meta-tags with the words you use in your page titles. Search engines check page titles, meta-tags, and page content for keywords. Your pages will be more relevant, and therefore will place higher in the search engines, for certain keywords if these keywords appear in each of these three sections. Position your keywords near the beginning of your page titles to increase your keyword relevancy.

Some of the search engines will retrieve your page, look at your title, and then look at the rest of your page for keywords that match those found in the title. Many search engines use title tags as one of the elements in their algorithm to determine search engine ranking. Among the search engines that use page titles in their ranking criteria are AltaVista, Excite, Google, HotBot, NorthernLight, WebCrawler, and Yahoo!. Pages that have keywords in the title are seen as more relevant than similar pages on the same subject that don't, and may thus be ranked in a higher position by the search engines. However, don't make your title a string of keywords like "cuisine, French cuisine, imported food, . . ." because this will likely be considered spam by the search engines and you will end up worse off in the rankings or removed altogether. Also keep in mind that people will see that title in the search results, and they're more likely to click on a site that has a title that flows and is descriptive—not a list.

Search Engines' Use of Alt Tags

Some search engines will include information within "Alt tags" when they form the description for your site and in the ranking of your site. Alt tags appear after an image tag and contain a phrase that is associated with the image. Ensure that your Alt tags contain descriptive keywords. This gives your page a better chance of being ranked higher in the search engines' directories. For example:

> *<image src="logo.gif" alt="Game Nation—Computer Games Logo">*

You do not want your Alt tags to look something like "Game Nation" or "Company Logo" because this does not include any keywords. Be sure you apply proper Alt tags to all images on your site to achieve best results. Keep in mind that users who browse with graphics disabled must be able to navigate your site, and proper use of Alt tags will assist them in doing so.

Significance of your URL

Where possible, apply keywords in your URL. Some search engines give higher rankings to sites that do.

Ensure that you own your own domain name. If your site is listed as a subdirectory on your ISP or Web host's domain, the search engines will not give you as much creditability. You don't want your site to be "http://www.yourhostsdomain/companies/yourcompany.htm." You want to be registered under your own domain, such as "www.yourcompany.com" or "www.keywordorkeywords.com". Google prefers domain names that match the keyword being searched for. Try searching for "mp3" on Google. What are the results? The number 1 result and likely most of the other top results all include mp3 in their domain name. Try a couple of other searches as well—maybe "real," for example. I'll bet Real Networks' home page is the one that comes up first.

Try to use keywords in your subpages where possible. For example, if you sell golf clubs, then you may want to have a subpage named "golf-clubs.htm" or "golf_clubs.htm." (It would appear in your URL as "http://www.yourdomain/directory/golf_clubs.htm" instead of a generic subpage named "page1.htm." An important thing to remember here is that some of the search engines can't tell that two keywords exist if you join the words together in your subpage, like "golfclubs.htm." Be sure you separate the keywords with either an underscore (_) or a dash (-). Using these little tips can go a long way in helping you achieve success among the search engines; it certainly helps with Yahoo!.

Site Content Revisited and Other Important Design Factors

To achieve optimum results, I recommend that you design your site content carefully. You want to apply the most important keywords near the beginning of your page because many search engines weigh the content near the start of a site as the most important.

Always have a descriptive paragraph at the top of your Web page. Search engines that do not use meta-tags will use this as their source for a site description and keywords on your site. In addition, search engines will use the content found within the opening paragraph in determining the ranking of your site among search results. Again, be sure to use the most important keywords first, preferably within the first two or three sentences. This is hugely important. Infoseek and AltaVista boost pages that use well-placed keywords near the top of the page content. Make sure that the keywords you use flow naturally within the content of the opening paragraph and relate to the content and purpose of your site. You don't want the search engines to think you're trying to cram in words where they don't fit.

Use your HTML <H1>headers</H1> effectively to indicate the subject and content of a particular page. Most people use them only as a method of creating large fonts. Some search engines, including Google, use the content included within the header text in their relevancy scoring.

As you can tell, textual HTML content is extremely important to the search engines, which brings me to my next point. Never create a page that is excessive in graphical content. For example, don't display information that should be displayed in text as a graphic file. I've seen this done numerous times. A site may have the best opening statement in the world, but the search engines can't use it because the information is presented in the form of a graphic. No matter how great it looks, the search engines can't read your graphics for content.

Do not make your home page excessively lengthy. The longer your page is, the less relevant the information on the page becomes to the search engines. I recommend that you keep your home page short and to the point. Of course, not every technique is going to work all of the time, so you might want to investigate creating doorway pages. AltaVista seems to like pages that are somewhat longer in length.

Little things like how often you update your site can have an effect on how well your site places in search engine results. Spiders can determine how often a page is updated and will revisit your site accordingly. This may lead to higher rankings in some of the major search engines. Remember, you can also resubmit your site manually once you have made changes; however, I don't advise doing so if you already have a high ranking. If the criteria used for ranking a site have changed, you may actually end up worse off.

Before you submit your site, be sure the content on the page you're submitting is completed. Yahoo!, for one, will ignore your submission if you have an "under construction" or similar sign on your page.

Additional Design Techniques

Doorway pages, also known as gateway pages and bridge pages, are pages that lead to your site but are not considered part of your site.

Doorway pages are focused pages that lead to your Web site but are tuned to the specific requirements of the search engines. By having different doorway pages with different names (e.g., indexa.html for AltaVista or indexg.html for Google) for each search engine, you can look back and see which page is bringing in the most traffic. Those pages that are not bringing in the traffic can then be edited and resubmitted until you get it right.

Due to the need to be ranked high in search engine results and the enormous competition between sites that are trying to get such high listings, doorway pages have increasingly become more popular. Each search engine is different and has different elements in its ranking criteria. Developing doorway pages allows you to tailor a page specifically for each search engine before submitting to achieve optimal results. Be careful, though; some search engines frown upon the use of doorway pages, so check before creating and submitting one. There are a number of sources online that offer advice for developing dynamite doorway pages. A good place to start is Search Engine Watch, listed in the resources section of this chapter.

Internet Resources for Chapter 6

Search Engine Watch
http://www.searchenginewatch.com
A Web site devoted to how search engines work, search engine news, search engine information, tips on using search engines, and more about search engines. More information than you can stand! Be sure to sign up for the Search Engine Report mailing list.

Search Engine World
http://www.searchengineworld.com
A great resource for everything surrounding search engines. Plenty of articles, tips, and information to help you achieve online success. This site also has in-depth information on the various search engine spiders.

Search Engine Matrix
http://searchenginematrix.com
Learn about search engines and search engine positioning to achieve greater positioning within any given search engine.

Search Engine Forums

http://searchengineforums.com/bin/Ultimate.cgi
Information pertaining to search engines and Web site promotion presented in the form of a bulletin board.

Internet InfoScavenger

http://www.infoscavenger.com/engine.htm
A monthly newsletter publication devoted to helping busy professionals market their products and services on the Web. Invaluable help, techniques, and tips for top search engine placement.

WebReference.com

http://www.Webreference.com/content/search
Search engines and examples, tips, and hints for getting the most out of your search engine, for people who work on the Web.

Submit It! Search Engine Tips

http://www.submit-it.com/subopt.htm
The purpose of this document is to provide you with background information on search engine technology and some tips on how to get your Web site to appear on the results pages of search engines and directories.

World of Design—Search Engine Secrets

http://www.globalserve.net/~iwb/search
References to monitor, submit, and improve search engine placements and positions.

Bruce Clay—Search Engine Optimization Tools

http://www.bruceclay.com/Web_rank.htm
Free search engine optimization, ranking, Web site promotion, keywords advice, and placement material for designers.

Net Promote

http://www.netpromote.com
Net Promote has Promotion 101, a Web Site Marketing and Promotion Info Center, where you can find all kinds of free articles, resources, tools, and links to help you promote your site. They also offer Web site registration, Web site consultation, press release distribution, site launch, banner advertising, consulting, and more.

JimTools.com Webmaster's Toolkit Command Center
http://www.jimtools.com/
A number of tools are available on this site that you can use for free. There's information on search engines and meta-tags, a link checker, and a link popularity tool.

LinkPopularity.com: The Free Link Popularity Service
http://www.linkpopularity.com/
A free service that queries AltaVista, Infoseek, and HotBot to check your link popularity.

Note: Resources found in the next chapter on search engine submissions are closely related to the information found in this chapter. I recommend reviewing the resources in the next chapter as many contain valuable information on designing your site to be search engine friendly.

7

Search Engine and Directory Submissions

There are an estimated billion-plus Web pages on the World Wide Web, so how can you increase your chances of being found? One method is submitting to the many search engines and directories. Once you've optimized your Web site to be search engine friendly, you are ready to face the challenge of submitting to the most important search engines. By "search engines," I'm referring to the combination of search engines, directories, spiders, and crawlers. You need to be within the first two pages of search results to ensure your best possible success online. This is no easy feat, and this chapter will provide you with the knowledge necessary to get on the road to success. This chapter covers

- Search engines, directories, and their ranking criteria

- An in-depth look at Yahoo!'s submission process

- An in-depth look at AltaVista's submission process

- The submission tools available to you

- Search engine and directory submission pointers

A Closer Look at Search Engines and Directories

The previous chapter discussed how search engines and directories differ. Although people use the terms search engine and directory interchangeably, there are subtle differences. In general, search engines have a much larger index and utilize spiders to add sites to their index. In contrast, directories typically have a smaller index and are maintained by humans. When you're submitting to a site, you can usually tell the difference between a directory and a search engine by the information they request. A search engine typically asks for the URL you wish to submit and sometimes your e-mail address. A directory will usually ask for much more, including your URL, the category you wish to be added to, the title of your site, a description, and your contact information.

When you do a search on the Internet, in seconds the search engine has digested what you are looking for, searches the millions of pages it knows about, and responds to your request with appropriate sites ranked in order of importance. Amazing! How do they do it?

Search engines use spiders to index your site. Usually a search engine's spider will index or include the pages on your site once you have submitted the request to be added to that database, but sometimes they can't for a number of reasons. They may have problems with frames on a Web site or image maps; they may simply miss a page; and so on. Even though a number of the spiders constantly crawl the Web looking for sites, I suggest you take a proactive approach and submit all appropriate pages on your site to the search engines to guarantee that all your important pages are properly listed. Also, before you submit, check the search engine's submission document to be sure submitting more than one page is permitted, because you don't want your site to be rejected. A search engine may also have restrictions on the number of pages you can submit in a single day—perhaps only 5 or 10 pages are allowed to be submitted. AltaVista has recently removed its restriction on the number of pages that can be submitted at a given time, but a kink has been added into the submission process as it pertains to automated submission software, which is covered in depth later in this chapter.

Some of the search engines share technology. Disney-owned Go.com no longer maintains its own index of sites; it now pulls all of its results from Goto. In addition, MSN Search uses Inktomi's technology for some of its results. However, all search engines have different ranking criteria to determine who gets top placement. Some search engines determine how often a keyword appears on the Web page. It is assumed that if a keyword is used more frequently on a page, then that page is more relevant than other pages with a lower usage of that keyword. Some search engines look for the keyword in the title of the Web page and assume that if the keyword is in the title, then that page must be more relevant than those that don't have the keyword in their title. Some search engines determine where keywords are used and assume that pages with keywords in the headings and in the first couple of paragraphs are more relevant. Some search engines use the number of links pointing to a particular page as part of their ranking criteria. Some search engines use information contained in meta-tags; others don't look at the meta-tags at all.

To summarize, search engines all have different ranking criteria, and this is why you receive different results when you search on the same keyword with different engines. You should learn as much as you can about each of the major search engines' ranking systems and adjust your submission or your site's content accordingly. One particularly useful site with this information is *http://searchenginewatch.com.*

Some of the more popular search engines are

- AltaVista (Figure 7.1)

- Excite (Figure 7.2)

- Google (Figure 7.3)

- Lycos (Figure 7.4)

Let's turn our attention to directories now. Because directories are maintained by human administrators, you can expect to wait a longer period of time before seeing your page appear in their index. In general, you can expect to wait between two and eight weeks. It takes longer because the administrators review every page submitted before adding it to their database. Make sure your page is easy to use, visually appealing, and rich in content, because it is the administrators who decide if your page is worthwhile before they include it.

When you submit to a directory, you will also have to take the time to find the best category for your site. Submitting your site to the wrong category could mean a minimal increase in traffic if no one thinks to look for you in the category you submitted to. Also, your site may not be added if you select an inappropriate category. LookSmart's Travel

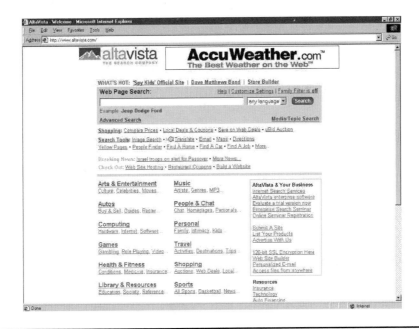

Figure 7.1.   AltaVista's home page.

Figure 7.2.   Excite's home page.

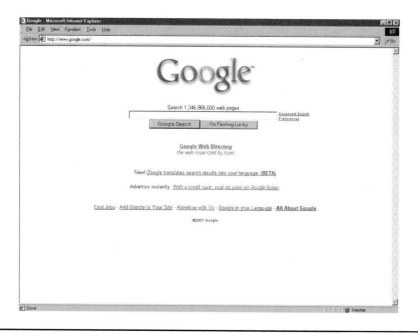

Figure 7.3. Google's home page.

Figure 7.4. Lycos' home page.

category contains subcategories including Activities, Destinations, Lodging, Transportation, and so on. These categories are then often broken down further into other categories within the subcategories. The deeper you go, the more specific the category becomes.

Unlike in a search engine, your site's position in directories depends much less on Web site design and more on the initial submission process itself, which is why it is important to review each directory's submission procedure and submission tips. You will be asked for a lot more information when submitting to a directory. The title, description, and any other information you give them during submission are what will be used to rank your site.

Here are some of the more popular directories

- LookSmart (Figure 7.5)

- Open Directory Project (Figure 7.6)

- Yahoo! (Figure 7.7)

Figure 7.5. LookSmart's home page.

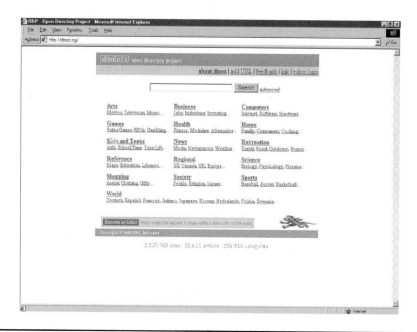

Figure 7.6. Open Directory's home page.

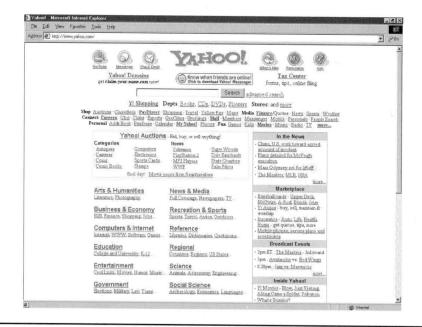

Figure 7.7. Yahoo!'s home page.

Search engines are known for their enormous databases of indexed Web sites. A couple of the leading search engines have over 500 million Web pages indexed. Google currently claims that it has the largest index, with over 1 billion indexed pages! Open Directory, Yahoo!, and LookSmart are popular directories, and each has approximately 2 million indexed Web pages.

Maximizing Exposure with Submission Pointers

Submitting to the search engines and directories is a very time-consuming but extremely important task. Don't rush! Take your time, do your research, know the ranking strategy employed, and prepare your submission for optimal results. It's very difficult to change your entry once it has been submitted, and the last thing you want is a typo. If the time available for indexing is limited, start by focusing on the most popular search engines and directories for individual submissions, and use a multiple submission site for the less important ones. Remember, 85% of all Internet users use search engines and directories to find what they are looking for.

When submitting to the search engines and directories, take the time up front to develop the submission material carefully. Organize the information in a logical order in a text file. Then, when you go to submit, you will be able to copy and paste the content to the appropriate fields on the submission form. Be sure to spellcheck, check, and recheck everything before you start. Spellcheckers won't pick up misspelled "works" if that word is also in the dictionary. The information prepared for each page on the site to be indexed should include

- URL

- Page title

- 10-word, 25-word, 50-word, and 100-word descriptions for the page (Different engines allow different lengths of description.)

- List of keywords for each page (See the next section, "Another Look at Keywords.")

- Description of the ideal audience for the site

- Contact information:

  - Company name

  - Contact name

  - E-mail address

  - Company address

  - Telephone and fax numbers

Print the submission forms for the various search engines and directories, and examine them to determine that you have all the information required for submission.

When submitting forms to directories, be very careful to fill in every field on the form. Some of the search engines will reject your registration automatically if you have not filled in all the blanks. When you have to choose categories, select them very carefully. It would be a shame to have a great product, great price, and a great site, but be listed in a place where your potential customer would never think about looking for you. Read the FAQs or instructions first to ensure that you understand exactly what information is being requested. Proofread your submission at least twice before you hit the Submit button. It isn't quick or easy to change listings if you make a mistake. Your listing may be wrong for quite a while before it gets corrected.

Another Look at Keywords

It's important to take another look at keywords. Keywords are the words used by your target customers when they do a search for your types of products and services in the search engines or directories. Your keywords will be used in everything you do and are the key determining factor in how you rank in the search results among many of the major search engines.

As a general rule, you should make sure you use keywords where appropriate. Keywords should be applied in your page titles, headers, Alt tags, keyword meta-tags, description meta-tags, hyperlinks, textual content information, and so on. Another rule of thumb is to apply keywords naturally, so that they flow with the information. For example, a description that is just a list of keywords is likely to get you bumped down in search engine results or removed altogether because some search engines consider this spamming. Finally, apply the most important keywords first. Many search engines place greater emphasis on keywords near the beginning of your keywords list, description, and so on.

Be sure to use different keywords and strings of keywords for different pages on your site. Each page is unique, with different content, so by using keywords specific to each page, you're increasing your chances of being found by your target audience. If you have the same keywords on every page, you're limiting yourself to the exact same range of keywords.

Review the keywords section in the previous chapter. It discusses how to develop your master keywords list and how to apply it to the appropriate sections of your site. The keywords you want to use are the ones individuals are likely to use when performing a search.

When applying keywords, the most important places to remember are

- Your page title

- Your page content—beginning, middle, and end of the page's text

- Your meta-tags—keywords and description

- Between your <NOFRAMES> tag if your site uses frames

- In Alt tags applied to your images

Great Descriptions Make the Difference

It is a good idea to create a number of different descriptions of varying lengths because the different search engines and directories allow different description sizes. Start off creating a description of 10 words, then 25, then 50, and then 100. Make sure that you use the right length description for each search engine, because you don't want it to be truncated when displayed in search results.

Your description should be compelling. When you get your site to appear in the first 20 to 30 top results of a search, the description is what differentiates your site from the rest. It is the description that will entice a prospective visitor to click and visit—or pass and go to a more exciting site.

Always use keywords in your description. Apply the most important keywords first because keywords used farther along in the description are generally given less weight by the major search engines. If possible, use keywords in combination with other keywords, but make sure your description flows naturally.

Be sure to use a call to action in your description. It's amazing how many people do what they are told. Perhaps your description could have a line that says "Visit us now and sign up for our free monthly newsletter."

Get Multiple Listings

One way to get your site listed many times is to submit many times. Because each page on your site is a potential entry point for search engines and each page has a unique URL, you can submit each URL (each page) in the various search engines, directories, and so on. Each page of your site should be indexed to improve your chances of having your site listed in the top 10 search engine results. And because every page on your site is different, each page should have a different title, a different description, and different keywords. In doing this, you're increasing your chances of being found by people searching for different criteria and keywords.

It is important to abide by netiquette. In some search sites, the previously discussed practice of submitting multiple times is acceptable and may even be encouraged. In others it is considered abuse and is discouraged. Use your judgment on this one!

Doorway Pages

Due to the need to be ranked high in search engine results and the enormous competition between sites trying to get listed on search engines, doorway pages have increasingly become more popular. Each search engine is different and has different elements in its ranking criteria. Developing doorway pages allows you to tailor a page specifically for each search engine before submittal to achieve optimal results. Be careful, though; some search engines frown upon doorway pages, so perform a background check before creating and submitting one.

Doorway pages, also known as gateway pages, are pages that lead to your site but are not considered part of your site. Do not include doorway pages on your site's site map! In fact, do not allow any pages within your site to link to the doorway pages you have created. If you do and a search engine spider finds these pages, it will likely consider them spam and you will be removed from their directory, or at a minimum your current ranking will fall.

Doorway pages are focused pages that lead to your Web site but are tuned to the specific requirements of the search engines. By having different doorway pages with different names (e.g., indexa.html for AltaVista or indexg.html for Google) for each search engine, you can look back and see which page is bringing in the most traffic. Those pages that are not bringing in the traffic can then be edited and resubmitted until you get it right. Make sure that the doorway page you create represents the page it leads to.

The various criteria search engines use in determining their rankings are always changing as the fight for top spot as search engine king (or queen) progresses; however, some general pointers always apply, and they always revolve around keyword use and placement.

Apply keywords or a keyword phrase in your title tag as well as a keyword or keyword phrase in your keywords meta-tag and description meta-tag. Many search engines consider your title tag when ranking sites. If you use a header tag, be sure you apply keywords or a keyword phrase here. Try to keep it a close match with what you use in your keywords meta-tag, descriptions meta-tag, and title tag. Stick with your keywords! Try to use the keywords you used in the preceding steps naturally near the start of the first paragraph on your doorway page. The farther down the page the keywords appear, the less emphasis the search engines will place on them. If your doorway page is going to include one or more graphics, then be sure to use those ever-important descriptive keywords once more in your Alt tags. This provides users who browse with graphics disabled the ability to understand what graphic you wanted them to see.

Perhaps more important is the fact that a number of the large and popular search engines reference keywords they find in Alt tags when ranking your site. Be sure to place keywords within your hyperlinks as well. This can also increase search engine rankings. Finally, use descriptive keywords throughout the content portion of your doorway page, with the most important keywords being applied first. The title and content of your doorway page are the two most important places, so take your time and do it right. For more details on what the major search engines use for ranking criteria, visit the URLs in the resources section of this chapter that relate to search engine feature charts. Also refer to Appendix C.

As one would expect, doorway pages have their drawbacks as well. Doorway pages are often easy to duplicate. Your competition may use your doorway page as a template and tweak or modify it to suit their purposes. If you create a doorway page, be sure not to use a fast meta-refresh tag as discussed in Chapter 6. In addition, if your competition copies and modifies your page to the search engine, it's likely that most of the content will remain very similar. If this is the case, the search engine may think you're trying to spam it by submitting duplicate sites, and you'll both get removed.

Keywords are the important thing to remember here. When you develop a doorway page, keep in mind the tips that were mentioned earlier. Place the most important keywords and keyword phrases first in your title tag, keyword meta-tags, description meta-tags, opening page paragraph, headers, hyperlinks, and so on.

A Closer Look at Yahoo!

Yahoo! is the most popular directory among Internet users today. Yahoo! was developed by David Filo and Jerry Yang around April 1994. Today millions of people use Yahoo! every day, and it is definitely a location where you want your site listed.

Yahoo! is not a search engine; it is a directory. Yahoo! has approximately 150 human administrators who review every site submitted. By default, Yahoo! displays information contained within its own directory; however, Yahoo! also allows you to perform searches outside its own database by referencing Inktomi's search technology. To view results returned by Inktomi's engine, click on "Web Pages" at the top or bottom of the page once you have performed your search.

Yahoo!'s directory is broken down into 14 major categories

- Arts & Humanities

- Business & Economy

- Computers & Internet

- Education

- Entertainment

- Government

- Health

- News & Media

- Recreation & Sports

- Reference

- Regional

- Science

- Social Science

- Society & Culture

Each of Yahoo!'s 14 major categories is broken down into subcategories that also contain sub-subcategories. The deeper you go into the categories, the more content-specific the directories become. When you are looking for categories appropriate for your site, take your time, because you want to be listed in the best location. If you submit to a category that is not appropriate, users may not think to look for you there, or Yahoo! may not even add your site at all. Check out your competitors and perform some searches using keywords you feel people would use when looking for your products or services. Observe the categories that are displayed. The category (or categories) you want to be listed in will likely be included in these. Pick the most relevant categories that apply to your page, but keep in mind that when searches are performed, the categories are displayed in alphabetical order. Once you find a category you wish to submit to, select "Submit a Site."

Before you go any further, is your site complete? Yahoo! won't add you if you have "Under Construction" signs on your site. Yahoo! likes sites that are complete, contain good and pertinent information, are aesthetically pleasing, and are easy to use. Also, check to see if you're already in their directory. You may not want or need to submit your site if you're where you want to be already. If you are in their directory but want to change the information displayed, then you can fill out a form located at *http://add.yahoo.com/fast/change* that is specifically used for changing information already listed in the directory.

Now that you are ready to submit, take your time to read all of the documentation on submitting. You want to follow their guide to the letter to ensure the best possible chance of being added to their directory. Yahoo! administrators are overwhelmed with submissions and will not take the time to review a site that has not followed their submission directions. Open up your text document where you've saved all of that relevant submission information I mentioned before. It will come in handy here. Fill out the submission form fully and completely. Before proceeding in the submission process, make sure your information is correct and you have made no errors. You do not want to make mistakes.

Once you have submitted your information, be patient. It takes an average of six to eight weeks for a submission to be reviewed and added to the directory if it's going to be added at all. If you feel you have done everything right, have been waiting for what seems an excessive length of time, and have not been added to the directory, resubmit. If you still aren't added, send a polite e-mail to Yahoo! discussing your situation and request assistance. As a side note, if you're a U.S. commercial company or business, you can pay U.S.$199 for express submission service. This service does not guarantee that you'll be listed faster or even that you'll be listed at all, however; it just means they'll put a priority on reviewing your Web site.

The following are some other tips to remember when submitting your site to Yahoo!:

- Remember, your submission counts for almost everything here, so do it right. Yahoo! is a directory, not a search engine. Designing your site to be "search engine friendly" means very little here.

- Make sure that what you submit is actually what your site is about. Yahoo!'s administrators will review your site, and if they feel the description you provided does not match up with your site, you will not be added to their directory.

- Keep your description to 25 words or less and use descriptive keywords that flow naturally within the description. Yahoo! reserves the right to modify your description if they see fit. You're the only one who knows what information is important to have included in your description, so you probably do not want Yahoo!'s administrators to modify your description, because you may lose an important part of your description, resulting in less traffic. Also remember that Yahoo! does not like submissions that sound like an advertisement—they like concise, pertinent information.

- Submit a short, relevant title, not something like "The Best Gardening Site on the Web." Also, be sure to use descriptive keywords in your title as well. When searches are performed, your page title will be referenced. In addition, when search results are displayed, they are displayed in alphabetical order. If possible, try to generate a title that starts with a letter near the beginning of the alphabet. If the title you submit is not appropriate, however, Yahoo! may consider your submission spam and your page will be rejected. For example, don't title your site "AAA Gardening Supplies" if that's not the name of your site just to appear near the top of the rankings. Like the description, make sure your title flows naturally.

- When submitting, develop your page title and descriptions to try to use keywords in combination with others as this can also give you a boost. Check out your competitors to see who's on the top and what they're doing right.

- If you're looking for local traffic, then submitting to a regional category may be appropriate for you.

- Don't fill out the submission form using ALL CAPITALS—they hate that. Use proper grammar and spelling. Before you submit, be sure to check and recheck your submission to be sure all is well.

- If your domain name contains keywords, you will benefit here. Keywords can help you out when a user performs a search on a keyword that is in your domain name.

- Don't forget to fill out Yahoo!'s submission form exactly as requested! Read the help documentation and FAQs, beginning with "How to Suggest Your Site" (see Figure 7.8), which can be found at *http://docs.yahoo.com/info/suggest.*

A Closer Look at AltaVista

Originally launched near the end of 1995, AltaVista is one the most popular search tools on the Web today. AltaVista is a true search engine whose spider, Scooter, indexes Web pages. Scooter is a "deep-search" spider, meaning it will visit all pages on your Web site as long as it is given the opportunity to. A fast meta-refresh or a dynamic page developed using CGI can cause problems for Scooter. I recommend reading

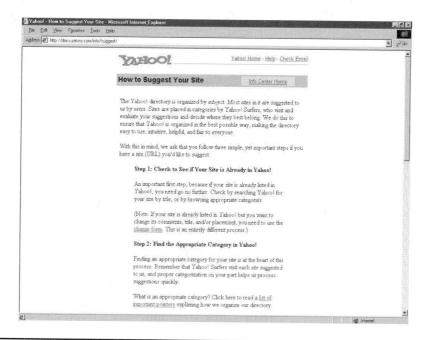

Figure 7.8.   How to suggest a site at Yahoo!.

Chapter 6, the search engine friendliness chapter, for more information, because it discusses Web site design and its effects on how your site is indexed by the major search engines. AltaVista also uses LookSmart for some of its results, so be sure to submit your site to LookSmart *(http:// www.looksmart.com)*.

Before you submit, make sure your page is complete. AltaVista wants quality pages and does not like to index pages that are incomplete or inappropriate. Every search engine wants quality sites indexed, because if they list a lot of "junk," then users will stop returning.

Submitting to AltaVista (see Figure 7.9) is a simple process. All you have to do is click on "Add a URL" from the home page. This will take you to the submission page, where you enter your URL into the designated field. AltaVista has recently added a submission code feature to its Web site submission page. For every URL you want to enter, you must enter the submission code. The submission code is generated automatically upon entering the submission section of AltaVista's site. The use of the submission code feature helps to block automated submission software and services, which means that you must add your site manually if you want to add it to AltaVista.

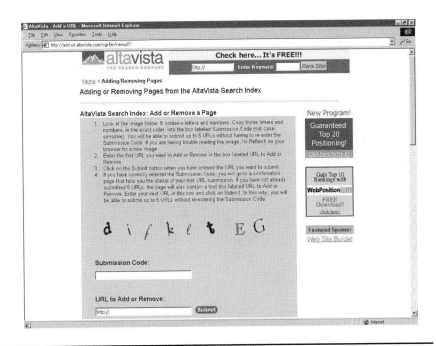

Figure 7.9.   AltaVista's URL submission page.

It typically takes 24 to 48 hours before your site is added to AltaVista's index. Scooter will then periodically revisit your site looking to add new and updated pages. If you feel you have done everything right but are not showing up in the index, then send them a polite e-mail asking if there's a problem and if anything can be done. It could be that your site is not optimized for AltaVista and that is why you're not appearing in the results.

AltaVista uses meta-tags. It will use your description meta-tag to formulate a description of your site, which is then presented to users when they perform a search. In addition, AltaVista uses your keyword meta-tag and your description meta-tag as factors in determining your site's ranking among its results. Keywords applied in your title are also a factor that affects your page's position. If you do not have a description meta-tag, AltaVista will reference your site's content and formulate its own description based on this. If you do not have a title tag, AltaVista will display "No Title" in the search results, if you're ranked at all. Here are some tips to improve your ranking in AltaVista:

- Your ranking on AltaVista is determined by your site's design, so be sure to make it easily accessible for AltaVista's spider, Scooter.

- Use keywords in your title, meta-tags, Alt tags, and page content. Make sure the most important keywords are used first because more weight is given to the keywords that appear first. Also, try to use keywords in combination with other keywords because this can boost your ranking.

- AltaVista is a case-sensitive search engine. For any of your keywords that are usually uppercase, you may want to include both the upper- and lowercase version of the word in your keyword meta-tag.

- Link popularity can influence your position. If possible, increase the number of links pointing toward your site.

- Search Engine World *(http://www.searchengineworld.com/)* mentions that older pages tend to perform better in AltaVista's rankings, as do pages with a lot of content.

- Do not spam AltaVista or your ranking will quickly drop or your site may be removed altogether. For example, AltaVista does not like multiple doorways or pages that repeat the same keyword over and over again (e.g., Gardening, Gardening, Gardening Supplies, Gardening, Gardening).

Effective Use of Submission Tools and Services

There are many search engine submission services available on the Net that will submit your site to varying numbers of indexes, directories, and search engines. They will register your URL, description, and keywords. Check them to see how comprehensive they are before using these services. Here are a couple of sites for you to look at:

Add-Me
http://www.addme.com
This site allows you to submit your page to 34 popular sites for free, using one form.

Submit It!
http://www.submit-it.com
Submit-It! is one of the oldest and most respected submission services.

SiteAnnounce.com
http://www.siteannounce.com
This is a search engine submission service.

GetSubmitted.com
http://www.getsubmitted.com
This site offers search engine submission and Web site promotion tools.

Although these services save a lot of time, it is essential that you be registered accurately in search engines and directories. For the best results, register individually in as many of the top search engines as you can before you resort to multiple-submission sites. There aren't that many search engines or directories that have long submission forms, so submit manually to ensure the best results. If you have taken the time to do the work described earlier, submit to the major engines yourself. This way you can take full advantage of the legwork you have done targeting the differences between the engines.

To summarize, each search engine is different. Know the unique qualities of each before you submit, and be sure to check out Appendix C of this book, where details are provided on many of the popular search engines and directories.

Complete Your Site Before You Submit

Before you submit to any of the search engines and directories, take the time to complete your site. Many of the major search engines and directories are not fond of receiving submissions from people who have pages that are not yet complete. You do not want to spend your time submitting your page only to find out it has not been added because it is "under construction." Also, be sure to validate your HTML before submitting. You want your site to be free of errors to ensure your success with submissions. A few of tools you can use to validate your HTML are

Web Site Garage
http://websitegarage.netscape.com

SiteInspector
http://www.siteinspector.com

W3C HTML Validation Service
http://validator.w3.org

NetMechanic
http://www.netmechanic.com/index.htm

Dr. Watson, v4.0
http://watson.addy.com

Is Your Page Already Indexed?

Before you submit or resubmit to a search engine, check to see if your page is already indexed. Perform a search using the most important keywords you think people will use to find your page. Also, perform a search using your company name. If your page is found and you're happy with the results, you will not need to submit or resubmit. In fact, if you do resubmit, you could end up worse off because you never know when a search engine is going to change its method of determining what pages receive a high ranking. If you are not listed or are not happy with your listing, you can submit your page. If need be, you can edit your page and then resubmit to achieve a higher position. To see if your URL is indexed by AltaVista, enter *url:yourdomain.com/directory/page.html* in the search field of each search engine. Check out the help files for each search engine for more information on how to verify that your URL is included in their index.

Check Out Your Competition

Using the techniques just mentioned, you can check out your competitors' rankings as well. By looking at the top results, you can see what they're doing right to achieve those top placements and learn from them to help you develop a successful submission strategy. You should look at your competition's keyword meta-tag, descriptions meta-tag, page content, page titles, and so on. They may have great keywords you missed. You might want to consider printing some of their pages or information so that you can use it for reference later. Do not copy their information— you just want to use their information for guidance and reference about what has given their site the high ranking. The top results for your keywords and your competitors can also be analyzed for link popularity, which you can then research to find appropriate links you may able to use to increase your link popularity. This is discussed in the next section.

The Link Popularity Issue

Now that you know who is appearing at the top of the search results, check out the number of links pointing toward their site. Link popularity is becoming more and more important among the major search engines, including AltaVista and Google. Perform a search using your most important keywords on Google to see who is appearing at the top of the results. Chances are the sites near the top contain the most incoming links. Look at the links leading to your competitors because they're likely appropriate links for you as well. If so, ask for a link, ask for a reciprocal link, or add yourself to their links if possible to build up your link popularity. This is a time-consuming task, but it will benefit you in the end. Keep in mind that link popularity is good, but link popularity from quality sites is better. Details on finding appropriate link sites, requesting links, and having your link stand out are all covered in Chapter 13.

It Doesn't Always Come for Free

Some search engines and directories are adopting various pay-for inclusion or submission policies. There are a couple general variations you should be aware of.

- Pay-per-click

- Paid inclusion

- Paid submission

The basic concept behind a pay-per-click search engine is that you bid for placement based on a specific keyword or keyword phrase. Every time someone clicks on your link and visits your site, you are charged the amount you have bid. If someone in your industry is paying $1.00 for a certain keyword and has the top ranking site, in theory you could bid $1.01 to overtake the number 1 position. Of course, if the second most popular site is paying only 10 cents for that position, it may be more cost-effective for you to target the position depending on your objectives, budget, and the amount of emphasis you want to focus on any given search engine.

Goto.com is the most well known example of a pay-per-click search engine. An important fact to note here is that search engines often reference other search engines for some of their results. Goto's listings appear in some form on AltaVista, AskJeeves, NBCi, Go, and Netscape Search, with others on the horizon.

SearchEngineWatch.com has a useful table on its site that provides an overview of information relating to the scope of paid processes used by a number of the leading search tools. I recommend you visit their site at *http://www.searchenginewatch.com/resources/paid-listings.html* for more details.

A paid-inclusion search engine or directory does not guarantee you a high-ranking position within a particular search tool; it simply means your site will be indexed assuming that your site conforms to the search tool's submission guidelines and that you will likely have a greater chance of appearing in the search results. Paid inclusion is used by such search tools as AskJeeves, LookSmart, and Inktomi. Details on their specific programs can be found on their respective sites.

Search tools that offer paid submissions as a service make no guarantees other than that your site will be reviewed for inclusion in that particular directory. Yahoo! offers a business express submission service to its users. On the site it clearly states that:

> *Payment does not guarantee inclusion in the directory, site placement, or site commentary. It only guarantees that Yahoo! will respond to your submission within seven business days.*

The key benefit of this type of program is that your site will be reviewed sooner rather than later. It can take months for some search engines and directories to review a site and either index it or reject it.

Purchasing advertising on the most popular search engines and directories will also get you in front of your target audience. Many search tools offer advertising based on targeted keyword buys or sponsorships. Google's new advertising program called AdWords, shown in Figure 7.10, is one such example.

Move to the Top of Search Engine Rankings with RealNames

The RealNames Corporation *(http://www.realnames.com,* see Figure 7.11) provides individuals, small businesses, and corporations with the opportunity to skirt the search engine mind games and instantly achieve top rankings using Internet keywords. In exchange for an annual fee, you can register an Internet keyword that is relevant to your online business from RealNames. Relevant keywords would include your company name, product names, brand names, or slogans.

The objective of RealNames' Internet keywords is to have the most deserving company's Web site appear at the top of the search engine rankings when a user searches on that company's keyword. For instance, if you search for "Nokia" in MSN Search, the RealNames' result for

Figure 7.10. Google's AdWords program.

Figure 7.11. RealNames' home page.

Figure 7.12. Nokia appears at the top of the MSN search list when searching for "Nokia."

"Nokia" is listed above the rest of the search results (Figure 7.12). Clicking on the RealNames link takes you directly to the Nokia *(http:// www.nokia.com)* home page.

Obviously, Nokia will have little trouble being found in the search engines anyway, but having a RealNames Internet keyword helps people find them more easily. However, what if your organization is the San Jose Sharks hockey team *(http://www.sj-sharks.com)*? Just imagine how many fan sites and sports news sites the San Jose Sharks would be competing with for high search engine placement. RealNames is a perfect solution for them. Instead of having to guess their domain name or wade through dozens of search results, a user can simply type San Jose Sharks into a search tool like MSN Search. The RealNames result is prominently displayed above the other search results (Figure 7.13), and the user can go directly to the San Jose Sharks' Web site (Figure 7.14).

By registering an Internet keyword with RealNames Corporation, you can generate more traffic to your Web site. As long as you maintain the registration for these keywords, you can have them forever. Keywords are also easier to remember and easier to type than a regular URL.

Individuals and small businesses can register a RealNames Internet keyword for U.S.$100 per year. In exchange, RealNames will issue (pending approval) a keyword within 72 hours and provide your site with up to 30,000 keyword-driven hits annually. RealNames will also provide you with keyword statistics and traffic reports.

Corporations must contact RealNames for subscription rates because RealNames customizes its services for larger business entities. RealNames will provide corporations with advanced keyword traffic analysis, marketing statistics, special RealNames promotions, and account management services. Typically, the subscription rate for corporations is determined by a performance-based pricing scheme related to the number of visitors or sales the RealNames keyword generates.

Of course, the scope of the RealNames Internet keyword system is limited by the number of major search engines that support it. MSN

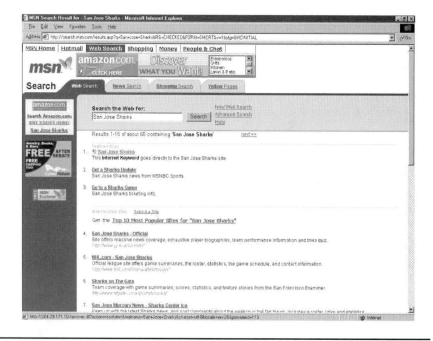

Figure 7.13. The San Jose Sharks' official Web site is the first URL displayed when searching for "San Jose Sharks."

Figure 7.14. The San Jose Sharks' home page.

Search and IWON are two search tools that support RealNames. Also, RealNames is built into the latest version of Microsoft Internet Explorer.

RealNames also has its own criteria and regulations for granting Internet keywords. They prefer that you use keywords that are specific to your company. If you do this, you are guaranteed the keyword(s). However, what if you want a keyword such as "Cooking?" "Cooking" is a general search keyword. Therefore, no single company, individual, or organization can have exclusive rights to it. However, RealNames will display a list of all Web sites with RealNames closely related to a common search term.

RealNames is very selective about the Internet keywords it issues and to whom the keywords are issued. To maintain the value of the RealNames directory, RealNames can deny the issuance of a keyword if it suspects any of the following conditions exist:

- Cybersquatting—This is a common problem with domain name registration. People will speculatively purchase a domain name (or keyword in the case of RealNames) with the hope that they can sell it at a considerable price to a more deserving company later.

- Use of others' intellectual property—RealNames will deny anyone but the rightful owner from buying the name of an actual company, brand name, or slogan as an Internet keyword (e.g., you could not register "McDonald's" or "Ford" as a RealName keyword unless you were a representative from either one of these respective companies).

- Misdirection—This situation arises when a commonly known word or phrase is misrepresented and leads visitors to a site containing content that is other than what was expected.

RealNames represents a new use for search engines and allows you to reinforce your company and brand identity. If there are keywords specific to your online business, strongly consider registering one, some, or all of these keywords with RealNames Corporation for increased exposure.

Don't Spam the Search Engines

If you want to achieve high rankings, then you should avoid spamming the search engines. A common name given to spamming the search engines is "Spamdexing." People often use these techniques to try and "cheat" their way to the top of the search engine rankings.

What is considered spam? (See Figure 7.15.)

- Keyword stuffing, which is repeating the same keyword or keywords over and over again hidden in your HTML and meta-tags.

- Repeating keywords over and over again by displaying them at the bottom of your document after a number of line breaks.

- Submitting multiple pages from the same domain during the same timeframe is considered spamming by some search engines, so be sure to do your research and check how many submissions per day they allow from a single domain. Some search engines want you to submit only your home page and allow their spider to do the rest; others say it's okay to submit as much as you want.

Figure 7.15. AltaVista's spam policy.

- Submitting identical pages but using different page names will also get you removed if it is discovered.

- Hiding keywords, often called tiny text, is also considered spamming. This is when you place keywords on your page by displaying them in your document using a very small font.

- Repeating keywords in your document by making the text color the same as the background color is considered spam.

- Making frequent and regular title changes so that the bots think your site is a new site and they list you again and again.

- Using page redirects or a meta-refresh can result in your site's being eliminated from a search engine's index.

- Using keywords that cannot be found on your page or are unrelated to your page.

- Altering the name of your site to have a space, exclamation mark (!), or A as the first character so that your site is displayed first in alphabetical lists.

Keep a Record

Keep a record of the directories and search engines to which you have submitted. The information recorded should include the following:

1. Date of the submission

2. URL of the page submitted

3. Name of the search engine or directory

4. Description used

5. Keywords used

6. Password used

7. Notes section for any other relevant information

8. Date listed

Some Final Pointers

Here are some important final pointers you should keep in mind. Always, always, always read the submission guidelines before submitting. Search engines and directories will also often provide a number of valuable tips that can help you to achieve better rankings.

Periodically review your rankings in the major search engines and directories. To make this manageable, I suggest you make a list of the search engines and directories to which you have submitted. Divide your list into four groups. Every week check your ranking with each of the search engines and directories in one group. If you have dropped in the ranking or don't appear in the first couple of pages of search results, then you want to resubmit to that particular search engine or directory. The next week you check your ranking with the next group. By doing so you can set a regular schedule for yourself, keep organized, and determine which search engines and directories you need to resubmit to and which you do not. Sometimes your site may be removed from an index because the search engine has flushed its directory, or maybe it is just one of those things no one can explain—either way you will be on top of things. If you make any significant changes to your site, you also may want to resubmit. You want to ensure that your content is fresh.

You also may want to consider submitting to country-specific search engines and directories. These search engines and directories often will give users the option of searching for sites from a specific country, which may benefit you if you are only looking for an audience in your country. A couple of examples are Canada.com *(http://www.canada.com)* Figure 7.16) and Yahoo! Sweden *(http://se.yahoo.com,* Figure 7.17).

Figure 7.16. Canada.com's home page.

Figure 7.17.   Yahoo! Sweden's home page.

Internet Resources for Chapter 7

AAA Internet Promotions
http://www.web-ignite.com
One of the first professional Web site promotion services on the Internet, and certainly the most reputable. AAA Internet Promotions manually submits your Web site to search engines and directories.

Web Themes Internet Consultants
http://www.webthemes.com
One of the most active submission and promotion services on the Net. They take a very active role in generating traffic to your site. Web Themes Advertising, Marketing, Promotion and Design (home of The Web Hitman) has been promoting new businesses on the Web since 1995. They have experience and the resources to promote your Internet Web site using a variety of tools to accomplish the task. Their Web page promotion services start with your standard professional submission services and extend to extensive programs for increasing traffic on a daily basis.

Submit-It!
http://www.submit-it.com
A very popular Web site promotion tool. You can use Submit-It! to register your URL with hundreds of search engines and directories.

AddMySite.com
http://www.addmysite.com
This is a free Web site search engine submission service.

SubmitWolf Pro
http://www.msw.com.au/swolf
With a database of over 2,500 sites to promote your URL and hundreds of fully automated submission scripts, SubmitWolf can dramatically increase your site traffic. SubmitWolf is loaded with features. It provides detailed submission reports, and it can generate meta-tags to help search engines correctly index your site. It even enables you to add your own engines.

Position-It
http://www.position-it.com
This site will show you how to use Internet search engines and directories to skyrocket your Web site traffic using search engine secrets for top positioning.

Position Agent
http://www.positionagent.com
This is a great utility that will check your ranking in the top search engines.

Promotion World
http://www.promotionworld.com
Lots of information surrounding online promotion, with some good information on search engine submission and preparing your site to be submitted to the search engines. This site also contains some tools you can use to generate meta-tags and check your position on search engines, and a free search engine submission service.

Search Engine Showdown
http://www.notess.com/search/
Detailed analysis of Internet search engines and their features, databases, and strategies.

Search Engine Tutorial for Web Designers
http://www.northernwebs.com/set/
Lots of valuable information on Web site design, search engine ranking methods, and policies.

Browser News
http://www.upsdell.com/BrowserNews/stat_search.htm
A weekly Web-based newsletter that provides a variety of browser news and search engine statistics.

Promotion 101—Web Site Marketing and Promotion Info Center
http://www.promotion101.com
A good resource with a search engine placement guide, free tools, and promotion articles.

PayPerClickSearchEngines.com
http://www.payperclicksearchengines.com
A list of pay-per-click search engines.

WebReference.com
http://www.Webreference.com/content/search
Search engines and examples, tips, and hints for getting the most out of your search engine—for people who work on the Web.

JimTools.com Webmaster's Toolkit Command Center
http://www.jimtools.com
A number of tools are available on this site that you can use for free. There's information on the search engines, meta-tags, link checker, and a link popularity tool.

Search Engine Matrix
http://searchenginematrix.com
Learn about search engines and search engine positioning to achieve greater positioning within any given search engine.

SEARCH ENGINE SEARCH FEATURES AND SUBMISSION CHARTS

Search Engine Chart
http://www.advance-training.co.uk/free/chart.htm

Search Engine Features for Webmasters
http://www.searchenginewatch.com/webmasters/features.html

Comparison of Search Capabilities of Six Major Search Engines
http://www.cyward.com/chart1.htm

SUBMISSION TOOLS

World Submit
http://www.worldsubmit.com
World Submit will submit your Web site to 1,550 of the World's search engine directories including Yahoo!, what's-new sites, and award sites in 90 categories.

SubmitPlus
http://submitplus.bc.ca
SubmitPlus helps you promote your Web site with two very effective Web site announcement programs. They offer free and pay services. Before you register your site, make sure you check out their "Free Promotion Tools" section for invaluable tips on how to make your Web site ready for the Internet!

The Broadcaster
http://www.broadcaster.co.uk
Broadcaster search engine submission and announcement services covers all aspects of Web site marketing, promotion, and search engine secrets.

MetaCrawlers Top Searches List
http://www.metaspy.com
Ever wonder what the rest of the world is searching for? Catch a glimpse of some of the searches being performed on MetaCrawler at this very moment!

SiteOwner.com
http://www.siteowner.com
Tools to help individuals submit their site to search engines, develop meta-tags, locate dead links, and so on.

Note: If you haven't already done so, be sure to review the resources for Chapter 6. The information contained in Chapters 6 and 7 is closely correlated, and their resources tie in well together.

8

Utilizing Signature Files to Increase Web Site Traffic

A signature file, or sig.file as it is commonly referred to, is a short memo at the end of your message. You can use your signature file in a number of clever ways, from just giving out phone numbers and addresses, to offering some substantial information. Sig.files can be used to let people know about a special event or to inform people about an award or honor your company has received. In this chapter we cover

- The appropriate size of sig.files

- Content and design of sig.files

- Creating sig.files to add statements to your messages

- The benefits of sig.files

Presenting Your e-Business Card

A signature file is your e-business card. It should be attached at the end of all your e-mails, those that are sent to individuals and especially those that are sent to Usenet newsgroups and mail lists. Most, if not all, e-mail programs allow for the use of a signature file. If yours doesn't, you should consider switching e-mail programs because sig.files can be very effective in drawing traffic to your Web site when used appropriately.

You can use your sig.file in a number of different ways, including providing basic contact information such as phone, fax, e-mail, and URL. You should provide every way possible for recipients to reach you; do not provide only the way in which you would like to be contacted. It is the recipients' choice if they would rather call than e-mail you. Some businesses also have a "click here" on their sig.file, which takes you directly to their Web site. This is a nice idea, but you must also remember to include your URL so that the recipients will have it. Sometimes people will just print their e-mail to take home that night, and they can't get to your Web site by trying to click on a piece of paper. You should also include details offering more substantial information about your company and its products and services. You can tell your readers about a current sales promotion, where you will be located at a trade show, a special event you are hosting, or an award your company has received. Sig.files are readily accepted online and, when designed properly, comply with netiquette.

How to Develop Your Signature File

In preparation for designing and developing your sig.file, you should decide what information you want to include and what you want your e-business card to look like. Create your sig.file using Windows Notepad and save it as a text file (with a .txt extension).

If you are using Netscape or Internet Explorer, the following are the steps to develop your sig.file:

Microsoft Outlook Express 5

1. On the menu bar, click "Tools."

2. On the drop-down box, click on "Options."

3. Click on the "Signatures" tab.

4. Click on "New" to create your sig.file.

5. Click on "Add sig.file to all outgoing messages."

Netscape Messenger

1. On the menu bar, click "Edit."

2. Click on "Preferences."

3. Go to the folder named "News Groups Folder."

4. Go to the folder named "Identity."

5. Choose a file to create your sig.file in. Be sure to always use a text file because you do not know what the other person is using. Therefore, you do not know how it will appear onscreen. After you have developed your sig.file, send an e-mail message to yourself with it attached to see what it looks like. Make sure to check and double-check for typos, errors, or omissions.

If you are using one of the online services, there are different ways to develop your sig.file:

America Online

1. Click on "Mail Center" on the toolbar.

2. Click on "Set Up Mail Signature."

3. Click on "Create," type in the name of the sig.file, and create the sig.file using the different options available.

4. Set the default to "On" so that your sig.file is added to your outgoing mail.

CompuServe

1. Click on "Mail Center" on the toolbar.

2. Click on "Set up Mail Signature."

3. Click on "Create," type in the name of the sig.file, and create the sig.file using the different options available.

4. Set the default to "On" so that your sig.file is added to your outgoing mail.

Prodigy

• Prodigy uses Microsoft Outlook Express for its e-mail service, so follow the instructions given earlier for Outlook Express.

The Do's and Don'ts of Signature Files

It is a good idea to develop several signature files to use with different groups of recipients. You can use an appropriate sig.file for each different group you are targeting. You should update your sig.file often to reflect current marketing-related information.

Some e-mail programs allow a maximum of 80 characters per line for sig.files. You should design your sig.file to fit well within the limits of all programs. Use no more than 70 characters per line to be assured that your sig.file will be viewed as you have designed it no matter what reader is being used. As a matter of fact, the fewer characters the better to ensure that what you have on one line appears on one line (and not two) in your viewers' browsers. Sometimes people open and view their e-mail in a small window and not the full screen.

Some people get really innovative in the design of their sig.files. They often include sketches, designs, or logos developed by combining keyboard numbers and punctuation. An example of this is "John Doe" of "Game Corporation," which is in the game software business.

```
>>>>>>>>>>>>>>>>>>>>>>>>>>>>>>>>>>>>>>>>>>>>>>>>>>>>>>>>>>>>>
John Doe, Director of Marketing              jdoe@gamecorp.com
                                              Tel: (800) 555-0008
 _____                                     Fax: (800) 555-0009
I GAME CORP I                                      290 Young St.
I   ____    I                                      New York, NY
I I        I I       "Free Trial Version @              81010
I_I___IIII___I_I     www.gamecorp.com"
GAME CORP.
>>>>>>>>>>>>>>>>>>>>>>>>>>>>>>>>>>>>>>>>>>>>>>>>>>>>>>>>>>>>>
```

Including graphics in your sig.file is not a good idea. This may look quite nice on your screen, but when you send it to other people who have a different e-mail program or different screen resolutions, it could look quite different on their monitors. You should also stay away from using icons or sketches in your signature files.

Check out sig.files attached to messages you receive or those posted to newsgroups to see what you like, what you don't, and what suits you best. You can always build it, test it on your colleagues, and then decide whether you will use it or not.

The use of sig.files offers a number of benefits to your company. If you use sig.files appropriately, you will be able to promote your company and your online presence in the following ways:

Tag line
Advertising message, usually included in your signature file attached to e-mail.

- The use of sig.files will increase your company's online exposure. By merely placing a sig.file at the end of a posting to a newsgroup, you ensure that your company name may be seen by thousands of people. A great **tag line** with a call to action will encourage people to visit your site.

- Like any advertisement, the design and content of your sig.file can be used to position your business and create or complement a corporate image.

- Using your sig.file can enhance the reputation of your company based upon the e-mail that it is attached to. If your postings to newsgroups and mailing lists are helpful and continually appreciated, this will become associated with your company name.

- Using appropriate sig.files, as shown below, will signal to the online community that you are a member that respects proper netiquette.

Sig.file DO's	Sig.file DON'Ts
Do list all appropriate contact information	Don't list prices of any kind
Keep it short, say 4 to 8 lines	Don't use a sales pitch
Keep it simple	Don't use too many symbols
Provide an appropriate and professional tag line	Don't list the company's products or services

Sig.files to Bring Traffic to Your Web Site

The major benefit of sig.files is that they can attract visitors to your Web site. Use your signature file as a mini-advertisement for your company and its products and services (called sigvertising). With sigvertising you can go beyond offering the basic contact information. Use your sig.file as a tool to bring traffic to your Web site. Instead of simply listing your company's phone number and URL, give the reader some insight into your company and a reason to visit your Web site.

One of the most important elements of your signature file from a marketing perspective is the tag line. Your signature file should always include a one-line tag line or catch phrase. A tag line is a small sentence that is used in branding and is often recognizable without even the mention of the company or product name. Does your tag line give the reader a real and compelling desire to visit your Web site?

Do you recognize any of these tag lines?

- "We try harder."

- "It's the real thing."

- "Like a rock."

- "Just do it."

- "Kills bugs dead"

A catch phrase may be something that catches the reader's attention and intrigues them to find out more. You should include a call to action in the catch phrase wherever possible to have your reader take action. I often include the catch phrase "Check out our Web Site Report Card" in my signature file with a hypertext link to my Web site, with very positive results. The recipients often do check out our Web site report card, ask for additional information, and often become clients. It works!

Consider some of the following tag line or catch phrase possibilities to increase the traffic to your Web site:

- Announce a sale or special offer. Briefly mention that your company will be having a sale, or inform people that there is a special offer available on your Web site.

- Offer something for free. Inform readers of free information or samples that they can access if they visit your site.

- Announce an event. If your company is organizing or sponsoring a special event, inform people through your sig.file, and invite them to your site for more information.

- Announce a contest. If your site is holding a contest, tell readers that they can enter by visiting your site.

- Announce an award or honor. If your company or your Web site has received special recognition, tell people about it through your sig.file.

Sig.files are accepted online in e-mail, newsgroups, mail lists, and discussion groups. However, be cautious when developing your sig.files to ensure that they will be well received. Sig.files that are billboards, or sig.files that are longer than most of your text messages, are to be avoided. Sig.files that are blatant advertisements definitely will not be appreciated. The online community reacts unfavorably to hard-sell advertising unless it is done in the proper forum. Here is an example of a sig.file that may offend Internet users:

xxxxxxxxxxxxxxxxxxxxxxxxxxxxxxxxxxxxxxxxxxxxxxxxxxxxxxxxxxxxxxxxx
Are you in need of a reliable vehicle?
If you are, come on down to Sunnyvale Volkswagen!
We have the best deals in town and will beat any of our competitors'
prices on new and used cars!
Money-back guarantee!
Great deal on a 1995 Diesel Jetta . . . . $2,995.
Talk to Jane Doe about our new lease incentives!
101 Main Street, Woodstock, New York 10010
Tel: (800) 555-0000
Cell: (800) 555-1010
Fax: (800) 555-1020
www.bug.com
xxxxxxxxxxxxxxxxxxxxxxxxxxxxxxxxxxxxxxxxxxxxxxxxxxxxxxxxxxxxxxxxx

Another mistake that people make is that they try to make their sig.files too flashy or eye catching. Using a lot of large symbols may catch people's eye, but the impression it leaves will not be memorable.

Here is an example of what not to do:

```
!Sunnyvale Volkswagen !
!Jane Doe, Marketing Assistant !
! jdoe@bug.com !
232 Main Street                    ☎800) 555-0000
Woodstock, New York                  (800) 555-0002
30210
              "Test drives @ www.bug.com"
```

Here are some examples of what sig.files should look like:

```
=========================================================
                    Sunnyvale Volkswagen
                Jane Doe, Marketing Assistant
                      jdoe@bug.com
101 Main Street                          Tel: (800) 555-0000
Woodstock, New York, 10010               Fax:(800) 555-0002
        "Our once a year sales event is on now @ www.bug.com"
=========================================================
```

```
                    Sunnyvale Volkswagen
                Jane Doe, Marketing Assistant
                      jdoe@bug.com
101 Main Street                          Tel: (800) 555-0000
Woodstock, New York, 10010               Fax: (800) 555-0001
        Charity Telethon sponsored by Sunnyvale Volkswagen
                info available @ www.bug.com
```

```
Jane Doe      Marketing Assistant      Sunnyvale Volkswagen
        "Enter to win a new 1999 Bug @ www.bug.com"
        101 Main Street, Woodstock, New York, 10010
              (800) 555-0000 jdoe@bug.com
```

>>>

Jane Doe, Marketing Assistant
Sunnyvale Volkswagen

101 Main Street   jdoe@bug.com
P.O. Box 101   Tel: (800) 555-0000
Woodstock, New York 10010   URL: www.bug.com
"1999 Winner of the Best Dealership Award"
>>>

Internet Resources for Chapter 8

123 Promote
http://www.123promote.com/workbook/plan1.htm
E-mail guide to e-mail styles, e-mail mail-merging, e-mail auto responders, e-mail auto reminders, e-mail netiquette, e-mail headers, signature files, announcements, press releases, business administration, free designs, mailing list announcements, newsgroup announcements, office automation, mass e-mailing, publicity, form letters, form folders, e-mailed databases, programs, software.

Siglets.com
http://siglets.com
Siglets are short notations, humorous or serious, placed at the bottom of an e-mail, usually in a sig.file. Siglets.com offers you thousands to use for free! As you browse the site, you'll find Siglets for all occasions.

Webnovice.com
www.Webnovice.com/sig_files.htm
"Everything You Wanted To Know About Signature Files. . . But Didn't Know Where To Ask."

Internet Strategist
http://www.techdirect.com/strategy/sigfiles.html
What to do and not to do on sig.files and mailing lists. Learn how to create your personal sig.file and what the different types are used for.

SquareOne Technology: How to Create an E-mail Signature
http://www.squareonetech.com/signature.html
How to create a sig.file with Notepad and import it to use with all your mail messages.

Signature Files
http://www.smithfam.com/news/n8.html
Signature files are an absolutely vital way of promoting your Web site. Learn how to market your product on the Internet from the leading Internet marketing experts, and it is all free.

GFOFN Help: How to Make and Maintain a Signature File
http://www.gnofn.org/info/help/ppp/makesig.html
A tutorial on designing and developing your signature file.

Esther's Massive Signature File Collection
http://www.contrib.andrew.cmu.edu/~moose/sigs.html
A massive collection of sig.files to review—the good, the bad, and the ugly.

Signature Museum
http://huizen.dds.nl/~mwpieter/sigs
The Signature Museum is a gallery of signature files sorted by category. At this site, you will also find a list of other sites that provide examples of lots and lots of signature files.

Workz.com
http://www.workz.com
Workz has a great tutorial on developing signature files properly. Check it out!

9

The E-mail Advantage

E-mail is rapidly becoming one of the most crucial forms of communication you have with your clients, potential customers, suppliers, and colleagues. E-mail is now a widely accessible and generally accepted form of communication. We are seeing a huge increase in commercial e-mail volume. The reason for this significant increase is understandable given that e-mail is a very cost-effective, time-efficient tool that has a high response rate. E-mail is used to build your community online, sell products and provide customer service, reinforce brand awareness, and encourage customer loyalty.

In the online community e-mail is an extremely efficient way to build and maintain relationships. As a marketing tool, e-mail is one of the most cost-effective ways to maintain an ongoing dialogue with your audience. In this chapter we cover

- Strategies for creating effective e-mail messages

- E-mail netiquette

- Information access with autoresponders

- Customer service and e-mail

- E-mail marketing tips

- Sending HTML versus ASCII (text-based) e-mail messages

Making the Connection

E-mail is a communication medium, and, as with all forms of communication, you do not get a second chance to leave a first impression. E-mail must be used appropriately. People receive large amounts of e-mail each day, and the tips in this chapter will help to ensure that your e-mail is taken seriously.

One of the greatest benefits of e-mail is the speed with which you can communicate. E-mail takes seconds rather than weeks to send a message around the world. The cost of this form of communication is negligible compared to making a long-distance phone call or sending a fax. The economies of scale are significant. One e-mail message can be sent to millions of people across the globe simultaneously. This type of mass mailing is done at a fraction of the cost and a fraction of the time (and internal resources) it would take with snail mail.

Snail mail
Slang term for the regular postal service.

All kinds of files can be sent via e-mail, including sound, video, data, graphics, and text. With an **autoresponder**, information can be sent to customers and potential customers 24 hours a day, 7 days a week, 365 days a year in response to their online requests.

Autoresponder
Program that automatically responds to incoming e-mail.

E-mail is interactive. Your current and potential customers can immediately respond to you and carry on an ongoing dialogue with you. E-mail is seen much more like a conversation than a text document. It is perceived as being more personal than snail mail and can go quite a long way in building relationships.

Effective E-mail Messages

Most people who use this medium get tons of e-mail, including their share of junk e-mail. The following tips will increase the effectiveness of your e-mail communication.

The Importance of Your E-mail Subject Line

When you receive e-mails, what do you use to determine which e-mail to read first or at all? The subject line, of course! Never send an e-mail message without a subject line. Subject lines should be brief, with the keywords appearing first. The longer the subject line is, the more likely it will not be viewed in its entirety.

The subject line is equivalent to a headline in a newspaper in terms of attracting reader attention. When you read a newspaper, you don't really read it; generally you skim the headlines and read the articles whose headline grabbed your attention. The same is true with e-mail. Many recipients, especially those who receive a significant number of e-mails daily, skim the subject lines and read only the articles whose subject line grabs their attention. The subject line is the most important part of your e-mail message because this phrase alone will determine whether or not the reader will decide to open your e-mail or delete it.

Effective subject lines will

- Be brief, yet capture the reader's interest

- Build business credibility

- Attract attention with action words

- Highlight the most important benefits

- Always be positive

- Put the most important words first

Effective headlines should grab the reader's attention, isolate and qualify your best prospects, and draw your reader into the subheadlines and the text itself. Remember to avoid SHOUTING! Using CAPITALS in your subject line is the same as SHOUTING AT THE READER! DON'T DO IT!!

E-mail "To" and "From" Headings Allow You to Personalize

Use personal names in the "To" and "From" headings whenever possible as this creates a more personal relationship. Most e-mail programs allow you to attach your personal name to your e-mail address. If you don't know how to do this, look at the help file of the e-mail program you are using.

Blind Carbon Copy (BCC)

Have you ever received an e-mail message in which the first screen or first several screens was a string of other people's e-mail addresses to which the message had been sent? Didn't you feel special? Didn't you feel the message was meant just for you? This sort of bulk mailing is very unpersonalized, and most often recipients will delete the message without looking at it.

It is advisable to use the **BCC** feature when sending bulk or group e-mails; otherwise, every person on the list will see that this e-mail was not sent just to him or her. The e-mail recipients will see the list of the other recipients first and not the intended message. They will be required to scroll down past the list of recipients to get to your message. This is not the best way to make friends and influence people. Make sure that you know how to use the blind carbon copy function in your e-mail program.

> **BCC**
> Blind Carbon Copy: all recipient names are hidden so that no one sees who else has received the e-mail.

Even better than blind carbon copy is using a software application that can send personalized messages to each recipient in your database. E-mail applications like this are far more flexible than the BCC method because there is no limitation on the number of messages you can send, and the field merge capabilities enable you to create a more personalized message.

Before you send any "live" bulk e-mail, do a test with a number of your colleagues and friends to make sure you are using the program and features effectively and that all of their addresses do not appear by mistake in each message.

Effective E-mail Message Formatting

The content of the message should be focused on one topic. If you need to change the subject in the middle of a message, it is better to send a separate e-mail. Alternatively, if you wish to discuss more than one topic, make sure you begin your message stating "I have three questions" or

"There are four issues I would like to discuss." People are busy; they read their e-mail quickly, and they assume you will cover your main points within the first few sentences of your message.

E-mail is similar to writing a business letter in that the spelling and grammar should be correct. This includes the proper use of upper- and lowercase lettering, which many people seem to ignore when sending e-mail. However, e-mail is unlike a business letter in that the tone is completely different. E-mail correspondence is not as formal as business writing. The tone of e-mail is more similar to a polite conversation than a formal letter, which makes it conducive to relationship building.

In general, you should

- Keep your paragraphs relatively short—no more than seven lines.

- Make your point in the first paragraph.

- Be clear and concise.

- Use http:// at the beginning of any Web address to ensure that you make it "live." Some e-mail readers recognize Internet addresses from the www, but most recognize Internet addresses from the http:// and automatically provide the hypertext link directly to the Web site.

- Give your reader a call to action.

- Avoid using fancy formatting such as graphics, different fonts, italics, and bold, because many e-mail programs cannot display those features. Your message that reads: "I loved the flowers. Love 'ya" could be viewed as "I <I>loved<I> the flowers. <B>Love ya<B>" if the recipient's e-mail software can't handle formatting. Kinda loses the impact!

- If your e-mail package doesn't have a spellcheck feature, you might want to consider composing your message first in your word-processing program. Spellcheck it there and then cut and paste it into your e-mail package.

- Choose your words carefully. E-mail is a permanent record of your thoughts, and it can easily be forwarded to others.

If you want to be really careful, test the e-mail in a number of the popular packages to ensure that your message will be received in the intended format.

A Call to Action

When you give your readers a call to action, it's amazing how often people will do as they're told. I'll give you an example through something we did at Connex Network. We ran a series of 10 Internet marketing workshops for a large organization. Their staff and selected clients were invited to participate in any, some, or all of the workshops. Their clients could include up to three employees. Since the workshops extended beyond noon, lunch was provided.

Since Connex Network was responsible for organizing and managing the project, we needed to know the approximate number of people who would be attending each of the workshops to organize the luncheons. When we contacted each company's representatives by e-mail looking for participation RSVPs, we conducted an experiment. We sent half the representatives one version of the message and the other half a slightly different version. The only difference between the two messages was that in one, we had a call to action. In that message we asked "RSVP before Wednesday at noon indicating if you will be attending as we must make arrangements for lunch," and in the other this same line read "Please let us know if you are planning to attend as we must make arrangements for lunch."

There was a 95% response rate from the group who received the first message. This is because we gave people a call to action and a deadline, and they felt obligated to respond more promptly. Meanwhile, fewer than 50% of the people in the second group responded to our message. What does this tell us? To improve your response rate, give your readers a call to action when you send them e-mail. People will respond when told to do something; they act with more urgency when there is a deadline.

Appropriate E-mail Reply Tips

Do not include the entire original message in your replies. This is unnecessary, is aggravating to the original sender of the message, and of-

Download
Transmission of a file
from one computer
to another.

ten takes too long to **download.** However, use enough of the original message to refresh the recipient's memory. Remember to check the "To" and "CC" before you reply. You would not want an entire mail list to receive your response intended only for the sender. The same applies for selecting "Reply to All" instead of "Reply."

HTML or Text?

Should you send e-mail messages as text or as HTML? HTML messages allow you to basically send a Web page via e-mail. These HTML messages are far prettier and eye-catching than text, and studies have shown that HTML messages deliver significantly higher click-through rates. However, not all e-mail programs support HTML, and therefore any HTML messages sent to users of noncompatible e-mail programs will not be able to be viewed. This issue will only be compounded as more and more people access their e-mail from e-mail enabled cell phones, Palm Pilots, and other devices.

Always Use Your Signature Files

As discussed previously, signature files are a great marketing tool. Always attach your signature file to your online communication. (See Chapter 8 for information on signature files.) Also, ensure that the signature files are appropriate for the intended audience.

Discerning Use of Attachments

If you are sending a fairly large volume of data, you may want to send it as an attached file to your e-mail message. However, only include an e-mail attachment if you have the recipient's permission to send an attached file. You would never consider going to someone's home, letting yourself in, finding your way into their living room, and then leaving your brochure on the coffee table. However, people do the online equivalent of this when they send an unsolicited attachment. The attachment is sent across the Internet to the recipient's computer and is downloaded and stored on the computer's hard drive. This is considered quite rude and, in most cases, unwanted.

Also, unless the recipient of your e-mail is aware of the file size and is expecting it, don't send an attachment that is larger than 50K. Although your Internet connection might be a cable modem or a T1 line and a 3MB file is sent in seconds, the person who is receiving your message and attachment might be using a 14.4 Kbps modem and a slow machine. If you send a 3 MB file, it might take the person with the 14.4 Kbps modem two hours to download the file. Needless to say, he or she won't be too pleased.

Another factor to consider when sending an unsolicited attachment is that the attachment you are sending may be incompatible with the operating system or the software on the recipient's system. Someone using a Macintosh with Corel WordPerfect installed may not be able to read a Microsoft Word 2000 document sent as an attachment. Thus, you will have wasted your time sending the file and the recipient's time downloading the file.

Viruses
Programs that contaminate a user's hard drive, often with unwanted results.

Finally, it is a well-known fact that e-mail attachments can act as carriers for computer **viruses.** You may unknowingly send someone an attachment with a virus, and even if the file you send is virus-free, you may still take the blame if recipients find a virus on their system just because you sent them an attachment. Basically, avoid sending e-mail attachments of any variety unless you have the recipient's permission. Be mindful of the size of the file you intend to send, compatibility with other platforms, and computer viruses. One alternative to sending a large attachment is to post the file on a Web server, and in your e-mail message direct users to a URL from which they can download the file.

Before You Click on "Send"

There are a number of things you should do before you send an important e-mail, especially if it is going to a number of people. Send a test message to yourself or a colleague so that you can check that the word wrap looks good, that the text is formatted properly, and that it displays as you want it to. Check that there are no typos, errors, or omissions.

Expressing Yourself with Emoticons and Shorthand

In verbal communication, you provide details on your mood, meaning, and intention through voice inflections, tone, and volume. You also give clues about your meaning and intention through facial expression and body language. E-mail does not allow for the same expression of feeling. The closest thing we have to this online is the use of **emoticons.**

> **Emoticons**
> Symbols made from punctuation marks and letters that look like facial expressions.

The word "emoticons" is an acronym for "emotions" and "icons." Emoticons are combinations of keyboard characters that give the appearance of a stick figure's emotions. They have to be viewed sideways and are meant to be smiling, frowning, laughing, and so on. Emoticons let you communicate your meaning and intentions to your reader. For example, if your boss gives you an assignment via e-mail and your response is, "Thanks a lot for unloading your dirty work on me," your boss may become upset at your obvious defiance. But if you replied with this: "Thanks a lot for unloading your dirty work on me :-)," your boss would understand that you were jokingly accepting the assignment.

Emoticons enable you to add a little personality and life to your text messages. However, their use is not universal and should generally not be used in business correspondence. Some of the more commonly used emoticons include

:-)	Smiling
:-@	Screaming
:-0 or :-o	Wow!
:-p	Tongue wagging
;-)	Wink
(-:	I'm left-handed
:-V	Shout
:-&	Tongue-tied
:-r	Tongue hanging out
;-(or ;-<	Crying
:-#	My lips are sealed!
:-*	Oops!

:-S	I'm totally confused.
8-0	No way!
:-	Skeptical
:-<	Sad or frown
~~:-(	I just got flamed!
%-0	Bug-eyed
:\	Befuddled
:-D	Laughing, big smile
}:->	Devilish, devious

E-mail shorthand is used in newsgroups and other e-mail to represent commonly used phrases. Some common abbreviations are

- BTW   By the way

- IMHO   In my humble opinion

- IMO   In my opinion

- IOW   In other words

- JFYI   Just for your information

- NBD   No big deal

- NOYB   None of your business

- TIA   Thanks in advance

- PMFJI   Pardon me for jumping in

- OIC   Oh, I see . . .

- OTL   Out to lunch

- OTOH   On the other hand

- LOL   Laughing out loud

- LMHO   Laughing my head off

- ROFL — Rolling on the floor laughing

- BFN — Bye for now

- CYA — See ya!

- FWIW — For what it's worth

- IAE — In any event

- BBL — Be back later

- BRB — Be right back

- RS — Real soon

- WYSIWYG — What you see is what you get

- <g> — Adding a grin

Since e-mail shorthand is most commonly used in newsgroups and chat rooms, you will be most successful when using these acronyms with others who are familiar with them.

Permission-based E-mail Marketing

Permission and privacy are critical to the success of any e-mail marketing campaign. Although unsolicited direct mail may be generally accepted or at least tolerated by many consumers, the rules are completely different online. Unsolicited e-mail runs the risk of damaging your company's reputation, not to mention the very real possibilities of flames, public blacklisting, hack attacks, and even having your Internet services revoked. Online consumers are very quick to let you know when you have crossed the line, and unsolicited e-mail (or spam) definitely crosses the line. Because of this, online marketers are using many techniques to get their customers, potential customers, and site visitors to give them "permission" to send them e-mail on a regular basis.

Permission marketing is really a win–win situation. Recipients receive information that they asked to receive, and the marketer is communicating with an audience that is genuinely interested in what is being marketed; otherwise the recipients would not have given their "permission" to receive the e-mail. Online marketers claim that permission e-mail marketing is one of the best ways to boost customer retention and boost sales. Permission e-mail marketing generally yields response rates 10 times that of banner advertising.

So how do you get this coveted permission? Generally you have to provide something of value and of interest to your target market. There are many opportunities on your Web site to ask for permission. The more repeat traffic generators on your site, the more opportunities you can provide for your Web site visitors to give you the permission (see Chapter 3 for repeat traffic generators). You should leverage repeat traffic generators with permission marketing and accelerate responses with a call to action. Let me provide you with some typical examples

- Click here to join our mail list and receive our monthly newsletter filled with great tips.

- Click here to be notified when we update our Web site.

- Click here to receive our weekly e-specials via e-mail.

- Click here to be notified when we update our online coupons.

- Click here to be notified when we introduce new products to our catalogue.

- Click here to be notified when we change our monthly free offer.

- Click here to be notified when we change our free sample offer.

- Click here to be notified when we introduce a new contest with great prizes.

- Click here to be notified when we update our What's New page.

- Want to receive our tip of the week via e-mail? Click here.

You get the picture. Almost every page on your Web site provides an opportunity for you to offer permission marketing. Of course, when site visitors click, they are taken to a screen where they add themselves to your mail list. Your mail list program should keep track of the element the visitor gave you permission to send.

Permission marketing enjoys its success because it is personal, relevant, and anticipated. Your messages should be personalized, enhancing the one-to-one relationship marketing element.

Privacy is a very big issue when a Web site visitor is deciding whether to give you an e-mail address or not. It is very important to assure your visitors that you will not pass on their e-mail address to others and you will not use it for anything but the purpose intended. Your privacy policy should clearly be evident on your Web site.

Using Automated Mail Responders—Mailbots and Infobots

Automated mail responders act like fax-back systems. They send requested information via e-mail automatically to the person who made the request. Having an autoresponder is like having a 24-hour, 7-day-a-week, 365-day-a-year online answering machine that provides information within seconds to anyone requesting information on your products or services. There are also autoresponders that can send multiple follow-up messages that can be scheduled. Having autoresponders send frequently requested information and follow up with your potential customers can save you time and money. One of the biggest benefits of these autoresponders is that your customers and potential customers are provided with an immediate response. Some of the better autoresponders provide personalization so that your response includes the requester's name in the subject line and throughout the response. This can be effective in making an impact and getting the recipient's attention.

You can ask your Internet service provider (ISP) for details on autoresponder services they may offer. Alternatively, you can also do a search on "mailbots" or "autoresponders" to find any third-party companies that can provide you with these services. When selecting an autoresponder, make sure it will allow you an unlimited number of responses and not something like 100 responses per month plus a charge per response over 100. Also ensure that there is no fee for updating responses from your autoresponder.

You can make information on your company, your products, your services, and your marketing materials easily accessible 24 hours a day, 7 days a week, 365 days a year through mailbots. Examples of information that you can easily provide through this service are

- Catalogue and price lists

- Product information, specs, white sheets

- Brochures

- Reviews and testimonials

- Press releases

- Newsletters

- Application forms

- Annual reports

- Award announcements

- Sample reports

These types of information could be placed on your Web site. However, you may choose to promote them by way of an autoresponder so that you can obtain customer data prior to providing the customers with the information they are requesting from you. Ask them for their e-mail address, mailing address, phone number, and answers to any marketing-related questions you may have. This type of data can be useful for targeting individuals in a future e-mail marketing campaign.

Autoresponders can also be used to personalize and build relationships and provide outstanding customer service. For instance, even if you are out of the office, you may set an autoresponder personal note that might consist of something like the following:

Thanks for your e-mail. Sorry, I am out of town and am unable to access my e-mail on a regular basis. If your message is time-sensitive, please contact my assistant Anne at 902/468-2578 or via e-mail at anne@connexnetwork.com. She has my itinerary and telephone numbers where I can be reached. I'll be back in the office Monday and will catch up on correspondence at that time.

Regards,
Susan

Obviously, it would be better to be able to respond immediately, but if you are unavailable, an "out-of-office" message such as the preceding one is an example of outstanding customer service. You are letting your customers know that they are important to you even though you are unavailable.

Autoresponders also provide an excellent means of promoting your company. Each time someone sends you a request for information, the autoresponder should include a short marketing blurb along with the requested information. This marketing technique will not be viewed as unsolicited e-mail because the person asked for it. Change the autoresponder message until you find the one that generates the best response. Autoresponders are easy to set up and easy to change, so your marketing message can be modified in an instant. See the Internet Resources at the end of this chapter for more information.

E-mail Marketing Tips

Be prepared. You will receive a number of e-mails requesting information on your company, your products, your locations, and so on, from people who have seen your e-mail address on letterhead, ads, business cards, and sig.files. Don't wait for the first inquiry before you begin to develop your company materials. Here are some tips. Following them will make you more prepared to respond.

Include a Brochure and Personal Note

Have an electronic brochure available that you can easily access and send via e-mail. Try to send a personal note in your e-mail along with any material requested.

Gather a Library of Responses

Different people will ask a number of the same questions, and over time you will be able to develop a library of responses to these frequently asked questions. You can save a lot of time by copying and pasting the answers to FAQs into your e-mail responses. Again, always make sure to personalize your responses.

Have More Than One E-mail Account

By having a number of different e-mail accounts, you can develop databases of all the people who have sent you a message—sorted by their interests. (You will know their interests by which mailbox they choose to send an e-mail to.) For example, you may be able to tell that a person is interested in your virus scanners but not your game software, or interested in your information on making animated GIFs but not in your virus archive.

GIF
Graphical Image File.

The tactic of using separate e-mail accounts and filtering them into different mailboxes can be used for many marketing purposes other than developing e-mail lists. An example would be to place the same advertisement in three different magazines. Associate a different e-mail address with each ad, and determine which ad generates the best response by reviewing the number of responses sent to the different e-mail addresses. You will then know which magazine to use in the future for the best response.

Have More Than One E-mail Folder

You want to be able to target your customers based on their interests and past purchases as much as possible. The more you can personalize your messages to your target audience, the greater success you will achieve with your Internet marketing campaigns. Organizing your e-mail inbox into distinct folders will assist you in sorting current customers from potential customers and further identifying these individuals by their interests.

For instance, if your online business sells books, music, and electronic equipment, create a separate folder in your e-mail program to contain all of the e-mail inquiries you have received from people interested in books. Then, create other folders for people who have written to you about certain music CDs, electronic equipment, and so on. In the future, you will be able to market to these individuals directly based on their specific, expressed interest from the past. This is the crux of opt-in e-mail marketing.

Run an Opt-In E-mail Marketing Campaign

An opt-in e-mail marketing campaign is perhaps the best means to reach your target audience. "Opt-in" refers to the fact that people can willingly subscribe and unsubscribe from your e-mail list. This is important because if people do not want mail from you and you send them unsolicited e-mail, you could be accused of spamming. Spam is the scourge of the Internet and a pet peeve of many people. If it is reported to your ISP that you are sending unsolicited bulk e-mail, you could lose your Internet account.

Send mail only to people who have expressed prior interest in your business, and allow them to unsubscribe themselves from your mailing list if they choose. As mentioned earlier in this chapter, you can use the blind carbon copy method or a specialized e-mail application to conduct an e-mail marketing campaign. Most e-mail marketing software packages will permit you to easily add or subtract new subscribers from your mailing list. These applications also create more personalized messages than can be achieved using blind carbon copy.

Following Formalities with E-mail Netiquette

When writing e-mails, remember these points.

- Be courteous. Remember your please's and thank-you's.

- Reply promptly—within 24 hours.

- Be brief.

- Use lowercase characters. Capitals indicate SHOUTING!

- Use emoticons where appropriate.

- Check your grammar and spelling.

- Use attachments sparingly.

- Do not send unsolicited bulk e-mail.

Reply Promptly

People expect an answer the same day or the next day at the latest. E-mail communication is like voice mail. If you do not respond within 24 hours, you send a very clear message to your clients, potential clients, and colleagues: "Your communication is not important to me." Respond within 24 hours even if the message is, "Sorry, I can't get to this immediately. I'll try to have a reply for you by the end of the week." This may be a response you will want to save in a readily available file from which you can copy and paste it into an e-mail message. A prompt reply is better than no reply at all. The people writing you for information will appreciate the fact that you felt their messages are important enough to respond to immediately.

The Heart of Customer Service

Although most customer correspondence via e-mail is very pleasant and businesslike, you will occasionally encounter people who are displeased with the service they have received from you. Very often, a series of courteous, prompt e-mail responses can turn a disgruntled customer into a customer for life. Taking a potentially disagreeable situation and reversing it to a positive one is the heart of customer service. Following is a real example of how a client turned such a situation around. This excerpt was provided to me by Donna Ross of the Shambhala Sun magazine at a recent seminar and has been included with the permission of

Donna and the Shambhala Sun *(http://www.shambhalasun.com)*. The name and address of the subscriber have been changed.

Customer's first message:

> *Dear Shambhala Sun Folk:*
>
> *I sent in a change of address form back a few months ago, but I have not been receiving the latest issues of your magazine at my new address. The last one I received was the January issue at my old address. So let's try again:*
>
> *Name: Joe Subscriber*
>
> *Old Address:*
> *100 Some Street*
> *Anaheim, CA 92999*
>
> *New Address:*
> *49494 Another Street*
> *San Jose, CA 92000*
>
> *My home phone number is (999) 999-9999.*
>
> *Thank you for your help and consideration on this matter.*
>
> *Sincerely,*
>
> *Joe Subscriber*

Shambhala Sun's Response:

> *Dear Joe:*
>
> *We do have your new address in our system. Your May issue should be arriving there any minute now. I will send you the missed March issue in this evening's mail. I notice that we have the city for your new address listed as Laguna Hills. In*

*your e-mail, you have it as San Jose. Please let me know which
of the two is more accurate. Thanks.*

Donna Ross
Shambhala Sun Subscriptions

Customer's second message:

*How did you know? The May issue arrived in my mailbox
this very day! As I was just in a fairly bad auto accident and
am laid up, it is most welcome. Thanks for your speedy reply.*

Sincerely,

Joe Subscriber

Shambhala Sun's Response:

*Actually, it is my job to know. :-) Sorry to hear you are hurt.
Heal well.*

Donna Ross
Shambhala Sun Subscriptions

Customer's final message:

*Thanks Donna for your concern. It's no surprise that
Shambhala Sun has folks like you working there. Consider me
a subscriber for life.*

Sincerely,

Joe Subscriber

*P.S.—Although my car was totaled, I am doing fine and
healing quickly.*

End of correspondence thread

As has been clearly demonstrated by the example, the value of strong customer relations is immeasurable. If you take great care to respond quickly and courteously to your customers' (even when they're not happy) e-mail messages, you can win them over for life. Nothing exceeds the value of a lifetime customer.

Internet Resources for Chapter 9

Everything E-mail
http://everythingemail.net
Information and links to make your e-mail account more productive and fun. Resources, guides, and a glossary make things easier for you to understand. This is an extensive Web site dedicated exclusively to e-mail and e-mail services.

123 Promote
http://www.123promote.com/workbook/plan1.htm
E-mail guide to e-mail styles, mail merging, autoresponders, autoreminders, netiquette, headers, signature files, announcements, press releases, business administration, free designs, mailing list announcements, newsgroup announcements, office automation, mass e-mailing, publicity, form letters, form folders, e-mailed databases, programs, and software.

A Beginner's Guide to Effective E-mail
http://www.Webfoot.com/advice/email.top.html
Help in writing the e-mail you need. Formats and why you need e-mail are all explained in detail.

Neophyte's Guide to Effective E-mail
http://www.Webnovice.com/email.htm
This site goes through, step-by-step, the important issues you should keep in mind from start to send.

I Will Follow.com E-mail Tips
http://www.iwillfollow.com/email.htm
This site offers advice to beginners on all aspects of using e-mail.

Smith Family Internet Marketing Support
http://www.smithfam.com/news/ap12.html
"The Secrets of E-mail Marketing Success," an article by Lesley Anne Lowe.

Windweaver
http://www.windweaver.com/emoticon.htm
Recommended emoticons for e-mail communication.

Dave Barry's Guide to Emoticons
http://www.randomhouse.com/features/davebarry/emoticon.html
Good resource for emoticons and shorthand. His site has an Emoticon Gallery with lots of examples (3,069 at last count) and an area where you can make your own.

EmailAddresses.com
http://www.emailaddresses.com
A directory of numerous free e-mail services including POP accounts, e-mail forwarding, newsletters, and so on.

Aaron's Emoticons
http://www.teleport.com/~rhubarbs/faces.htm
Another extensive source of emoticons.

E-mail—The Mining Company
http://email.miningco.com/internet/email/
Updated weekly, this site consists of articles and links to e-mail resources on many topics: beginning e-mail, finding people, free e-mail, greeting cards, privacy, and much more.

10

Effective Promotional Use of Newsgroups

It is estimated that over 10 million people read newsgroups, making newsgroups an ideal marketing vehicle. The number of newsgroups is increasing, with over 100,000 different topics now estimated. People participate in newsgroups by "posting" or e-mailing comments, questions, or answers to other participants' questions, thus taking part in a conversation or thread. Using proper netiquette is important. To do this, read the FAQ files and rules, "lurk" first, and stay on topic. In this chapter, we cover

- The benefits of using newsgroups in your marketing plan

- Newsgroup netiquette

- Reading the FAQ files, abiding by the rules, and lurking

- How to advertise if advertising is not allowed

- Developing your Usenet marketing strategy

- Identifying your target newsgroups

- Participating in this online community

- How to respond correctly to messages

- How to start your own newsgroup

- Cross-posting and spamming

- Using signature files

Newsgroups—What Are They?

Every day, millions of people from all over the globe enter a virtual community that they share with others who are interested in the same topic. These people are brought together by their common interest in the topic of discussion. While they are in this virtual community, only that specific topic is discussed. There are many communities that are discussing different topics. You can visit and participate in as many of them as you wish.

These virtual communities are called Usenet **newsgroups**. They have their own section of the Internet. There is the World Wide Web part of the Internet where there are many Web sites that you can visit and read, and there is the e-mail part of the Internet where you can send and receive messages, and there is the Usenet newsgroup part of the Internet where discussions are taking place about many different topics.

> **Newsgroups**
> A discussion group on the Internet that focuses on a specific subject.

Usenet newsgroups are hierarchical and are arranged by subject. Each newsgroup is dedicated to a discussion of a particular topic, such as antique cars, home schooling, artificial intelligence, or the latest hot band.

Visitors to these virtual communities, or newsgroups, can "post" messages. These messages may be questions or comments or answers to other participants' questions. Everyone who visits the newsgroup views these "postings." Often many visitors participate in these discussions, and every side of the issue is presented.

Usenet has been defined as follows:

Usenet is the Internet's public forum, comprising thousands of newsgroups, each of which is devoted to the public discussion of a narrow, chartered topic such as microbrews, baseball cards, arthritis research, or traveling in Africa.

There are three types of newsgroup visitors

- People asking questions or advice

- People providing answers or advice

- People who read the discussion without taking part

The Changing Face of Newsgroups

Usenet newsgroups started out as places where academics conducted discussions on research and quickly expanded to include newsgroups on every topic imaginable, with participants having wonderful conversations relevant to the topic. Then the commercialization of the Web hit, and today there are many newsgroups that are overrun with advertisements with very little topical discussion taking place. However, there are still many newsgroups that have vibrant discussions with loyal participants that provide a great opportunity for reaching and communicating with your target market.

Every visitor to a newsgroup made an effort to get there. He or she chose the specific newsgroup for a reason, usually an interest in the topic being discussed. If your business's products or services are related to the topic of discussion, you have found a group of your target market (they have prequalified themselves) in one place interested in discussing what you have to offer.

Newsgroups—An Ideal Marketing Vehicle

Usenet facilitates the exchange of an abundance of information on every topic imaginable. Many newsgroups are tight-knit communities with very loyal residents. Each group's readers are interested in the newsgroup topic, so when you find a newsgroup related to your product or service, it is likely you have found members of your target market.

The number of newsgroups is steadily increasing. Currently it is estimated that more than 100,000 topics are available. Different newsgroups have varying numbers of readers. Some are read by hundreds of thousands of readers a day, and others see very little traffic. The newsgroups you decide to participate in may be read by a relatively small number of people or have a large number of participants. Large isn't always better. A smaller group may provide you with a better chance of having your message read by your ideal target market; a larger group will provide you with better exposure by sheer volume.

Whether you pick a large group or a small group depends on your objectives and also on your product or service. For example, even though a posting to alt.politics may be seen by 300,000 readers, if what you are trying to sell is reproduction Model T Fords, it will not likely generate more potential business than a posting to a Usenet group such as rec.antiquecars.misc with only 1,000 readers. Not to mention that if your posting to alt.politics is inappropriate for that group, you will have done more harm than good. Newsgroup readers do not appreciate messages unrelated to their topic posted to their newsgroup, especially if they are advertisements.

If you use an online service, you can still participate in newsgroups because they have similar services. CompuServe has forums or special-interest groups, AOL has forums and clubs, and Prodigy has forums and bulletin boards. The same rules regarding participation, acceptable messages, and marketing activities generally apply. Not only are newsgroups helpful marketing tools, they can also help you identify competitors and trends in your industry, find valuable information from experts in your field, and perform market research activities.

The Benefits of Newsgroups

There are many ways online marketers can benefit from participating in newsgroups:

- Reaching prospective customers. You can immediately reach thousands of your targeted potential customers with a single message.

- Communicating with existing customers. You can provide your loyal customers with valuable information.

- Market research. You can use newsgroups to find out the latest trends, customer needs, what people are looking for, and what they are talking about. These newsgroups can be beehives of information where you can check out your competition and gather invaluable data on your market.

- Reputation building. By answering people's questions and helping to solve their problems, you will build your reputation as an expert in the field.

- Increased Traffic. You can direct people to your commercial Web site if you do it in an informative way.

Thousands of Newsgroup Categories

Newsgroups are organized into different types of discussions or categories. Each of the major categories has lots of individual newsgroups in which you can participate. Major newsgroup categories include

- **alt** Discussions on alternative topics.

- **biz** Discussions on business topics. You may find groups that allow advertising here.

- **comp** Discussions on computer hardware- and software-related topics.

- **humanities** Discussions on fine arts, literature, and philosophy topics.

- **misc** Discussions of miscellaneous topics that don't have their own categories such as employment, health, and other issues.

- **news** Discussions on Usenet news and administration.

- **rec** Discussions on recreation topics like games, hobbies, and sports.

- **sci** Discussions on science.

- **soc** Discussions on social issues.

- **talk** Making conversation.

Each of the major categories has a number of subgroups, and each of the subgroups has a number of sub-subgroups. For example, under the rec major group you will find a subgroup rec.sports. Here the discussion revolves around all kinds of sports. Under the subgroup rec.sports you will find sub-subgroups and sub-sub-subgroups, for example:

rec.sports

rec.sports.hockey

rec.sports.hockey.NHL

rec.sports.hockey.NHL.BostonBruins

As you can see, the longer the name, the narrower is the discussion that is taking place.

Target Appropriate Newsgroups

With the large number of Usenet newsgroups that currently exist and the additional groups that are being introduced every day, it is a formidable task to identify appropriate newsgroups for your company's Internet marketing activities. First, you need to determine which newsgroups your prospective customers frequent.

Look for a close fit between a newsgroup and the product or service you are offering. For example, if your company sells software that aids genealogical work, then one appropriate newsgroup for your business might be soc.genealogy.methods. Try finding newsgroups that your target market may enjoy reading or ask your clients or customers which newsgroups they participate in or find interesting. Find and make note of appropriate newsgroups that might be of interest to your target customers.

There are many ways to find appropriate Usenet newsgroup listings: More than 80,000 mailing lists and 30,000 newsgroups are located at the Liszt Web Site, *http://www.liszt.com.* You can also do a search using the newsgroup functions of the two leading browsers, Netscape Navigator and Microsoft Internet Explorer.

Most newsreader programs have a search capability. Search the newsgroups for keywords that relate to your target market, your product, or your service to identify possible appropriate newsgroups for your marketing effort. Another good place to start is Google.com *(http://groups.google.com).* Here you can conduct a keyword search of the Usenet newsgroups. The search results are displayed in chronological order, with the results at the top being the most recently used. You should choose keywords appropriate for your target customer or client. These methods will identify a fairly large list of potential newsgroups that may be included in your marketing activities.

If your company specializes in providing exotic vacations to Mexico, you may want to search Deja.com for keywords like "Mexico, vacation, travel, tropical, resorts, beaches," and so on, to find potential newsgroups for your marketing effort. A benefit of the Deja.com site is that you can post to the newsgroups directly from the site. You don't have to go through alternative software to do so.

Once you have done your preliminary research and compiled a long list of what you think are the most appropriate newsgroups related to your target market, you are ready to investigate further and qualify your list. The next step is to go to the Usenet Info Center Launch Pad at *http://sunsite.unc.edu/usenet-i/home.html.* There you can look up the newsgroups on your list. From this site you will be able to find out where the FAQ files for each newsgroup are located. The FAQ files will usually provide information on the newsgroup's stance on advertising. Info Center Launch Pad will also provide you with details on the number of people participating in the group.

Read the FAQ Files and Abide by the Rules

Charter
Established rules and guidelines.

Read the FAQ files, **charter,** and rules about posting and advertising for each of your target newsgroups. It is very important that you abide by all the rules. If the FAQ files do not mention the group's stance on commercial advertising and announcements, then go back to Deja News. Conduct a search based on the group's name and charter. This will tell you where the newsgroup stands on commercial activity.

Lurking for Potential Customers

Once you have narrowed your potential newsgroup list, you will want to visit each and every one to determine if the participants of the newsgroup are, in fact, potential customers. Spend time **lurking**. Monitor the types of messages that are being posted. Is there likely to be an opportunity for you to contribute? Are the participants your target market? Research the newsgroup to ascertain if it will appeal to your customers. The name of the newsgroup may not reveal what the newsgroup is about, so take your time and make sure.

Lurking
Browsing without posting.

Tips on Posting Messages

After you have become familiar with the rules of your selected newsgroup, have spent some time lurking, and have decided that the newsgroup is one where your target market is participating, you may begin to post messages. Remember to abide by the rules! If the rules do not allow advertising, then do not blatantly post an ad. To take full advantage of the newsgroup, you have to gain the trust of its members. With one wrong message, you could outrage all of the potential customers who participate in the newsgroup.

It is a good idea to run a test before you post a message to a newsgroup. Doing a test will show you how the posting works and will prevent you from making a mistake when it comes to the real thing. For a test mechanism, go to the newsgroup misc.test.

Becoming a respected member in a newsgroup is a way to promote yourself as well as your company. Provide valuable responses— the readers can tell when you are making a valuable contribution and when you are just advertising. In time you may forget that you began reading the newsgroup to promote your business. You will find yourself reading newsgroups in order to participate in stimulating discussions. You will be discussing anything and everything about the newsgroup subject. Only mention your Web site when you find an appropriate opportunity to bring your business knowledge into the conversation.

Newsgroups exist for specific purposes. They can be designed for discussions, news announcements, postings related to particular topics, and even buying and selling goods. They may have hundreds of messages sorted and available for access at any point in time. Newsgroup participants will decide whether to open or pass up your posted message based on the words in the subject area. Make your subject short and catchy so that your message will be read and not be passed over. Try to put the most important words of the subject first. This is a very critical part in posting a message to a newsgroup. Some people adjust the screen to see only the first few words in the subject area. When deciding on the text for the subject area, think about what keywords someone would use to search for information on the content of your message. The worst thing that you can do is post a message to a newsgroup with no subject at all. This will definitely receive no attention and is basically a waste of your time.

Start your message with a short description of how it relates to the group's main topic. People are looking for answers to specific questions, so it is rude to jump into the conversation with a topic that doesn't match the one in the subject line. You should attempt to get your message across right away. You should get to the point of your message in the first sentence. By doing so you will catch the readers' attention and ensure that they will read the entire message.

Message length should be short, no longer than 24 lines. Messages should briefly discuss main points and ask if readers would like to have more information. Once people show an interest in the information you are offering, your message can be as long as needed.

When responding to a message in a newsgroup, you have the option of privately responding to the individual who posted the message or responding through the newsgroup. Determine which is more appropriate under the given circumstances. If your message will be of value to the entire group or will appropriately promote your company's capabilities, then post the response to the newsgroup for all to see. If you think that your company has a solution for the individual and would like to provide details to the "target customer," but feel that it would not benefit the other members of the group, then deliver a private response. Often you will choose to do both because once the answer to a question has been received, the original poster may not visit the newsgroup for awhile and you want to make sure he or she has the benefit or your posting. Whichever approach you take, make sure that you respond as quickly as possible so that the first message is still fresh in the mind of the recipient.

Tips to Ensure That Your Messages Will Be Well Received

Here are some basic rules to help you post well-received messages.

Keep to the Newsgroup Topic
Make sure you always stay on the newsgroup topic of discussion. People participate in specific newsgroups because of that subject and don't appreciate off-topic postings.

Stay on the Thread
When responding to a message, use the Reply option to stay on the same thread. When you reply without changing the subject line, your message will appear immediately below the message you are responding to in the newsgroup. This makes it easy for others to follow the discussion. For an example of this, see Figure 10.1.

Figure 10.1. It is very important to stay on thread. As you can see in this travel newsgroup, the Painted Desert messages are staying on thread. The message has been replied to, keeping the same subject line.

Make a Contribution

Informed, quality responses to people's questions will give you credibility with the group and will reflect well upon you and your company. If you post positive and informative information, visitors will return to the newsgroups and look for your posts.

Don't Post Commercials or Advertisements

Advertising is not welcome in most newsgroups, and many charters specifically disallow the posting of ads. Read the FAQ files before posting a message. If the newsgroup does not allow commercial messages or ads, don't post them.

You Don't Have to Have the Last Word

Don't post gratuitous responses in newsgroups. Never post a message with just a "Thanks" or "I like it" if you have nothing else to contribute. If you feel such a response is warranted or would like to discuss the issue privately, send a private e-mail to the person to convey your appreciation or opinion.

Signature Files as Your e-Business Card

A **signature file**, or sig.file as it is commonly referred to, is your e-business card. It is a short message at the end of an e-mail. Most, if not all, e-mail programs allow for the use of a signature file. Sig.files can be attached at the end of your message when you post to a Usenet newsgroup or a mailing list, even if the group does not allow advertising.

Signature file
An e-business card usually attached to e-mail.

You can use your sig.file in a number of clever ways. Sig.files can be simple—listing only phone numbers and addresses—or they can be virtual ads for your company. They can be very useful in providing exposure for your company. You can use your sig.file to offer some substantial information, such as letting people know about a special event, informing people about an award or honor your company has received, or promoting a specific product or service your company has to offer.

You can design and use different sig.files for posting to different newsgroups. A particular sig.file may be appropriate for one newsgroup but not for another. Always ensure that the message in your sig.file is appropriate for its audience.

Keep your sig.file short. Usually four to eight lines is a good size. There is nothing more annoying than a sig.file that is longer than the text of the message to which it is attached, or one that resembles a brochure.

Sig.files should include the following:

- Contact name

- Business name

- URL

- Address

- E-mail address

- Telephone number

- Fax number

- A brief company tag line or a company slogan

This is an example of what a sig.file looks like:

Jane Doe, Marketing Assistant
jdoe@bug.com
Sunnyvale Volkswagen
101 Main Street
Woodstock, NY 10010
Toll-Free Tel: (800) 555-1001; Fax: (800) 555-1000
Visit *www.bug.com* to see our latest models

For a complete discussion of sig.files and how to use them, see Chapter 8.

Newsgroup Advertising Hints

Newsgroups have been developed for different audiences and different topics. Some newsgroups are dedicated to posting advertisements. If advertising is appropriate for your company, the following newsgroup types might be included in your Internet marketing strategy. Most of the newsgroups that allow advertising are readily identifiable. The newsgroup name itself might include one of the following:

- biz

- classified

- for sale

- marketplace

Again, read the FAQ files and lurk to determine if the newsgroup is appropriate for your target market before you post. Use a short, catchy subject line with keywords at the beginning—the subject will determine whether your message warrants a read or a pass. Avoid ALL CAPI-TALS. This is equivalent to shouting on the Internet. Stay away from !!!!, ****, @@@@, and other such symbols.

When you have found a newsgroup whose participants include your target market but the newsgroup does not allow advertising, don't de-spair. By responding to queries or providing information that is of genuine interest to the newsgroup, you have the opportunity to attach your sig.file. A sig.file can be as effective as an ad if it is designed properly. Your message should offer substantial information to the discussion. (A thinly veiled excuse to get your sig.file posted will not be appreciated.) If your information is relevant and of value to the participants of the newsgroup, the fact that your sig.file is an advertisement will not mat-ter—in fact, it may add credibility to the information you have pro-vided and enhance your company's reputation.

Cross-Posting and Spamming

Cross-posting is posting identical messages to a number of relevant newsgroups. Doing this is considered to be inappropriate because of the number of common users in associated newsgroups. Spamming is posting identical or nearly identical messages to irrelevant newsgroups without care or regard for the posting guidelines, the newsgroup topic, or the interests of the group. Cross-posting and spamming will annoy the readers of the newsgroup. Doing these things will reflect badly on you and your company and will prevent you from achieving your online marketing objectives.

If you disobey proper newsgroup netiquette, you may quickly learn what a flame is. A flame is a reply that may be posted into a newsgroup, or sent to you by e-mail, that contains extremely negative feedback. In the worst cases, people have been sent e-mail that contain 100 copies of a 16MB file, which could take their computer hours to download or even crash the server. Although these acts are very immature, you must remember to obey newsgroup netiquette to make sure that this does not happen.

Sometime in your online postings, no matter how careful you are, someone is bound to get upset. Accept this as fact and learn how to handle flames appropriately. Be sensitive to complaints. Learn from them, but do not worry unnecessarily. If someone posts a message that reflects badly on your company, you have three options: Defend your comments in the newsgroup, send the person a private e-mail, or do nothing. Responding to the person via e-mail is the most appropriate response, even though in most cases your message will be ignored.

Earning Respect with Newsgroup Netiquette

Following are ten rules for netiquette. Incorporating them in your newsgroup posting will gain you respect by the other participants:

1. Don't use CAPITALS. They are akin to shouting on the Internet.

2. Don't post ads where they are not welcome.

3. Do provide valuable, on-topic information for the newsgroup.

4. Don't be rude or sarcastic.

5. Don't include the entire message you are replying to in your response. Only quote relevant sections of the original message.

6. Do a thorough review of your message before you post. Check your spelling and grammar. Check your subject; it should be short and catchy with the keywords first.

7. Do provide an appropriate sig.file.

8. Don't post messages that are too lengthy. Online communication tends to be one screen or less.

9. Don't spam or cross-post.

10. Don't post replies that contribute nothing to the discussion (e.g., "I agree" or "Thanks").

Have Your Own Newsgroup

You can start your own newsgroup if you feel it is warranted and appropriate. All group creation requests must follow set guidelines and are first met with discussion. If you need help, you can always find a body of volunteers who are experienced in the newsgroup creation process at *group-mentors@acpub.duke.edu*. They assist people with the formation and submission of good newsgroup proposals.

The Discussion

A request for discussion on creation of a new newsgroup should be posted to *news.announce.newsgroups* and *news.groups*. If desired, the request can also be posted to other groups or mailing lists that are related to the proposed topic. The name and charter of the proposed group and whether it will be moderated or unmoderated should be determined during the discussion period.

The Vote

The Usenet Volunteer Vote Takers (UVT) is a group of neutral third-party vote takers who currently handle vote gathering and counting for all newsgroup proposals. There should be a minimal delay between the end of the discussion period and the issuing of a call for votes. The call for votes should include clear instructions on how to cast a vote. The voting period should last for at least 21 days and no more than 31 days. Only the votes that are mailed to the vote taker will be counted.

The Result

At the completion of the voting period, the vote taker must post the vote tally to the applicable groups and mailing lists. The e-mail addresses and names (if available) of the voters are posted along with the tally. There will be a five-day waiting period, beginning when the voting results actually appear. During the waiting period there will be a chance to correct any errors in the voter list or the voting procedure. In order for a proposal to pass, 100 more YES/create votes must be received than NO/do not create votes. Also, two-thirds of the total number of votes must be in favor of creation. If a proposal fails to achieve two-thirds of the vote, then the matter cannot be brought up for discussion until at least six months has passed from the close of the vote.

The following locations will help you should you wish to create your own newsgroup:

- How to Format and Submit a Newgroup Proposal: *news. announce.newgroups, news.groups*

- How to Write a Good Newsgroup Proposal: *news. announce.newgroups, news.groups*

- Usenet Newsgroup Creation Companion: news.groups, *news. announce.newusers, news.answers*

Internet Resources for Chapter 10

Newsgroups
News.newusers.questions
News.announce.newusers
News.newusers

These provide information to new Usenet users on posting, finding appropriate newsgroups, netiquette, and other frequently asked questions new users are faced with.

Google—The Source for Internet Newsgroups!
http://groups.google.com
The Web site where you can read, search, participate in, and subscribe to more than 50,000 discussion forums, including Usenet newsgroups. Google has recently bought Deja.com, a resource for finding people, getting noticed, and getting answers to all sorts of questions. You can find discussion forums on any topic imaginable.

Liszt of Newsgroups
http://www.liszt.com/news
A complete listing of newsgroups organized by different categories. Has listed over 30,000 newsgroups and is the largest directory of newsgroups on the Web.

How to Advertise on Newsgroups
http://www.nsmi.com/noflames.html
How to Advertise on Newsgroups shows step-by-step techniques to follow so you won't get blacklisted. Everything you need to know about how to advertise in newsgroups and mailing lists without getting flamed.

Open Newsserver Search
http://www.muenz.com/sdienst/html/sgroup_e.html
English/German search engine that finds open news servers that carry newsgroups matching your search terms.

NIC—Master List
http://www.engl.uvic.ca/OnlineGuide/News/newsGroupsWel.html
See this master list for a description of newsgroups.

Talkway
http://www.talkway.com
This membership site attempts to provide a friendlier interface to the arcane structure of Usenet newsgroups.

11

Effective Promotion Through Publicly Accessible Mailing Lists

Internet mailing lists are quick and easy ways to distribute information to a large number of people. There are thousands of publicly available online lists. You can also create your own Internet mailing lists to keep your clients and prospects informed of company events, product announcements, and press releases. In this chapter, we cover

- How to identify appropriate publicly accessible mailing lists (discussion lists)

- Subscribing to the mailing list

- Writing messages that will be read

- Mailing list netiquette

- Creating your own mailing list

Connecting with Your Target Audience

Discussion mailing lists are publicly accessible and are focused on a particular subject matter. Participating in a discussion list relevant to your line of business can help you attract new customers. Discussion lists are organized hierarchically by subject matter in a way similar to Usenet newsgroups. Likewise, the membership rate of each discussion mailing list varies. People subscribe to particular lists to participate in that list and receive all of the postings that are sent to the group, generally because they have an interest in the topic. When you post a message to a mailing list, the message is sent out to everyone who has subscribed to the list by email.

Discussion mailing lists are quick and easy ways to distribute information to a large number of people interested in a particular topic. The difference between discussion mailing lists and newsgroups is that anyone on the Internet can visit newsgroups at any time and read any articles of interest, whereas a discussion list delivers all messages posted directly to the subscribers' email. Only discussion list subscribers can receive these messages. Newsgroups can be viewed by anyone with access to a news server. All they have to do is log onto the news server and enter the name of the newsgroup they wish to peruse, and they can view all postings made to that group. To subscribe to a discussion list, you have to send a subscription message to the list administrator and request permission to join the mailing list. Newsgroup postings can be viewed anonymously, but permission is required to receive and view postings to mailing lists.

Types of Publicly Accessible Mailing Lists

Publicly accessible mailing lists can be one of several types, each with varying degrees of control. Following is a discussion of the two major types of lists.

Moderated Discussion Lists

This type of list is maintained by a "gatekeeper" who filters out unwanted or inappropriate messages. If you try to post an advertisement where it is not permitted, your message will never make it out to the list of subscribers. Similarly, flames (i.e., publicly chastising another list member) are screened out. The gatekeeper will also keep the topic of discussion on track if a few members get off-topic.

Unmoderated Discussion Lists

An unmoderated list is operated without any centralized control or censorship. Many publicly accessible lists are of this type. All messages are automatically forwarded to subscribers. Unmoderated lists tend to have more blatant advertisements and flame wars because there is no gatekeeper to guide the discussion. It is then the responsibility of the list members to police their own actions. If the list participants aren't rigidly abiding by the rules and reprimanding others who stray, the list could end up being a landfill for spammers. When this happens, a lot of members will simply leave the list.

Targeting Appropriate Discussion Mailing Lists

There are thousands of publicly accessible lists online and a number of sites that provide lists of these mailing lists. Several of the most popular and comprehensive are

- Liszt at *http://www.liszt.com* (Figure 11.1)

- The List of Publicly Accessible Mailing Lists at *http://www.paml.net* (Figure 11.2)

- Tile.net at *http://tile.net/lists* (Figure 11.3)

- Topica at *http://www.topica.com* (Figure 11.4)

There are also companies online that specialize in providing targeted lists for a fee, much like purchasing a direct-mail list in the offline world. One company that provides this type of list is Post Master Direct Response at *www.postmasterdirect.com*. This company rents e-mail lists of people who have requested information on a particular topic. However,

Figure 11.1.   Liszt has a searchable index of publicly accessible mailing lists.

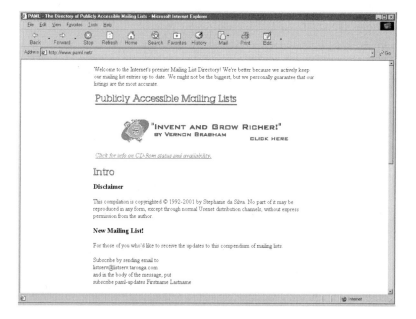

Figure 11.2.   The List of Publicly Accessible Mailing Lists.

Figure 11.3. Tile.net offers more publicly accessible mailing lists.

Figure 11.4. Topica provides access to thousands of mailing lists and discussion groups.

these differ from the discussion mailing lists that we described earlier in this chapter. E-mail lists are simply that—lists of e-mail addresses. If you subscribe to one of these lists, you are not entering into a discussion; you are placing yourself on a mailing list that will receive e-mail advertisements. However, from a marketing perspective, e-mail lists can be useful tools if they are targeted.

Bulk e-mail

A group of identical messages e-mailed to a large number of addresses at once.

Spam

Sending the same message to a large number of people who didn't ask for it. Sending people annoying mail.

Another option is to develop your own mailing list. This concept is discussed in the next chapter. Still another option is to purchase **bulk e-mail** lists. This is a questionable practice because it involves **spam**. Bulk e-mail lists are generally sold without the permission of the addressees, much like junk mailing lists. The recipients did not ask to be put on a mailing list. They are not aware of the fact that they are on a list and often do not appreciate being sent unsolicited e-mail. Another drawback is that usually these lists are not targeted. By using bulk e-mail lists, you run the risk of not reaching any of your target market. You also risk annoying those addressees who under other circumstances may have been interested in what you were trying to sell.

The correct choice depends on the market you are targeting. Some people use the shotgun approach to reach as many people as possible. We've all received e-mails that say, "Reach 5 million with our mailing list available for $29.95." After all, one of the major benefits of the Internet is reaching large numbers of people quickly. There is no excuse for this kind of "marketing." Even if someone is marketing a product with broad-based appeal, it does not grant him or her a license to spam the world with a marketing message. If it isn't "opt-in," don't send it. Nobody is going to be too impressed by receiving spam. Either the message will be deleted without being read or some of the recipients of the spam could complain to the sender's ISP and have the sender's Internet access revoked.

The best approach is to choose a list whose subscribers fit your target market as closely as possible. For example, if you are selling geographic information systems to municipalities, a shotgun approach is a waste of both your time and your resources. By using bulk e-mail, you raise the ire of thousands of recipients of your e-mail, destroy your corporate image, and potentially damage your professional credibility. In this case, a targeted list, even though it will likely be much smaller, will get a much higher-quality response rate. Less is sometimes better.

Finding the Right Mailing List

Whether you join a publicly accessible discussion mailing list or choose to purchase an opt-in e-mail list from one of the many online sources, you want to find a mailing list whose members are your target market. You will have to do your homework here, because there are thousands of mail lists to choose from.

There are various meta-indexes of publicly accessible mailing lists where you can search by title or by subject. Some of these sites provide detailed information on the mail lists, such as their content and the commands used to subscribe. We have provided information on a number of these resources in the Internet Resources section at the end of this chapter.

Once you have identified mail lists that have your target market as members, you will subscribe to those lists. To confirm that the list is appropriate for your marketing purposes, lurk a while to monitor the discussion taking place. Once this has been confirmed, you can begin participating in the list by providing valuable content. If advertising is not allowed, abide by the rules. However, signature files are generally allowed, and you can always have that one-line tag line or mini-ad to advertise where advertising isn't allowed.

Subscribing to Your Target Mailing Lists

Liszt *(http://www.liszt.com)*, tile.net/lists *(http://tile.net/lists)*, Topica *(www.topica.com)*, and the List of Publicly Accessible Mailing Lists *(www.paml.net)* are great resources and will provide you with not only a huge list of accessible mailing lists but also specific instructions for joining the particular lists you are interested in. Most lists are subscribed to by sending an e-mail message to the given address with "subscribe" in the subject line or the body of the message. There are variations on this theme, so you must check the instructions for joining each specific mailing list. After you subscribe, you generally will receive an e-mail response with the rules, FAQs, and instructions on how to use the list.

For the most part, all of the rules for posting to newsgroups apply to mailing lists as well. Read the rules carefully and abide by them. A lurking period should be considered before you post a message. This will help you observe what types of messages are posted and the commonly accepted practices for that particular group.

List Digests

When subscribing to a mail list, quite often you are given the option to subscribe or to subscribe-digest. When you subscribe, you receive each message to the mail list as it is posted. When you subscribe-digest, the messages are accumulated and sent in one e-mail, usually on an overnight basis. The compilation of many individual messages is sent to each subscriber as one bulk message. Many digests contain a table of contents. The good thing about a digest is that you do not receive as many separate e-mail messages and your mailbox doesn't become clogged up. Also, the digest administrator chooses all or only the best postings to include in the list digest. Therefore, blatant advertisements, flames, and postings containing repetitive subject matter are filtered out. In an unmoderated list, you would receive every single message posted to the list. Many of these postings may not be of interest to you and would be deleted anyway. The digest format simplifies things so that you get the information you need without filling your e-mail box.

Composing Effective Messages

As discussed in the previous chapter, your e-mails must be carefully prepared before you post to a mailing list. Remember to make your subject line relevant, keep your messages short and to the point, and always include your sig.file. If you are unsure whether your posting is appropriate for the group, you can send a test message to the moderator asking for advice.

Unlike newsgroups, the members of mailing lists receive all the messages directly into their mailbox every day. Some people prefer to receive the postings in digest form; that is, all the messages for that day are compiled into one e-mail sent to the recipient at the end of the day. At the beginning of the e-mail, the digest provides a listing of all the messages with the "From" and "Subject" identified, followed by the complete messages. Just as individuals who visit a newsgroup don't read all the messages, subscribers to publicly accessible discussion lists do not read every posting. They decide which messages to review based on the subject line. Thus, the content of the "Subject" field is extremely important.

You must never repeat the same or similar messages to a mailing list, as you might do in a newsgroup. Once members of a mailing list have seen your posted message, they will not appreciate seeing it again, whereas a newsgroup has different readers all the time and similar postings are acceptable if they are timed appropriately. The following tips on mailing list postings will assist you in becoming a respected member of their online community:

- Make sure that your messages are "on the subject." List subscribers don't want to receive announcements unrelated to their topic.

- You should be a regular contributor to your list before making any commercial announcement. If your mailing list does not allow advertising (most do not), use your sig.file. Sig.files are generally accepted. Ensure that you make effective use of your tag line to get your mini-ad into discussion mailing lists where blatant advertising is not permitted. (See Chapter 8 for advertising when advertising is not allowed.)

- Track and record your responses when you use a new mailing list. You should have a call to action in your posting, encouraging the readers to visit a specific page on your site or to send e-mail to an e-mail address designated solely for this purpose. Only by employing an appropriate mechanism to track responses will you know with any certainty which mailing lists are successful and which are not. It's amazing how well calls to action work. For some reason, people tend to do what they're told.

- Set reasonable and achievable goals. As a benchmark, in most e-mail marketing campaigns, a 1% to 3% response rate is considered a good response. However, if your mailing list is very targeted and you are offering something of interest or value to a particular group, your response rates should be significantly higher.

Building Your Own Private Mailing Lists

You may want to build your own mailing lists. Generating your own mailing lists is often beneficial because of the many marketing uses the lists have. They can be used to maintain an ongoing dialogue with existing customers regarding updates, support, specials, and so on. They can also be used to communicate with current and prospective customers through distribution of corporate newsletters, price lists, new catalogues, product updates, new product announcements, and upcoming events. A full discussion of private mail lists is provided in Chapter 12.

Starting Your Own Publicly Accessible Mailing List

You can create your own publicly accessible Internet mailing list. This is something you will want to give careful consideration to before you make your final decision. It takes lots of time and effort to do this right, so be sure you're ready and that there will be sufficient return on your investment. First you must give it a name that reflects the discussion that will take place and is enticing for your target market. You will have to draft a FAQ file or charter containing information on what the list is all about. You will have to develop guidelines for participation.

You should create a Web page for your list to provide information about the list as well as its charter and guidelines. You should provide an opportunity to subscribe from the Web site as well. This will add credibility to your mailing list.

Once the list is up and running, you will have to advertise it so that people will actually subscribe. You can promote your list by participating in newsgroups that relate to your mail list topic. Remember not to post blatant ads where advertising is not allowed. Contribute to the newsgroup with your postings and use a tag line in your signature file to promote your mail list. You can also trade e-mail sponsorships with other mailing lists for promotion purposes.

There are a number of places to appropriately announce your list. Get your mail list linked from the many lists of lists on the Internet.

We provide some of these in the Internet Resources at the end of this chapter. Make your list worth reading by ensuring that you and others have valuable information on the topic to share. You should make sure you include an opportunity for your subscribers to spread the word or to recommend your mail list to others. You can do this in your mail list messages and also through the companion Web page. In the newsletter or announcement mail lists where messages go only one way, it is easy to encourage your subscribers to send a copy to a friend who they think might be interested. If you encourage viral marketing in this way, you want to make sure you have included the how-to-subscribe information in the messages as well. When encouraging viral marketing through the companion Web page, make sure you include an appropriate call to action. It's amazing how well this works!

Escape the Unsolicited Bulk E-mail Trend

Bulk e-mail is any group of identical messages sent to a large number of addresses at one time. In some cases, bulk e-mail lists have been developed from opt-in lists, and the names are continually filtered through all of the universal remove lists. These lists are often categorized by subject and provide an acceptable marketing vehicle. If you are using opt-in lists and are removing unsubscribe requests from your database, this is considered a legitimate marketing campaign.

However, many bulk lists have been developed by unscrupulous means, and the people on the lists have no interest in or desire to receive unsolicited e-mail. Unsolicited bulk is the single largest form of abuse we have seen to date.

Over the last couple of years, more and more businesses on the Internet focus on services and software products catering to the bulk e-mail market. Software products have been developed that collect e-mail addresses from Usenet newsgroups, online service members' directories and forums, bots that look for "mailto:" codes in HTML documents online, publicly accessible mailing list subscribers, or even your site's visitors. Service companies that collect e-mail addresses and perform bulk mailings abound today on the Internet. Be very careful when considering bulk e-mail for online marketing purposes.

Internet Resources for Chapter 11

LISTS OF MAILING LISTS

AOL, Prodigy, and CompuServe
All have their own areas where you can search for mailing lists.

HTMARCOM
A mailing list that discusses high-tech marketing. To subscribe send the message "subscribe htmarcom your name" to the e-mail address listserv@usa.net.

Internet Marketing Mailing List
http://www.o-a.com
The Online Advertising Discussion List focuses on professional discussion of online advertising strategies, results, studies, tools, and media coverage. The list also welcomes discussion on the related topics of online promotion and public relations. The list encourages sharing of practical expertise and experiences among those who buy, sell, research, and develop tools for online advertising, as well as those providing online public relations and publicity services. The list also serves as a resource to members of the press who are writing about the subject of online advertising and promotion.

I-Sales Digest
http://www.mmgco.com/isales
Formed in November 1995, the goal of the Internet Sales Moderated Discussion List is to provide a forum for meaningful and helpful discussion of online sales issues by those engaged in the online sale of products and services. The list is moderated by John Audette, president of Multimedia Marketing Group, Inc.

The List Exchange
http://www.listex.com/imark.html
The Internet's one-stop mailing list resource. It links to a number of list sites and sites with information on building your lists.

List of Publicly Accessible Mailing Lists
http://www.paml.net
The List of Publicly Accessible Mailing Lists is posted on this site and once each month to the Usenet newsgroups news.lists.misc and

news.answers. The Usenet version is the definitive copy—this Web version is generated from the database and is uploaded several days after the Usenet version is posted. They continually post to Usenet so that the PAML will be archived at *rtfm.mit.edu*.

Liszt, the Mailing List Directory

http://www.liszt.com

A very big directory of mailing lists—over 90,000 to date. Liszt has organized its lists into subject categories. Liszt provides details on how to subscribe to each of the mailing lists in its database and provides information on content as well.

L-Soft's CataList

http://www.lsoft.com/lists/listref.html

CataList, the catalog of listserv lists! From this page, you can browse any of the 19,516 public listserv lists on the Internet, search for mailing lists of interest, and get information about listserv host sites. This information is generated automatically from listserv's lists database and is always up-to-date.

E-MAIL LIST BUILDER PROGRAMS

Campaign E-mail Marketing Software

http://www.arialsoftware.com

This is e-mail marketing software used to conduct legitimate e-mail marketing campaigns. Campaign can import your contact database information and send personalized e-mail messages to all of your contacts.

The Direct E-mail List Source

http://www.copywriter.com/lists/index.htm

Thousands of e-mail lists where you can advertise without spamming.

Elmed Targeted E-mail Software

http://www.yug.com/tools/itools.htm

Information on, and links to, many e-mail marketing tools and software programs.

ListBot

http://www.listbot.com

ListBot makes starting your own free e-mail list quick and easy. Use a ListBot e-mail list to stay in touch with friends and family; notify customers of new products and specials; find out who is visiting your Web site and send updates; let your clubs, teams, classes, and so on, talk by e-mail; create a forum for discussing a favorite topic; publish an electronic newsletter; or connect any group of people by e-mail.

MailKing
http://www.mailking.com
MailKing is similar to Campaign in that it can import your contact database information and send personalized e-mail messages to all of your contacts.

12

Establishing Your Private Mailing List

Private mailing lists enable you to create one-way communication to your Web site visitors and are a tremendous vehicle for building relationships and a sense of community with your target market. Generating your own mailing lists is highly recommended because of the many marketing uses a targeted opt-in list has. The list can be used to maintain an ongoing dialog with existing customers and potential customers regarding updates, support, specials, and so on. It can also be used to communicate with current and prospective customers through distribution of corporate newsletters, price lists, new catalogues, product updates, new product announcements, and upcoming events. You have seen how you can join a publicly accessible mailing list, but what if you wanted to establish your own private list? In this chapter, we cover

- Why have your own mailing list?

- Establishing your list

- The issue of privacy

- Managing your mail list

- Promoting your mail list

Why Have Your Own Mailing List?

There are numerous reasons why it would be appropriate to administer your own list. In fact, some of the same reasons that make it imperative to join someone else's list are also benefits for running a list of your own. Running a private mailing list can be beneficial in other ways, too, including

- Permission-based marketing

- Establishing yourself or your business as an expert in your field

- Networking

- Conserving contacts

- Building repeat traffic to your Web site

- Branding

- Promotion of your business's products and services

- A potential source of revenue

You can use a number of methods for soliciting and collecting e-mail addresses, including an online guestbook or other type of registration form to be filled out on your Web site. However, you will have better results if you provide people with an incentive to leave their e-mail address with you.

Place a form with a "Subscribe here" button on your site where visitors can sign up for the mailing list. Calls to action such as "Sign up now to receive our free newsletter" or "Click here to receive our informative newsletter and be included in a drawing for great prizes" might be useful in convincing people to subscribe. Having people register for your mailing list by offering an informative newsletter is a great way to stay in touch with your target market. If you have valuable information that your current and potential customers want, they will gladly give you their e-mail address to obtain your newsletter.

A prime example of this would be my mailing list that is accessible when you visit my Web site (*http://www.susansweeney.com*). Through my private mailing list I regularly send out valuable Internet marketing tips, tools, techniques, and resources to my subscribers. When visitors come to the site and see that we have a mailing list, they need little encouragement to sign up because they know that they will be receiving valuable information that can help them strengthen their online marketing plan. Other mailing lists provide freebie incentives such as T-shirts, software, or games. If you sign up for the newsletter at Lobster Direct (*www.lobsterdirect.com*), your name will be put in their drawing for live lobsters (see Figure 12.1).

Encourage customers and potential customers to subscribe to your private mailing list through traditional marketing techniques including press releases, offline newsletters, advertising, letters, and so on. If you use hardcopy direct mail, you can design a response system that requests the e-mail addresses through a fax-back, business reply card, or 1-800 number, or by asking respondents to go to your Web site or e-mail you directly. You can also ask people to sign up for your mail-

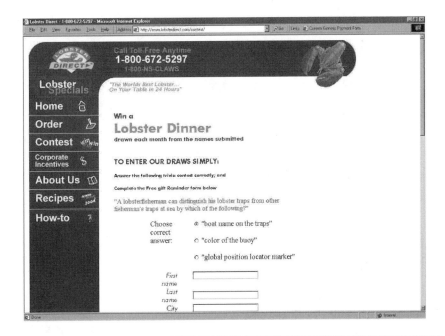

Figure 12.1. Lobster Direct (*http://www.lobsterdirect.com*) offers Web site visitors the chance to have their name entered in a drawing for free lobster if they sign up for their newsletter.

ing list through newsgroup and mailing list postings, an appropriate tag line in your signature files, banner advertising, links from appropriate sites, and other online advertising techniques.

Permission-Based Marketing

There are many opportunities from your Web site to encourage visitors to give you permission to send them e-mail on an ongoing basis. You want visitors to subscribe to your mail list and should exercise every opportunity to accomplish this from your site. The more often you are in front of your target market's eyes through e-mail and site visits, the more they feel a part of your community. Subscribers to your mail list willingly give you their e-mail addresses and are obviously interested in the issues you are discussing. You have acquired their permission to send them e-mail, and you have established yourself as a respected member of the industry. For more information on permission marketing, refer to Chapter 5.

Benefits of Private Mail Lists

The benefits derived from having a private mail list are numerous.

- *Establish **Yourself** as an Expert.*   By operating your own private industry-specific mailing list and offering your advice to members of your list, you will establish yourself as an expert in your field. As a result, you can quickly earn the respect and admiration of your peers and develop new business contacts and clients.

- *Networking.*   Having your own private list permits you to network closely with others in your industry and with clients and potential clients. Very often, new business relationships and opportunities develop when people with similar interests are brought together. Utilize your mailing list to facilitate the creation of these sorts of relationships. It could be that you find new business partners, establish new clients, or start another business venture.

- *Conserving Contacts.*   You develop many great contacts every day in business. Often businesses develop a relationship with a firm, complete a project with the firm, and then lose contact with the client as time goes on. Starting your own private mailing list enables you to stay in constant contact with these individuals. This will help you to maintain the relationships that you have developed with your clients in the long term, and will ultimately result in more business and a stronger reputation for your business.

- *Branding.* Once you have developed your own private mailing lists and have generated a loyal list of subscribers, people will relate the value of your mail list to your company's products or services. Mailing lists are an effective way to brand your business's products and services online. If you send messages to your mail list subscribers on a regular basis, they will be exposed again and again to your business's corporate ID and products and services. This is an effective way to increase the brand awareness for your business.

- *Promotion of Your Business's Products and Services.* It is important to remember that people are subscribing to your mail list to receive valuable information that will help them in some way. It is for this reason that your mail list messages should not be full of blatant advertising; if it is, the retention rate of your subscribers will drop dramatically. However, since launching your own mailing list is such a good branding tool, you should always include a call to action that would encourage a subscriber to click through to your Web site and learn more about your products and services. This is a great way to generate exposure for your products and services.

- *Potential Source of Revenue.* Once your list becomes established and has many subscribers, you may be able to sell advertising to people interested in marketing to your list members. Needless to say, a mailing list becomes an excellent revenue source as its credibility and membership numbers expand. In the end, the time and effort you exert nurturing your list to prominence will pay for itself and more. If you are already a member of a publicly accessible mailing list, take note of the number of advertisements that appear in each posting you receive from the list. Administer your own private mailing list and earn advertising revenue for yourself. However, you have to be ever mindful of the number and type of ads you have in your mail list. The ads should not detract from your message or your credibility.

The Issue of Privacy

Privacy is a growing concern among many online users. You will be able to boost your mailing list's sign-up response rate by guaranteeing that subscribers' e-mail addresses will be kept confidential and not be sold to anyone else. People are concerned about the privacy of the information they provide you with. If you cannot assure them that your company will use their e-mail address solely for your correspondence with them, they will not feel comfortable giving their e-mail address to you. Provide people with your privacy policy statement. Make them feel comfortable about divulging their e-mail address to your business. To do this, you should place a link to your business's privacy policy in a prominent location on your Web site, especially on your mailing list sign-up page.

You should never add someone's name to your mailing list without his or her permission. People really resent receiving unsolicited mail, even if you give them the option to unsubscribe. However, one method of obtaining more e-mail addresses is to suggest to your subscribers that they recommend your mailing list to a friend (or a few friends). Let your subscribers spread the word about your mailing list. If your list provides useful information, your subscribers will recommend the list to their friends. Some of these people will then subscribe and tell others about your mail list, and so forth. You remember the old commercial: "They told two friends and they told two friends and they told two friends." This viral marketing technique is a quick and cost-effective way to increase the amount of people who subscribe to your mailing list. For more information on viral marketing, please refer to Chapter 4.

Managing Your Mail List

There are a large number of mail list management software programs available to help you better organize your mail list distribution. This software enables you to easily add and remove subscribers to your mail lists.

Mail list management software enables you to draft and send properly formatted messages to your subscribers directly from within the software. Mail list software often provides you the opportunity to personalize your e-mails quickly and easily. Many of these programs can be integrated with your Web site so that people can add themselves to your list right from the site. You can also use this software to set up notification mechanisms to reply to subscribers confirming that they have been added to the list. This makes running your mail list less time-consuming, as the software does most of the work for you.

At Connex Network Inc., we use a dynamite mail list management software program called Mailworkz (*http://www.mailworkz.com*) to manage our Internet marketing newsletter. Mailworkz's flagship product, Broadc@st HTML (see Figure 12.2), is a dynamic e-mail marketing solution that enables you to create and send important e-mail messages—personally and individually to thousands of your mail list subscribers. This tool has been invaluable to us in delivering our mail list to our

Figure 12.2. Mailworkz (*http://www.mailworkz.com*) offers a dynamite mail list management software program called Broadc@st HTML.

subscribers on a timely and professional basis. Other recommended mail list software resources can be found in the Internet Resources section at the end of this chapter.

Promoting Your Private Mail List

You will promote your private mail list wherever you can reach your target market. You will promote it on your site, online through various online marketing techniques, and offline. You will

- Encourage visitors to your Web site to join your mail list by making sure you have "Join our mail list—click here" calls to action throughout your site. You might enhance this with an incentive "Join our mail list to receive our bi-weekly tips, tools, and techniques and to be included in our drawing for a Palm Pilot—Click here."

- Include a viral marketing element as previously described to encourage your subscribers to recommend your mail list.

- Publicize your mailing list in postings to other mailing lists and newsgroups if it is appropriate. There is a moderated mailing list devoted to helping new list owners promote their list. To subscribe, send a message containing the line "Subscribe new-list firstname lastname" to *listserv@vm1.nodak.edu.*

- Invite your friends, colleagues, current clients, and potential clients to join your list.

- Remember to mention your mailing list in your e-mail signature file. This is an easy way to promote the list.

- If you are looking for a large distribution list, you might even register your mailing list with Topica *(http://www.topica.com)*, Liszt *(http://www.liszt.com)*, tile.net *(http://tile.net/lists)*, and the Publicly Accessible Mailing Lists index *(http://paml.net).*

Where to Go from Here

In this chapter, we discussed reasons you might want to administer your own mailing list, how you can set up your mailing list, and other issues you will likely face once your list goes live. Private mailing lists are prime marketing vehicles if you manage them correctly and actively promote them. You can reach out to your target market with a mailing list. This technique of permission, or opt-in, e-mail marketing is the key to your success. If you have something to offer to people in your industry and it is feasible for you to establish and administer a mailing list, give the idea strong consideration.

Internet Resources for Chapter 12

E-mail List Management Software
http://www.catalog.com/vivian/mailing-list-software.html
This is a list of e-mail list management software packages provided by Vivian Neou.

LISTSERV
http://www.lsoft.com
LISTSERV e-mail list management software is renowned for its flexibility, scalability, and performance. Start your own Internet mailing discussion list.

Lyris—E-mail List Server
http://www.lyris.com
Lyris is a powerful e-mail list server that automatically delivers your newsletters, announcements, and discussion lists.

MailWorkz
http://www.mailworkz.com
Broadc@st HTML facilitates your online communications campaign; from building quality customer lists through designing and sending your key messages, to handling the responses and requests for more information.

Majordomo

http://www.greatcircle.com/majordomo

Majordomo is a program that automates the management of Internet mailing lists. Commands are sent to Majordomo via electronic mail to handle all aspects of list maintenance. Once a list is set up, virtually all operations can be performed remotely, requiring no intervention from the postmaster of the list site.

13

Developing a Dynamite Link Strategy

The more appropriate **links** you have to your site, the better! Expand your horizon by orchestrating links from related Web pages to increase your traffic. In this chapter, we cover

- Developing a link strategy

- How to arrange links

- Getting noticed—providing an icon and tag line hypertext for links to your site

- Link positioning

- Tools to check your competitors' links

- Using links to enhance your image

- Web rings and meta-indexes

- Getting links to your site

Links
Selectable connections from one word, picture, or information object to another.

- Reciprocal link pages

- Associate programs

- How links can enhance your search engine placements

Links Have an Impact

Developing your link strategy is one of the most crucial elements involved in Internet marketing. It is a very time-consuming task, but it is time very well spent. Links are important for a few reasons.

1. Appropriately placed, they can be a real traffic builder.

2. A number of the frequently used search engines use link popularity as one of their ranking criteria. The more links to your site, the more popular it is; so the number of links you have to your site can significantly impact your placement with the search engines.

3. The more links you have to your site, the more opportunities the search engine spiders have to find you.

Links Have Staying Power

When you post a message to a newsgroup where you promote your Web site through your brilliant contribution and your signature file, you will receive increased traffic while the message is current and is being read by participants in the newsgroup. As time passes, your message appears farther and farther down the list until it disappears, and then your traffic level returns to normal. The same goes for a promotional effort in a mail list. You can expect increased traffic for a short period of time after your mail list posting, but as soon as everyone has read your posting and has visited your site, traffic levels return to normal.

This is not the same for links. Traffic from links does not go away as easily as other forms of Internet marketing. Links generally stay active for a long period of time. When a link to your site is placed on another Web site, people will see it and be enticed to click through to visit your site. As long as the site that hosts your link has new traffic, you will continue to receive traffic through it. The beauty of links is that in three months' time that link will still be there, and people will still be clicking through!

Links are very important because if you have links placed appropriately on a high-traffic Web site, they can turn into traffic builders for your own Web site. They are also important because they can have a major impact on your ranking in some of the major search engines, because some search engines use link popularity in their ranking criteria. Some of these search engines include

- AltaVista *www.altavista.com*

- Excite *www.excite.com*

- Google *www.google.com*

Once your link strategy is implemented and you begin to see an increase in the number of sites linking to your Web site, you will see your ranking in the previously mentioned search engines improve. For more information on search engines and their ranking criteria, see Chapters 6 and 7.

Everything Links to You

The more links you have to your site, the better chance you have that someone will be enticed to visit. However, a quid quo pro usually applies, and this means providing reciprocal links, giving people the opportunity to leave your site with the click of a button. To minimize this "flight effect," make sure you place outbound links two or three layers down in your site. Never place outbound links on your home page. You want your visitors to come into your site and see everything you want them to see and do everything you want them to do before they have the opportunity to go elsewhere.

Regularly test all of the links from your site to ensure that they are "live" and are going to the appropriate locations. Dead links reflect poorly on your site. There are tools available online that can help you determine whether or not you have dead links. These tools include

NetMechanic at *www.netmechanic.com* (see Figure 13.1), Web Site Garage at *www.websitegarage.com*, and SiteOwner.com at *www.siteowner.com*. These tools analyze your page, detecting any dead links that may be on your site. Each of these tools is discussed in more depth in the Internet Resources section at the end of this chapter.

Strategies for Finding Appropriate Link Sites

Ideally, you should be linked from every high-traffic site that is of interest to your target market. You have to develop a strategy to find all of these sites and arrange links.

The first place to start is with the popular search engines. Most people use search engines and directories to find subjects of interest on

Figure 13.1.   The NetMechanic site provides many valuable tools. Its HTML Toolbox can be used to find out if you have dead links on your site or if you have any HTML errors that need correcting.

the Internet. Most of the people searching never go beyond the first 20 to 30 results the search engine returns. Thus, these top 20 to 30 sites returned by the search engines must get a lot of traffic. Make sure you search relevant keywords in all the popular search engines and directories, and investigate these top sites for appropriate link sites. Some of these sites will be competitors and may not want to reciprocate links. The best opportunity for links is with noncompeting sites that have the same target market. I suggest you take your most important keywords, do a keyword search in the 20 most popular search engines and directories, and review the top 30 sites in each for potential link sites.

Another strategy to find appropriate link sites is to see where the leaders in your industry and your competitors are linked. I use the term "competitors" very loosely. It would include your direct competitors, your industry leaders, companies selling noncompeting products to your target market, companies selling similar types of products or services to your target market, and companies that compete with you for search engine ranking. See what your competition is doing. Determine where they are linked from, and decide whether these are sites that you should also be linked from. Learn what they are doing well, and also learn from their mistakes. You should be linked everywhere your competition is appropriately linked, and then some.

Explore These URLs

There are many tools on the Internet to help you identify a Web site's links. This is a great way to research where your site could be linked from but isn't—yet!

When determining which sites you should be linked from, you first have to develop a lengthy list of competitors. A competitor can be any business or site that offers the same products or services as you do or anyone targeting the same demographic group as you. Since the Internet creates a level playing field for all businesses, you are also competing against people in other countries. Someone using a search engine to find information on services that your company can provide may see results from companies from all across the world in the top 10 results.

Once you have developed your extensive list of competitors and have gathered their URLs, you must then find out what sites they are linked from. Tools have been developed to assist you in finding who is linking to your site. In most cases you enter your URL, and then these tools provide you with the list of sites linking to your URL. However, these tools can be used just as easily to determine which sites are linking to your competition and industry leaders by entering *their* URL instead of your own.

The more organized you are for this exercise, the better. I suggest that you

1. Gather an extensive list of competitors and their URLs.

2. Choose the tool(s) from the next section that you are going to use for this exercise.

3. Enter the first competitor URL to find the sites linking to it.

4. Copy and paste the results into a Word, Notepad, or other file that you can access later.

5. Enter the next competitor URL to find the sites linking to it.

6. Copy and paste the results into the same Word, Notepad, or other file, adding to your list of potential link sites.

7. Repeat steps 5 and 6 until you have found all the sites linking to your competition. When this is done, you have your Potential Link Sites list.

8. Now develop a link request (see the next section for details) and keep it open on your desktop so that you can copy and paste it into an e-mail when you find a site you'd like to have a link from.

9. Next, visit every one of the potential link sites to determine whether the site is appropriate for you to be linked from. If the site is appropriate, then send your link request. If the site is not appropriate for whatever reason, delete it from your list.

10. Follow through and follow up. Follow through and provide an appropriate link to those who have agreed to a reciprocal link. Follow up to make sure that they have provided the link as prom-

ised to your site, that the link works, and that it is pointing to the correct page on your site.

11. Submit the Internet address of the page that has provided the link to you to the popular search engines so that they know it's there. This will ensure that your link popularity score increases with that particular search engine.

Tools to Identify Your Competitors' Links

The following tools can be used to obtain a list of locations on the Internet that are linked to your competitors' Web sites:

AltaVista
http://www.altavista.com
To find out where your competitors are linked using AltaVista, simply enter the competitor's URL in the search area like this: *link:yourcompetitorsdomain.com.* This will return all pages in AltaVista with a link to your competitor's Web site.

Excite and Other Search Engines
Just enter your competitors' URLs and see what comes up. (Be sure to include *http://*.) If anything, the search query will include all indexed Web sites that contain the URL searched.

Google
http://www.google.com
Enter your competitor's URL in the search box like this: *link: yourcompetitorsURL.* The results will contain all Web sites linking to your competitor's Web site.

Hot Bot
http://www.hotbot.com
Enter your competitor's URL in the search box and change the default from "all the words" to "links to this URL." When you type in the URL, remember to include *http://*. The results will contain all Web sites linking to your competitor's Web site.

WebCrawler
http://www.webcrawler.com/WebCrawler/Links.html
Enter your competitor's URL into the search query box to find out how many links are provided to that page. WebCrawler provides the names of all the referring sites.

Other Potential Link Strategies

Another strategy for finding potential competitors is to visit the many different search engines and do a search on the keywords you feel people would search on if they were looking for your site. The top results can also be considered your competition. You should add them to your list, and repeat the procedures discussed earlier to find out where they are linked from and to see if they are appropriate links for your site.

Now you have a starting list of sites you want to link from. Your next activity is to request the link. Remember that although this is a time-consuming exercise, it is also one of the most important activities. Developing a strong link strategy is critical if you want a large volume of traffic to your Web site and if you want high placement in those search engines that give heavy weighting to link popularity.

Winning Approval for Potential Links

Now that you have a list of Web sites you would like to be linked from, the next step is to identify the appropriate company contact from whom to request the link. Usually this can be found on the site. Titles such as Webmaster@ or any variation on the theme are usually a pretty safe bet. If the site does not have an appropriate contact, then try *feedback@*. You can either send the request there or ask for the e-mail address of the appropriate person.

If you cannot find an e-mail address on a Web site, and you feel that you will benefit a great deal from being linked on that site, you can visit a domain registration service like Network Solutions *(www.networksolutions.com)* to find out contact information for that domain name. Click on the *"WHOIS Lookup"* link and submit the URL in the WHOIS search to do a search on the domain in question. The results will include the contacts, both technical and administrative, for that Web site. The technical contact will most likely be the person that you are looking for, because that person is the one who most likely looks after the Web site. The administrative contact is usually responsible for the renewal of the domain name, and the billing contact is usually the bill payer for the domain name.

Generally, a short note with the appropriate information in the subject line is most suitable. Your note should be courteous, briefly describe your site's content, and provide the rationale for why you think reciprocating links would result in a win–win situation. It doesn't hurt to compliment some aspect of the site that you think is particularly engaging.

It is a good idea to develop a generic "link request" letter that you can have on hand when you are surfing. You should always keep this letter open on your desktop when surfing the Internet so that you can quickly and easily copy and paste the letter into an e-mail. If you don't have a link request ready and you find a site that you are interested in requesting a link on, you usually jot the site down as a reminder to go back to request a link. Quite often it just doesn't happen. But if you have the request open on your desktop, when you find a site that is appealing from a link perspective, you can simply copy and paste the link request into an e-mail, do a little editing or customizing, and hit the "Send" button.

Here is an example of a link request e-mail:

Dear Web Site Owner,

I have just finished viewing your site and found it quite enjoyable. I found the content to be very valuable, particularly [customize here]. My site visitors would appreciate your content as I think we appeal to the same demographic group. My site, http://www.mysitename.com, focuses on [my site content] and would likely be of value to your visitors. If you have no objection, I would like to add a link to your site.

Sincerely,

John

When you get a response, it will usually say that they would appreciate the link to their site and will offer to provide a reciprocal link. To facilitate this, you should either have the HTML for the link ready to send or have it available on your site, or both.

Make sure to follow through and follow up. If you said you would provide a reciprocal link, follow through and do so within 24 hours. Follow up to make sure that your site has been linked from theirs, the link works properly, and it is linked to the appropriate page on your site.

Then remember to send a thank you. Since they are doing you a favor by adding your site to their Web page, you should strive to develop a good relationship with them. This way they may be more generous with the link that they give you. They may place it higher on the page, or even offer you the opportunity of having a small graphic link on their page, which would be dynamite for increasing traffic to your site. These graphic links are explained in more detail later in the chapter.

Another way to get links is to ask for them on your site. In a prominent location on your site, place a link that says something like, *"Would you like to provide a link to this site? Click here."* Link this message to a separate page that holds several options for links. You can provide viewers with several different sizes of banner ads they could place on their Web site. See Figure 13.2 for an example. You can also provide them with a thumbnail icon, the HTML, and your tagline, which they could simply copy and paste into the HTML code on their Web site. Quite often, if you offer viewers these opportunities for links, you will have a better chance of receiving these enhanced link features. If you make it easier for them to add the link, they would be more willing to provide the link, for they can do it at their convenience. Figure 13.2 shows an example of a site that provides the relevant coding and images for people who want to provide a link to the site.

You might want to consider offering an incentive to people who will provide you with a link. It could be something that can be downloaded or a free sample of your product in exchange for a link. This also provides you with another opportunity to market your site because you are giving something away for free, and thus you can be listed on the many Internet sites that identify sites for freebies. Another tactic that you can use is that viewers who provide a link to your site will be included in a drawing for a prize.

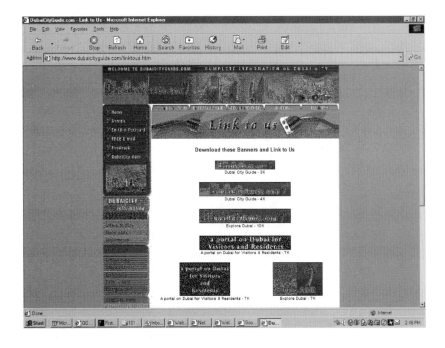

Figure 13.2. By providing the HTML text and icons on your site, you can make it very easy for viewers to add your link to their site. It is best to supply them with the option of placing a text link, a small button, a large button, or a banner advertisement on the Web site.

You might want to consider running a contest such as "Provide a Link to Us and Win," where you include all those sites linking to you in a drawing once a week or once a month, depending on the size of the prize. There is even free software to help you run this type of contest; it's called ClicksContest. This software will track all the sites that link to a specified Internet address and will even pick your winner at random. The software also tracks and reports the amount of traffic you get from each link. ClicksContest can be downloaded from *http://www.web-reviews.com/clickscontest/*.

Meta-indexes and **Web rings** are other sources for links. For a complete discussion of meta-indexes and Web rings, see Chapters 15 and 21, respectively.

Web rings
Interlinked Web sites.

You may need to prompt sites to provide promised links. If you have made an arrangement for a link and, on following up, find that the link is not there, it is appropriate to send an e-mail reminder. When sending the follow-up e-mail, include your icon, HTML, URL, and any other information that may be helpful.

Making Your Link the Place to "Click"

There are links and then there are links. Usually links are your company name hypertext-linked to your home page, and your company's site link is listed with a number of other companies' links. Sometimes, if you are lucky, there is a brief description attached to the link.

You should take a proactive approach with linking arrangements. Explore every opportunity to have your link placed prominently and, if possible, to have it *differentiated* from the other links on the page. Figure 13.3 demonstrates how having an image associated with your link can make your link stand out among all of the other links.

Once you have an agreement with a site willing to provide a link, you should ask if you could send them an icon and the HTML for the link. The **icon** (GIF or JPG format) should be visually pleasing and representative of your company. Within the HTML, include a tag line that entices people to click on the link. With the icon or logo, the tag line, and your company's name, your link will stand out from the rest. Since another Web site is going to be generous in providing a link to your site, your image should be only a thumbnail, for you don't want to take up too much space on the host Web site. This image could be your corporate logo or a graphic that is being used in the current promotion for one of your products or services. By having this image and tag line strategically placed on a Web site, the chances that a viewer will click through to visit your Web site are much higher. Here is an example of what it should look like:

Icon
An image that represents an application, a capability, or some other concept.

<IMG SRC=*"your gif/tif/bmp name"*>
<A HREF=*"http://www.yourdomainname.com"*>Catchy tag line here </A>

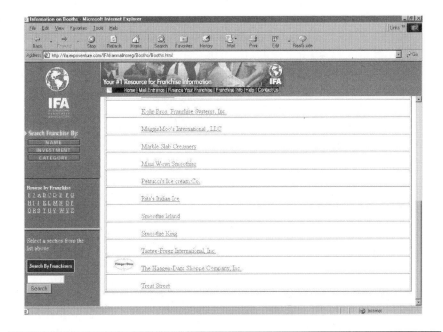

Figure 13.3. By adding a small graphic to your link, you can definitely make your link stand out from the others.

To Add or Not to Add with Free-for-All Links

There are thousands of free-for-all links on the Net. These sites allow you to add your URL to a long list of links, but they provide little in the way of traffic unless you can have your link stand out from the rest. One advantage you can get from being linked from these sites is in search engine ranking. As mentioned previously, some search engines use the number of links to your site in their ranking criteria.

Add Value with Affiliate Programs

Another way of benefiting from links to your Web site is by developing an associate program. Associate programs (also called reseller or partnership or affiliate programs) are revenue-sharing arrangements set up by companies selling products and services. When another site agrees to participate in your associate program, it is rewarded for sending customers to your business. These customers are sent to your site through links on your associates' or affiliates' Web sites. By developing and offering this type of program, you generate increased revenue and increased links to your site. Associate programs are explained in more depth in Chapter 14.

Maintaining a Marketing Log

Record all new links to your site in your Internet marketing log. It is important to maintain this log and review it on a regular basis. You must periodically check to make certain that links to your site are operational and are going to the appropriate location. Along with the URL where your site is linked from, you should also keep track of all contact information you may have gathered when communicating with the Web master.

A Word of Caution with Link Trading

You must be aware when trading links that all links are not created equal.

- If you provide a prominent link to another site, make sure you receive a link of equal or greater prominence.

- Be aware, when trading your links with sites that receive substantially less traffic than you do, that you will probably have more people "link out" than "link in" from this trade. Consider trading a banner ad and a link from their site for a link from your site, thus making it more of an equal trade. If their site has more traffic than yours, don't mention it unless they do.

- Never put your outbound links directly on your home page. Have your outbound links located several levels down so that visitors to your site will likely have visited all the pages you want them to visit before they link out from your site.

- Sometimes when people update their site, they change the Internet address or delete a page altogether. If you have placed a link on your page to that page, and one of your viewers tries to link out to that page and receives an HTTP 404 error, this reflects badly on your site. You should always check your Web site for dead links.

Internet Resources for Chapter 13

TOOLS THAT CHECK FOR DEAD LINKS

NetMechanic
http://www.netmechanic.com
To find out if you have any dead links with NetMechanic, simply enter your URL into the query box and view the results. The site will generate a detailed report, which will outline whether or not you have any dead links, and if so, where.

Site Owner
http://www.siteowner.com
When using Site Owner, you can check your site for various Web site criteria. To check for dead links, you must enter your URL into the query box, then select "Dead Link." The results will outline any dead links that are on your site.

Web Site Garage
http://www.websitegarage.com
This site has a dead-link check in its Web site diagnosis. It has a link popularity tool as well, which tells you how many links a particular site has pointing to it and also from where a URL is linked.

RECIPROCAL LINK INFORMATION

Virtual Promote
http://www.virtualpromote.com/guest6.html
This tutorial covers how to promote traffic to your Web site with reciprocal links. This is a free service for all Web site developers who want to learn more about announcing their Web site and promoting more traffic to the Internet.

FREE-FOR-ALL LINK SITES

AutoLink/MasterLink

http://www.career-pro.com/autolink/index.cgi?autolink

AutoLink allows you to type in your site's URL, and with one click automatically list it on over 350 FFA pages, directories, and search engines. MasterLink is a brand-new tool, and you must see it to truly appreciate this new concept in Web site promotion. Highly recommended.

Entrepreneurial Trend

http://www.angelfire.com/ct/suremoney/page2.html

Links to hundreds of places to list your site! Free-for-all link pages and search engines. Free classifieds and message boards. Free newsletters and reciprocal links.

FFA Net

http://www.ffanet.com/links/list.pl

This page has a detailed listing of thousands of free-for-all link pages. It also offers you the opportunity to set up your own free-for-all link pages on the FFA network.

Link-O-Matic

http://www.linkomatic.com/index.cgi?10000

This site allows you to submit your URL to over 450 quality promotional sites with one click, driving traffic to your Web site and saving you loads of time.

Mega Linkage List

http://www.netmegs.com/linkage

An exhaustive listing of over 1,500 directories, classified ad sites, little-known search engines, FFA pages, and more. . . all compiled for you alphabetically. Although there are some dead or broken links here, a large majority are active, and you will be hard-pressed to visit each one.

14

Affiliate Programs

It is a well-known fact that referral business is the easiest and most efficient business to generate. When doing business online, affiliate programs enable you to capitalize on this concept. The concept of setting up a referral business model was first started in 1996 when Amazon.com started paying other Web site owners for referring customers to their Web site. This referral business model caught on, and now many sites are incorporating this model into their everyday business activities. The idea and the corresponding software technology have come a long way since 1996. The software available today makes the process so simple that anyone with basic Web skills can set up an affiliate program or join one within 10 or 20 minutes.

There are many different affiliate programs available on the Internet. These programs all vary in terms of reliability, quality, and the amount of commissions offered. E-tailers have these programs to develop repeat business and increase sales. A side benefit to having an affiliate program is that every affiliate provides a link to your site, which in turn improves link popularity, which in turn improves search engine ranking in a number of the popular search engines. On the downside, developing and implementing the affiliate program takes time and effort, and you have to be competitive with other affiliate programs to encourage participation. In this chapter, you will learn

- How to distinguish among the different types of affiliate programs

- How to pick the appropriate affiliate program for your Web site

- Tips to succeed with affiliate programs

- The benefits of affiliate programs

- How to start your own affiliate programs

- Important features for affiliate-tracking software

- Affiliate program resources

Affiliate Programs: Increase Traffic to Your Web Site

To understand the opportunities available, you must first understand the different types of affiliate programs. All pay for referral business, but in different ways. Before you decide to participate in an affiliate program, you must first look at your objectives, your products and services, and your target market, and then decide whether an affiliate program is appropriate for your site. Once this has been affirmed, you then choose the type of program that works for you.

Commission-Based Affiliate Programs

The most common type of affiliate program is the commission-based program. This type of program offers a Web site a chance to make a percentage of sales resulting from the referral. Commissions typically range from 1 to 15%. Some programs offer a two-tier commission structure, and some offer an increased amount of commission for those who have higher-traffic sites. Some examples of commission-based affiliate programs include

- Amazon.com: *http://www.amazon.com*

- One and Only: *http://www.oneandonlynetwork.com*

- WebPosition: *www.webposition.com* (Figure 14.1)

Flat-Fee Referral Programs

Flat-fee referral programs will pay a Web site a fixed amount for every new visitor who links from the referring site to the host site and takes certain predefined actions. The required action quite often is making a purchase on the host site. Other flat-fee programs do not require the purchase of an item. The predetermined actions might be downloading a free demo, ordering a catalog, requesting a quote, or taking another action desired by the host site. A good example of this is NextCard (Figure 14.2). NextCard offers consumers a co-branded VISA credit card that is targeted toward Internet users. If you join the NextCard affiliate program and place a link on your site that encourages your viewers to apply for a NextCard Visa, you will receive a flat fee for your

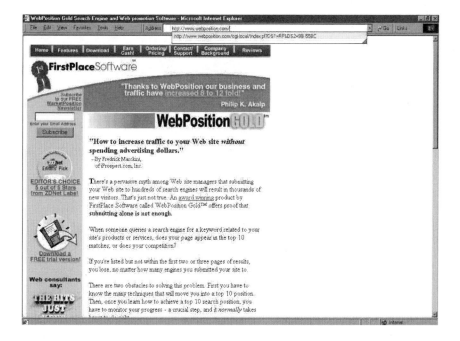

Figure 14.1. WebPosition Gold (*http://www.webposition.com*) has a very popular affiliate program.

Figure 14.2. NextCard (*http://www.nextcard.com*) has a dynamite flat-fee affiliate program.

efforts. Following you will find URLs for NextCard and two other companies that offer flat-fee affiliate programs from their Web site:

- NextCard: *http://www.nextcard.com*

- BizBuyer.com: *http://www.bizbuyer.com*

- eBay: *http://www.eBay.com*

Click-Through Programs

A click-through program is one in which affiliates receive a fee for every unique visitor who clicks through on the host's banner ad that has been placed on the host Web site. There are many click-through programs available on the Internet. For example, ValueClick (*www.valueclick.com*)

is a click-through program that eliminates the problems of finding individual advertisers and allows you to place various banner advertisements on your Web site. Whenever a visitor links out from your site through one of these banner ads, you receive a flat fee. Two other popular click-through programs are

- AllClicks: *http://www.allclicks.com* (Figure 14.3)

- SearchTraffic.com: *http://www.searchtraffic.com*

Selecting an Affiliate Program That Is Right for You

The first thing that you should do when deciding whether to start an affiliate program is to ask yourself if this fits in with your Web site objectives and if the program is something that would be of interest to

Figure 14.3. AllClicks has one of the top click-through affiliate programs on the Internet.

your target audience. Click-through programs can serve to increase traffic to your Web site as long as your banner ad is designed with your target market in mind and the banner ad is placed on sites that are of interest to your target market. Commission-based and flat-fee affiliate programs can go further in having the referred visitors do what you want them to do when they get to your site. The referring site knows that they only receive their commission when a certain action has been taken by the visitor, whether that action be a purchase, a quote request, or something else. The referring site has a vested interest in having the referred visitor take the desired action and is in a position to suggest or recommend that the visitor take that action.

How to Succeed with Your Affiliate Site

You may have an affiliate program, but are you really doing all that you can to exploit it? There are several things that you can do to be successful with an affiliate program. You should go out of your way to help make the links stand out on your affiliates' sites. Provide different-sized icons that grab visitors' attention and are designed with the target market in mind. Also prepare the proper HTML coding and a tag line linking to your Web site, and you will help your affiliates get the attention of their visitors. You can also inspect your affiliates' Web sites regularly to determine whether or not there is anything you can do to help them add value to the links on their pages. You could offer them advice about where they should locate their links if they are in an obscure place on their Web site. Remember that you don't run their Web sites, so make it clear that you are simply offering advice and not trying to run their site.

Other affiliate program operators offer more advanced tools to their affiliates. For example, a program operator may offer affiliates a generic e-mail newsletter, which the affiliate could easily download, personalize, and send out in its mailing list. This generic newsletter is written in an enticing manner and will encourage the affiliate's mail list subscribers to visit the affiliate Web site and click on the affiliate program link. The key point is that you should take advantage of as many opportunities as possible to leverage the power of your affiliate program. Through providing your affiliates with these value-add services, you not only strengthen the power of your affiliate program, but you also show your affiliates your commitment to seeing that they are successful with your program.

You should also make sure that you, the affiliate program administrator, do your best to be prompt with reporting and referral payments. People will not want to participate in your program if you are late with payments or don't provide them with detailed reports of their referrals from the previous reporting period. By sticking to the program schedule and doing the best you can for your affiliates, you not only will keep your affiliates happy, you will also advance the interests of your affiliate program.

Benefits of Creating an Affiliate Program

There are many benefits to participating in an affiliate program, especially if you decide to create your own. There are also some not-so-obvious advantages that you can benefit from. By creating your own affiliate program, you may generate a significant increase in traffic to your own Web site. When your affiliates place links on their Web sites linking to your site, you will increase your link popularity. This generates a significant amount of traffic to your site, but also helps to increase your search engine rankings. Some of the major search engines use link popularity in their search engine ranking criteria. Once you have successfully launched your affiliate program and have developed a wide sales force on the Internet, you may be surprised by the amount of new traffic that is coming to your Web site.

Your greatest advantage is the opportunity to expand your sales force to thousands of people. If you run a good affiliate program, your sales force could consist of people all over the world, thus expanding your target market into different cultures your personal sales force otherwise might not have been able to penetrate.

Another benefit of launching an affiliate program on your Web site is that you will increase the brand awareness for your business. For example, how many times have you seen an Amazon.com logo on a personal or commercial Web site? Over 500,000 people have subscribed to Amazon.com's affiliate program, making it one of the largest programs on the Internet. All of Amazon.com's affiliates place banner ads, buttons, text links, and other promotional tools on their Web site in an effort to encourage their visitors to click through to the Amazon.com

Web site and make a purchase. Even though everybody may not click through to the Amazon.com site, their Web site visitors are still exposed to the Amazon.com brand, thus increasing the brand exposure for Amazon.com's products and services. This may ultimately result in those visitors' going directly to the Amazon.com Web site in the future to make a purchase, thus bypassing the affiliate's Web site and the need to pay that affiliate a referral for their business.

Starting Your Own Affiliate Program

If you have a product or service that you are trying to sell online, you should consider starting your own affiliate program. It is an easy way to generate a wide sales force for your products or services, while continuing to retain most of the profits. But what is involved in starting your own affiliate program?

First you must decide which type of program you want to offer to your affiliates. If you expect a high amount of interest in your affiliate program, perhaps click-through and flat-rate programs are not for you. Your program could be very successful in getting visitors to your site, but they may actually never purchase your products or services. With a commission-based program, you don't pay affiliates for referrals that did not produce any sales. Your affiliates have an incentive to recommend specific products to encourage the sale.

The second, most important step in setting up your affiliate program is deciding which type of tracking software you are going to use to monitor your affiliate program. This is important because, like any other part of your Web site, you want it to be as user-friendly as possible. You should make it easy for your affiliates to verify how well they are doing with your program. There are three options for tracking your affiliates' success.

Developing Mirror Sites for Each of Your Affiliates

This is one of the original ways of tracking affiliates. It is a more cost-effective way to track your affiliates, yet it is very time-consuming and has a number of faults. What you actually have to do is set up a mirror site for each of your affiliates. This is a separate page for each of your affiliates to use when directing consumers to your site.

For example, let's say that you are developing your mirror page for your first affiliate. Your site is *http://www.yourdomain.com*, but you can assign your first affiliate the URL of *http://www.yourdomain.com/index1.html*. Your first affiliate would be indexed as affiliate number one, and all sales that came from that mirror page would be traced to that affiliate. You would repeat this process for the next affiliate, and so on.

The problem that occurs when using mirror sites to track your affiliates is that they are aimed more specifically at people who have only one product to sell. If you have more than one product, you would have to design multiple mirror pages for your affiliates, and this would be very time-consuming. With more pages for each of your affiliates, it may become confusing when tracking sales due to sheer volume. When changes are made to any of the pages (e.g., a graphic is updated), you would have to modify the graphic on each of your affiliates' mirror pages. This too is very time-consuming. If you don't host your site on your own server, you would also have to be concerned with the cost for hosting. With more pages on your ISP's server, you will have to pay more, and if each of these pages is receiving high amounts of traffic (as you hope), you will have to pay for more bandwidth.

Paying an Affiliate Program Service to Track Your Affiliates' Success

Another avenue you can explore when starting your own affiliate program is to pay an affiliate program service to track your affiliates' traffic and their activities. The affiliate program service can provide everything you need to have a good affiliate program. Full-tracking services provide real-time statistics for your affiliates so that they know how they are doing with sales, and the tracking service takes care of the accounting side as well. They calculate the amount due to your affiliates at the end of every reporting period. The affiliate program service providers charge a fee for their services.

Some of the more popular affiliate program services are

- ClickTrade: *http://www.clicktrade.com*

- My Affiliate Program: *http://www.myaffiliateprogram.com* (Figure 14.4)

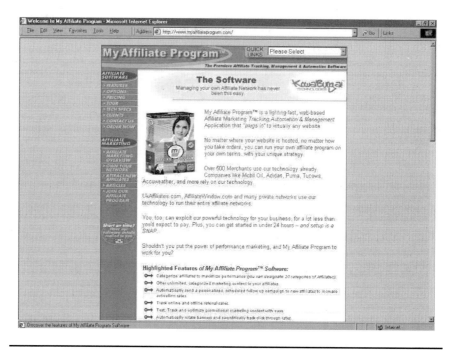

Figure 14.4. My Affiliate Program (*http://www.myaffiliateprogram.com*) is a terrific affiliate tracking software program.

These services take care of everything for you from developing and implementing the program to providing you with activity reports. However, if your objective for starting your affiliate program was to make more money, you might want to do a few calculations to determine the cost. With the affiliate program service, you not only have to pay your affiliates, you also have to pay for the tracking service, which in turn cuts into your profits.

Purchasing Affiliate-Tracking Software

If you want to avoid the problems involved in tracking your affiliates, your best bet is to purchase affiliate-tracking software. Companies have developed comprehensive tracking software that can allow you to provide maximum service to your affiliates. Depending on what features you would like to provide to your affiliates, the cost of tracking software ranges anywhere from $300 to $15,000.

There are many varieties of affiliate-tracking software. Some software programs are quite unsophisticated and offer very few features, and others offer them all. There are some features that you should watch for when purchasing your software. They can help you to run a very smooth affiliate program and can save you a lot of time. Here are some of the more important features available:

- *Automated Signup.* You should always look for this feature because you want to make it as easy as possible for your affiliates to sign up for your program. It should not take them days to officially sign up; they should be able to do so automatically. You want them to get started as quickly as possible, so as soon as they sign up, they should automatically be sent all information that you feel is necessary for them to quickly incorporate your program on their Web site.

- *Automated Tracking System.* This is one of the most important features that you must look for. You want to make sure that your software is capable of tracking all sales made so that you can reward your affiliates with the appropriate commission. You don't want to have to calculate which Web sites the sales came from at the end of the month. You want to be able to let the software do all of the tracking for you and at the end of the reporting period provide you with a report outlining payment due to your affiliates.

- *Automatic Contact Systems.* You should be able to contact all of your affiliates whenever you find it necessary. Some software allows you to send messages to all of your affiliates at the click of a button. It compiles their e-mail addresses in a database.

- *Real-Time Statistics.* Real-time statistics allow your affiliates to view their current sales statistics. This will let them know how many people clicked through from their site and how many of those people actually purchased something. This is a very good feature because it is important to keep your affiliates informed about their current sales status in your program.

- *Variable Payment Option.* Another important feature that you should look for is the variable payment option. Some forms of affiliate software will only let you work with so many variables, meaning the fixed fee, percentage, or flat rate per click-through that you multiply by the referrals from your affiliates' sites. Some software is only designed for certain types of programs. You might purchase software designed to calculate payments for a click-through program. If you wanted to have a commission-based program that pays a percentage of sales resulting from each click-through, this software would not be good for you. It would not be able to comprehend and manipulate data to calculate the payments, for it is incapable of using the percentage of sales variable. You should remember to check this out before you purchase any software.

- *Automatic Check Payment.* As soon as your affiliate program is up and running, and you have developed an extensive list of affiliates, it can become a hassle to write checks at the end of each payment period. Some software comes equipped with an automatic check payment option that allows your computer to print the checks payable at the end of the payment periods. This can make your affiliate program run very smoothly and can also save you lots of time.

- *Automatic Reporting-Period Statistic Distribution.* Some of the more advanced affiliate-tracking software will automatically e-mail each of your affiliates at the end of the reporting period, which is usually one week. This keeps your affiliates informed as to how much success they are having with your program, and allows them to adjust their marketing strategy to help them to succeed with your program.

Some of the more popular affiliate-tracking software programs available to people wanting to start their own affiliate program are

AffiliateLink
http://www.affiliatezone.com
AffiliateLink enables you to do everything from signing up affiliates to checking on both administrative and individual affiliate statistics.

My Affiliate Program
http://www.myaffiliateprogram.com
Kowabunga! Technologies provides affiliate-tracking software that allows you to manage all of your affiliate members and track impressions, click-throughs, and online sales.

The Amazon Example

Amazon.com is a pioneer in the affiliate program game. For this reason, we will now walk through how its affiliate program is set up. The Amazon.com affiliate program model is a good one for you to follow if you intend to establish an affiliate program of your own.

Amazon describes its affiliate program as follows (the following excerpt is taken directly from *http://www.amazon.com*):

> *Amazon.com Associates is free to join and easy to use. As an Associate, you simply place links to Amazon.com on your Web site. Each time a visitor clicks from your site to Amazon.com to purchase items, you earn generous referral fees. We take care of their entire shopping experience: fulfillment, customer service, and shipping, and we track the sales generated from your site. All you have to do is decide how you want to link to Amazon.com.*
>
> *We provide you with a wide and colorful selection of links that can be easily added to your site. You can choose to link to any of the millions of items across our expanding selection of stores. Or, simply select a home page graphic and let us take care of merchandising to the customer. However you choose to set up your links, you'll benefit from the values offered on our site, great selection, and the convenience of online shopping. No matter how you choose to link to us, you get paid on all sales.*

As Amazon describes it, the affiliate program sounds easy for both the affiliate and Amazon. Upon further inspection, we can see that this truly is the case. Prospective affiliate members can link through to the Amazon affiliate program information page directly from Amazon's home page (see Figure 14.5). You should make your affiliate program this easy to find on your site.

Like Amazon, you will need an information page or section of pages explaining the details of your affiliate program to visitors. The Amazon.com information page (shown in Figure 14.6) is well written and walks potential affiliate members through a series of steps that describe the details of the program (what the affiliate program is, the commission rate, how commissions are paid, and so on). Current affiliate program members can also login to their account from this page and inspect their sales statistics. Be sure that you provide a place on your site for potential affiliate members to log in and find adequate information about your affiliate program so that they understand its potential.

Next you will require a signup form for your affiliate program. Figure 14.7 displays a portion of Amazon's associate program application form. Ask applicants for necessary information only. This will keep the length of your signup form brief and will encourage more new members to join.

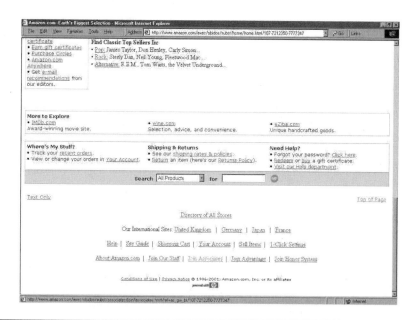

Figure 14.5. Visitors can access the Amazon.com affiliate program directly from Amazon.com's home page by clicking on "Join Associates."

Figure 14.6. Amazon.com provides visitors with detailed information about its affiliate program opportunity.

Figure 14.7. Like Amazon.com, you should make it easy for new members to join your affiliate program by providing a concise application form on your site.

Once a person completes and submits the affiliate program application form, Amazon immediately sends the linking code to the new member to include on their site. SusanSweeney.com is a member of the Amazon affiliate program, and when we joined, we were sent the following code:

```
<url1>
<A HREF="http://www.amazon.com/exec/obidos/ASIN/1885068379/
susansweeney.com">Title of book or image goes here
</A>
```

As you can see, the URL to the SusanSweeney.com affiliate page is quite lengthy. However, there is no need to memorize it. The affiliate member (in this case, SusanSweeney.com) simply has to copy and paste this linking text into the HTML code of the pages of his or her site. As described earlier, you should provide affiliate members with tips on where to include and how to present the affiliate link on their site. On the SusanSweeney.com site, we simply link to our Amazon affiliate page by inserting the linking text around a graphic of the book we're selling (see Figure 14.8). The affiliate link is prominently displayed on our site, so if visitors want to purchase the book, they click on the book graphic and are linked through to Amazon.com, where they can proceed with the transaction (see Figure 14.9).

Thus, Amazon receives the sales request, processes the order, and delivers the book to the customer, and SusanSweeney.com receives a 15% commission from the order. Amazon sends SusanSweeney.com a weekly sales report and a check for the commissions earned after our affiliate sales reach a certain level.

Once again, the point of presenting this example of how the Amazon affiliate program operates is to give you some ideas for what you should include in your affiliate program and how you should present the information. With this example and the other details provided in this chapter in mind, you should now be sufficiently informed to initiate an affiliate program of your own.

The Connex Network Inc. Example (shameless self-promotion :-)

Similar to Amazon.com, but on a much smaller scale, Connex Network Inc.*(http://www.connnexnetwork.com)* has a successful affiliate

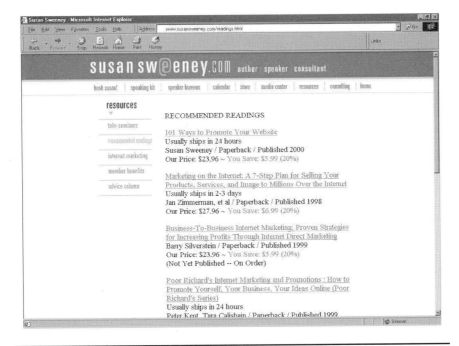

Figure 14.8. Amazon.com can provide listings for one product or an assortment of products, similar to how SusanSweeney.com provides a detailed listing of recommended readings on a section of the SusanSweeney.com site.

program on its Web site that offers affiliates the opportunity to sell a variety of e-business and Internet marketing-related books written by yours truly. Powered by the My Affiliate Program™ affiliate software, the Connex Network affiliate program is easy to join and is set up in a similar fashion to the Amazon.com affiliate program. When a visitor first arrives at the Connex Network Web site, he or she is immediately presented with the opportunity to join the Connex Network affiliate program, as can be viewed in Figure 14.10.

Connex Network describes its affiliate program as follows (the following excerpt is taken directly from *http://www.connexnetwork.com/ affiliateprogram.htm*):

> *We have a great deal for affiliates because we've implemented a two tier system!*
>
> *The two tier system allows primary affiliates to sign up secondary affiliates under their ID. The first tier affiliate earns*

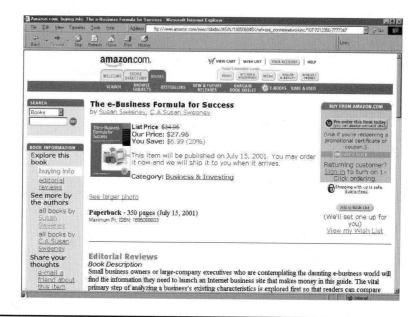

Figure 14.9.   Visitors to your affiliate members' sites can link through to your site. The affiliate members receive a commission for each sale they generate. In this image, a visitor had clicked through from the SusanSweeney.com site to the Amazon.com site. SusanSweeney.com will receive a commission if a sale is made.

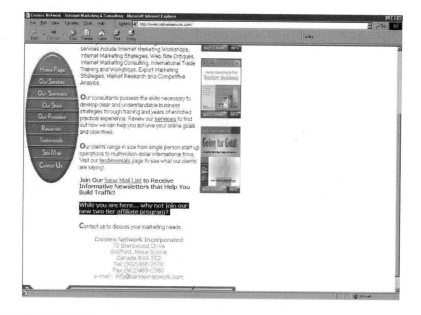

Figure 14.10.   Connex Network (*http://www.connexnetwork.com*) prominently displays its affiliate program opportunity directly on its home page.

10% of all sales that come through to our Shopping Cart from their links as well as 2% of all the second tier affiliate sales that have joined under their affiliate ID.

The second tier affiliate earns 10% on all sales as well so it's an attractive proposition to make to partners and friends and a great way to earn an extra 2% on their sales without dipping into their commissions.

Connex Network does a dynamite job at outlining the benefits of joining its affiliate program. From this page, visitors can immediately sign up for the affiliate program, and current members are given the opportunity to log in and check their account status. Once a visitor decides to sign up for the Connex Network affiliate program, he or she is presented with the "affiliate program agreement" which outlines the rules for joining the affiliate program. This can be viewed in Figure 14.11.

The visitor is then presented with a brief signup form for the Connex Network affiliate program (see Figure 14.12). This page collects all of the necessary contact information for the affiliate, the Web site, and

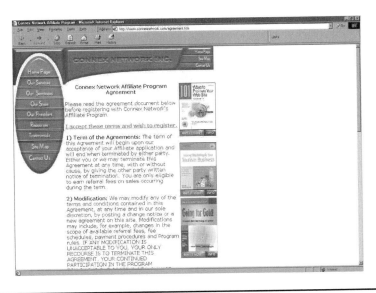

Figure 14.11. When a visitor decides to join the Connex Network affiliate program, he or she is asked to read and accept the affiliate program operation agreement.

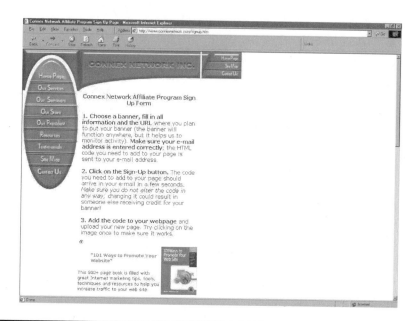

Figure 14.12.   Connex Network has a very brief signup form, which enables visitors to sign up for the affiliate program quickly and with little hassle.

asks the visitor to select which product(s) will be promoted on his or her Web site. The form will then generate the code for the individual to place on the site. The signup form also provides the visitor with the option to tell up to five friends about the affiliate program via e-mail, with the incentive that if the visitor's friends sign up for the affiliate program, they will become a part of the visitor's second tier. This means that the visitor would earn a commission on all sales resulting from his or her own efforts, and also from the efforts of those individuals who sign up for the affiliate program as a result of this referral. This viral marketing technique is a dynamite way to increase the exposure for the Connex Network affiliate program.

Once people complete the affiliate signup form and submit the application, they are immediately sent the code that they will need to place on the Web site in order to participate in the affiliate program. This can be seen in Figure 14.13.

Similar to how SusanSweeney.com placed links to Amazon.com, Bells Alaska Travel Guide (*http://www.bellsalaska.com*) is participating in

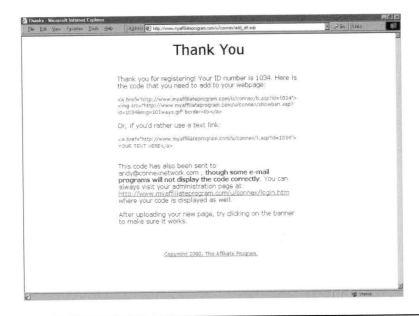

Figure 14.13. Once the affiliates complete the affiliate program application form, they are automatically provided with the code that they need to place on their Web site to link to the Connex Network affiliate program.

the Connex Network affiliate program (see Figure 14.14). The affiliate link is prominently displayed on this site, so if visitors want to purchase the book, they click on the book graphic and are linked through to the Connex Network Web site where the transaction takes place. Once the order has been processed, the affiliate is rewarded a commission for his or her efforts.

Internet Resources for Chapter 14

AssociateCash.com
http://www.associatecash.com
AssociateCash.com reviews different associate and affiliate programs and rates them. Learn which affiliate programs earn Web masters' money.

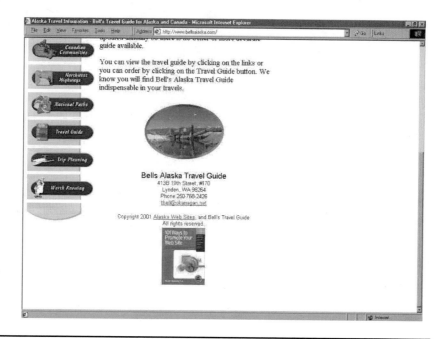

Figure 14.14. Bell's Alaska Travel Guide prominently displays a link to the Connex Network affiliate program directly on its home page.

Associate-It
http://www.associate-it.com
Claims to be the "Web's biggest directory of associate programs."

AssociatePrograms.com
http://www.associateprograms.com
The AssociatePrograms.com directory helps you find the best associate programs—also known as referral, partner, revenue-sharing or affiliate programs—to earn money from your Web site.

AssociatePrograms.co.uk
http://www.associateprograms.co.uk
A UK guide to affiliate marketing and associate programs. Listings and ratings of many programs by category—Fox Tucker, managing director. Includes headlines, tips, advice, and free weekly news update.

CashPile.com

http://www.cashpile.com

Comprehensive directory/search engine for revenue-sharing (affiliate, associate, referral, and bounty) programs.

ClickQuick: Affiliate and Pay-per-Click Program Reviews

http://www.clickquick.com

ClickQuick provides in-depth reviews of Web master affiliate, associate, and pay-per-click programs that offer opportunities to make money on the Internet. Also reviews of banner ad networks and helpful articles on improving affiliate program performance.

I-Revenue.net

http://www.I-Revenue.net

Claims to be one of the largest affiliate program directories on the Internet.

Refer-it.com

http://www.refer-it.com

Refer-it.com is the authoritative guide to Internet affiliate programs, associate programs, and referral programs. Refer-it is a great resource for merchants with affiliate programs and Web masters with affiliate Web sites.

MORE POPULAR AFFILIATE PROGRAMS

Amazon.com

www.amazon.com

A pioneer in the affiliate program industry, Amazon.com claims to have the earth's biggest selection of products, including free electronic greeting cards, online auctions, and millions of books, CDs, videos, DVDs, toys and games, and electronics.

CDNow

www.cdnow.com

CDNOW is the world's leading online music store.

Reel.com

www.reel.com

Reel.com is one of the biggest places online to buy movies.

Barnes and Noble

www.barnesandnoble.com

BarnesandNoble.com offers a wide selection of books and has over 120,000 Web sites participating in its affiliate program.

Tunes.com

www.tunes.com

Steal Our Sites is Tunes.com's affiliate program. Tunes.com is the Internet's definitive music hub, combining the Web's largest collection of music content with programming and content from RollingStone.com, TheSource.com, and DownBeatJazz.com.

15

Maximizing Promotion with Meta-Indexes

Meta-indexes are intended to be useful resources for people who have a specific interest in a particular topic. Meta-indexes are a large and valuable resource for reaching your target audience and should be utilized to their full potential. In this chapter, we cover

- What meta-indexes are

- Why meta-indexes are useful

- How to make the links to your site stand out

- How to create your own meta-index

What Are Meta-Indexes?

Meta-indexes are lists of Internet resources pertaining to a specific subject category and are intended as a resource for people who have a specific interest in that topic. These lists, like the one for Internet shopping sites shown in 15.1, consist of a collection of URLs of related Internet resources and are arranged on a Web page by their titles. The owners or creators of meta-indexes put a lot of effort into compiling these lists and are eager to find new sites to add to them. They often will list your site for free because they desire to have the most meta of the meta-indexes—they strive to have the largest of the large indexes, and more sites means a larger index. So if you come across a meta-index that is associated with the topic of your site, feel free to ask for a link.

Some of these meta-indexes have a "Submit to add your site" area; for others, you have to develop an inclusion request e-mail and send it to the owner of the site. In your inclusion request e-mail, you would let the owner know that you had visited the site and feel that your site would be appropriate to be included. Give the reasons you think your site appro-

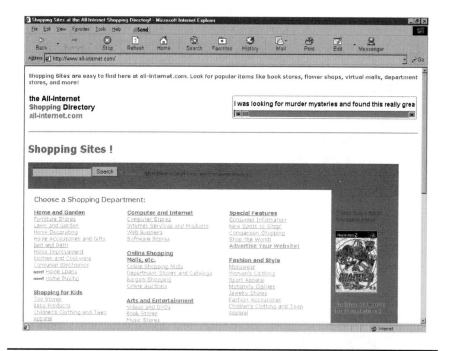

Figure 15.1. All-Internet Shopping Directory—a meta-index of malls, stores, products, and services on the Web.

priate and request the link. You should provide the HTML for the link as well. Review the techniques discussed in Chapter 13 to have your link stand out with the graphical icon, hypertext link, and tag line.

Meta-indexes are directed at a specific topic, such as "pets" or "cars." Meta-indexes provide easy access to a number of sites on a specific topic, and they are a great way to draw targeted, interested people to your Web site. In addition, some users may rely on meta-indexes as their only search effort. They may not use a search engine to perform a query on Mexican resorts, for example, if they know a certain meta-index contains 200 sites on Mexican resorts. Meta-indexes can increase your chances of being found by people who are interested in what you have to offer. You may want to consider placing a banner ad on one or some of the meta-indexes you find, given that the target audience you want to reach will be the people using these indexes. Choose carefully, though; you don't want to buy a banner ad on a meta-index that is not up to par and doesn't provide you with the traffic you want to acquire. Take your time and investigate the meta-index before advertising on it. Does it appeal to the eye? Is it of good quality? Are there a lot of dead links? Is it updated frequently? Does it have sufficient traffic?

How to Find Appropriate Meta-Indexes

Now that you know what a meta-index is, how do you find one? You might be browsing on the Web and happen to come across one. If you do, bookmark it for future use or add it to a document that you can look at and print off at a later time. A better way to find meta-indexes is through the search engines and directories on the Web.

When you're looking for meta-indexes, we recommend you create a more focused search by adding an extra word such as "directory," "list," "index," "table," "resource," "reference," or "guide." By adding one of these words in conjunction with another word—for example, "travel"—you're increasing your chances of finding appropriate meta-indexes. Performing a search on "travel" alone will return far less-targeted results. Looking for a travel directory alone may not work for you. Why not? A search for a travel directory on the search engines often means looking for all sites that contain the words "travel" and all sites that contain "directory." You should refine your searches to achieve more accurate results. Some general techniques using the words "travel" and "directory" as examples you can apply in your search for meta-indexes are

- Entering *travel directory* generally means: Look for all sites containing the words "travel" or "directory," but try to gather those sites with "travel" and "directory" together.

- Entering *"travel directory"* (with quotation marks) often means: Look for all sites containing the words "travel" and "directory" next to each other.

- Entering *+travel directory* generally means: Find all sites with the word "travel" and preferably the word "directory" as well.

- Entering *+travel+directory* generally means: Find all sites with both words.

Search engines look for information in different ways and allow different techniques to be applied in order to narrow or broaden the search criteria. This information can be obtained by looking at the respective search engine's help page (Figure 15.2).

Many search engines and directories have or give you the option to use an "advanced" search or search "options" page that presents you with the ability to perform more detailed searches without using the parameters outlined above. Yahoo! (Figure 15.3) and Google (Figure 15.4) are two such sites.

Enlisting Meta-Indexes for Optimal Exposure

To ensure that you are taking full advantage of meta-indexes, do the following:

- Source appropriate meta-indexes

- Request a link

Figure 15.2. AltaVista's help page and quick-search guide.

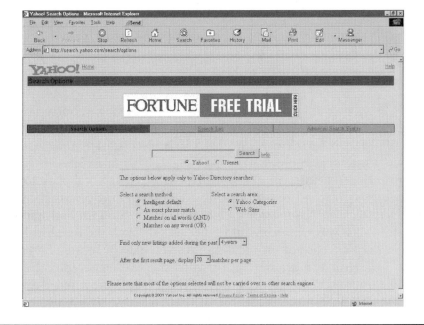

Figure 15.3. Yahoo!'s advanced search.

Figure 15.4. Google's search options.

- Provide the details necessary

- Look at sponsorship or banner advertising opportunities

Meta-indexes can be arranged by subject (sites that provide information on book publishing) or by geography (tourist sites in Alaska). As mentioned before, the major search engines are a good place to start. For example, to find tourist sites in Alaska, conduct a search by entering *+Alaska+tourist+directory*. Once you find a good list and start to check the links, you will likely find other lists through the first list. Bookmark or keep a record of the meta-indexes you like for future reference.

Even if you are not sure if your site will be accepted by a certain meta-index, send a request anyway. Meta-lists draw more traffic when they provide more resources to their readers, so list owners may be fairly lenient on what's acceptable and what's not.

When requesting a link to your site, send an e-mail with "site addition request" in the subject area of your message. Include the following in the body of the message:

- URL

- Description of your site

- Why you feel your site is appropriate for the list

- Your contact information in your signature file (see Chapter 8)

Once you have identified indexes that appeal to your target market, determine whether additional opportunities might exist for sponsoring or purchasing banner advertising on the site. Meta-indexes that relate to your market are a great place to advertise because they are accessed by your target customers.

Keep in mind that the compilers of meta-indexes are motivated by noncommercial reasons and are under no obligation to add your site to their list or process your request quickly. However, because of the banner-advertising revenue potential, more and more meta-index sites have a commercial focus.

To make your link stand out among the many others listed, inquire about adding a prominent link or icon to the meta-index page along with a short tag line, in addition to your company name. If you provide the GIF and the HTML, the meta-index owner may be happy to include it.

Review the Work of Some Meta-Index Giants

Achoo Healthcare Online (Figure 15.5)
http://www.achoo.com

Buzzle.com Travel and Tourism Meta-Index (Figure 15.6)
http://www.buzzle.com

GIS Resources on the Web (Figure 15.7)
http://www.gsd.harvard.edu/~pbcote/GIS/web_resources.html

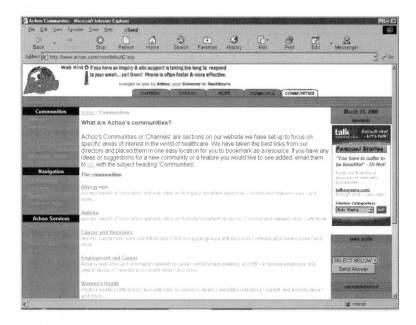

Figure 15.5.   Directory of healthcare-related sites.

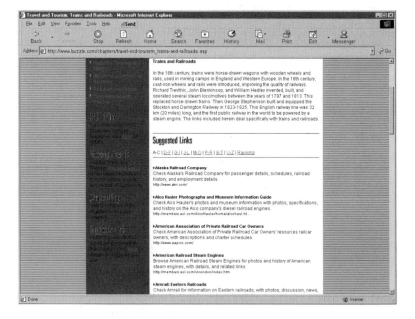

Figure 15.6.   Meta-index of trains and railroads, a subset of Buzzle.com's.

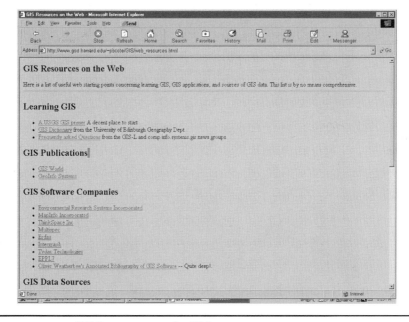

Figure 15.7. GIS Resources on the Web.

Hotels and Travel on the Net (Figure 15.8)
http://www.hotelstravel.com/homepage.html

Hyde's Travel Agent Resource (Figure 15.9)
http://www.infomatch.com/~hyde/newindex2.htm

Jim Gaston's Fountain Pen Sites Meta-Index (Figure 15.10)
http://www.jimgaston.com/sitelink.htm

Internet Resources for Chapter 15

Essential Links: Portal to the Internet
http://www.el.com
Essential links to the Internet and the World Wide Web—Essential Links is a portal to the Internet portal sites, news headlines, search engines, Web directories, references, and utilities.

Figure 15.8. A list of links to all kinds of Web sites for hotel chains worldwide.

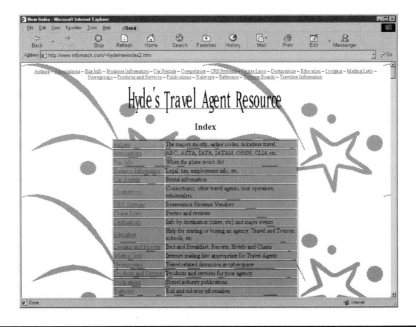

Figure 15.9. Hyde's Travel Agent Resources.

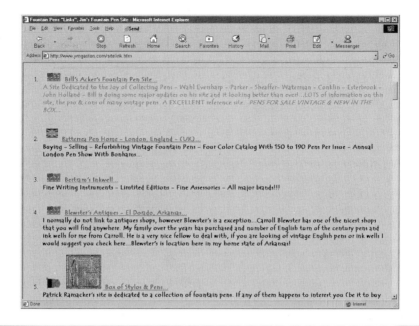

Figure 15.10. Jim Gaston's Fountain Pen Sites Meta-Index for the collector.

Internet Resources Meta-Index

http://www.ncsa.uiuc.edu/SDG/Software/Mosaic/MetaIndex.html
A meta-index of the various resource directories and indexes available on the Internet.

@LinkPad

http://www.referthem.com/pad/links.htm
A meta-index of meta-indexes—this site has indexes ranging from advertising, e-zines, and e-mail to Web graphics and real estate.

Metaplus

http://www.metaplus.com
A meta-index of the directories and essential sites.

Virtual Library

http://vlib.org/Overview.html
The Virtual Library is the oldest catalog of the Web, started by Tim Berners-Lee, the creator of the Web itself. Unlike commercial cata-

logs, it is run by a loose confederation of volunteers, who compile pages of key links for particular areas in which they are experts. Even though it isn't the biggest index of the Web, the VL pages are widely recognized as being among the highest-quality guides to particular sections of the Web.

WWW Meta-Indexes and Search Tools
http://www.fys.ruu.nl/~kruis/h3.html
A Library of Congress Internet resource page.

16

Winning Awards, Cool Sites, and More

There are literally hundreds of Cool Sites, Sites of the Day, Hot Sites, and Pick-of-the-Week Sites. Some of these sites require you to submit; others are selected based on such things as

- Awesome graphics

- Dynamite content that is useful and interesting

- Uniqueness

- Fun features

If you are selected for one of these sites, it can mean a huge increase in the number of hits to your site. You must be prepared for the increased traffic flow as well as the increased demand for online offerings. In this chapter, we cover

- Where to submit your site for award consideration

- How to win Site of the Day—tips, tools, and techniques

- Getting listed in What's New

- Posting your awards on your site

- Hosting your own Site of the Day

It's an Honor Just to Be Nominated

There are sites that find and evaluate other sites on the Internet and recognize those that are outstanding by giving them an award. The award sites are generally very discriminating in terms of which sites are selected to be the recipients of their award. They have established criteria defining what is considered "hot" or "cool" and base their award selection on those criteria. Figure 16.1 shows a variety of awards.

What's New Web sites are designed to inform Internet users of new sites and updates to existing sites, and are often selective in which new sites they will promote. The owner of each site also selectively chooses awards for Site of the Day, Week, Month, and Year. As men-

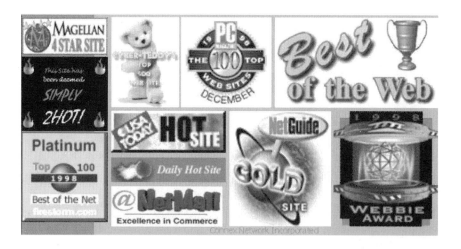

Figure 16.1.   A collage of some of the more popular award sites.

tioned earlier, some of these sites require you to submit an announcement or site description, and the awards are granted based on criteria such as graphics, dynamic content, uniqueness, and the "fun" quality of your site. Other sites grant their awards based solely on the personal likes and dislikes of the owner of the site and do not adhere to any criteria at all.

Some awards are taken just as seriously as the Academy Awards. The Webby Awards have a very comprehensive nomination procedure. The following information regarding the Webby is available on that Web site:

THE WEBBY AWARDS

The International Academy of Digital Arts and Sciences (IADAS) is responsible for nominating and awarding each year's Webby Award and People's Voice Award winners. In each category there are 2 awards given: The Webby Award and The People's Voice Award. Judges from The International Academy of Digital Arts and Sciences decide on the winners of The Webby Awards. Popular vote by the online community determines the winners of The People's Voice Awards.

Members of The Academy are luminaries in their areas of expertise: evangelists, visionaries, journalists and top-notch Web developers dedicated to the creative, technical, and professional progress of new media. The Academy brings together their wealth of knowledge to select 5 nominees in each category.

*The 2001 Webby Awards will feature 29 categories, including two **new** categories, Government & Law and Spirituality. The complete list of categories is: Activism, Arts, Broadband, Commerce, Community, Education, Fashion, Film, Finance, Games, Government & Law, Health, Humor, Kids, Living, Music, News, Personal Web Sites, Politics & Law, Print & Zines, Radio, Science, Services, Spirituality, Sports, Technical Achievement, TV, Travel, and Weird.*

From online galleries and up-to-the-second news sources, to interplanetary exploration and cyber-communities, The Webby Awards nominee exemplify the kinds of sites that Internet users should visit every day for information and entertainment.

In addition to these annual awards, The Webby Awards and The Academy, in conjunction with the San Francisco Museum of Modern Art, are now offering a brand new prize for online art. It's called the SFMOMA Webby Prize and is the first of what we hope will be many new honors for outstanding online achievements.

When you win an award, you post the award on your site for all to see. The award icon is usually a link back to the site that bestowed the honor on you.

Choosing Your Awards and Submitting to Win

There are different levels of prestige associated with each of the different award sites. Some are an honor to receive. Some are highly competitive because of the number of submissions they receive.

Some awards are easier to receive than others, such as those from commercial sites that give out awards in an attempt to increase the traffic to their own site. Traffic increases because the award is a graphic link displayed on the winner's site that visitors can follow back to the award giver's site. Other Web masters give out awards to anybody and everybody who makes a submission. The award is granted with the sole purpose of building traffic.

The bottom line is that awards are valuable assets. The average Web user cannot tell which awards are the prestigious ones and which are given to anyone who submits. So, submit for any awards that you choose to, as long as your site is ready. (A sample submission form is shown in Figure 16.2.)

Where you place these awards is important. If you win a lot of awards, you will be expected to place a promotional graphic and a link on your home page for each award you win. Your home page can become quite cluttered and will load more slowly as a result. If you have

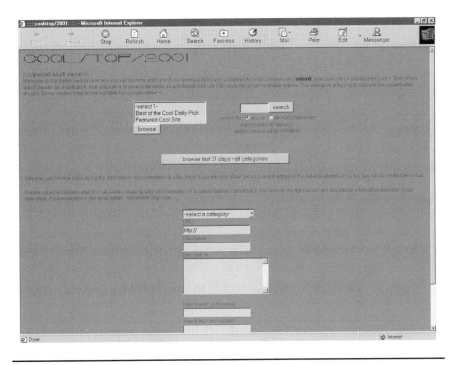

Figure 16.2. Sample award submission form. This one is for Coolstop.

been fortunate enough to be in this situation, consider developing an awards page with a link from your navigation bar to house them.

Another item to determine before you submit for an award is whether the huge amount of new traffic will benefit your site. If you sell t-shirts emblazoned with WWW cartoons, then any traffic is good traffic, and awards will benefit your site. On the other hand, if you are a marine biologist specializing in red tides in the Arctic, then the traffic that "Site of the Day" would bring may be more of a hindrance than a help in marketing your services. Always determine if the marketing tools and techniques will increase hits from your target market before deciding whether to include them in your online marketing strategy.

Getting mentioned on one of the Cool Sites lists is probably the single biggest way to draw traffic to your site. The traffic they send to your site is like a flash flood—fast and furious. Be careful what you wish for—you might just get it! The traffic will be swift and plentiful after you win one of these awards. Be prepared! Have a plan that you can implement on a moment's notice. If you offer something free from your site, ensure that you can access a huge volume of whatever it is and ensure that you have a plan to distribute quickly. If you offer a free download from your site, plan to have a number of alternate **FTP sites** available to your visitors. If you have a "call-in" offer, make sure you have a telephone response system in place and staff to handle the huge volume of calls you may get. You will need a plan to handle the huge volume of e-mails you will get as well.

FTP (File Transfer Protocol)
The simplest way to transfer files between computers on the Internet.

What's New sites accept submissions for sites that they review. The best of the best are then placed prominently on their home page for all to see. It is considered to be quite an honor to develop or own a site that has been selected by some of the more discriminating What's New sites.

Once you have decided that the type of traffic that comes along with winning the award fits with your marketing strategy, you should make sure your site has the makings of a winner and then submit to as many award sites as you can.

- First, make a list of the URLs of these award sites.

- Understand the submission form and guidelines. Review a number of forms to determine the common information requested.

- To save time, develop a document with the answers to the various questions from which you can copy and paste into the different submission forms.

- Submission forms will capture the following types of information:

  - URL

  - Title of your site

  - Contact person (name, e-mail, phone, address)

  - Owner of the site

- Submission guidelines will tell you what types of sites can be submitted. (Some awards do not accept personal pages; others do not include commercial sites.) The submission guidelines will also tell you what meets the definition of "cool" or "new" and what doesn't.

- Some award sites require that you display their award icon on your site. Posting an award on your site can provide a number of positive results—including enhanced credibility.

There are different levels of prestige associated with each of the different award sites. Some of these awards are highly competitive because of the number of submissions they receive.

What's Hot and What's Not in the Name of Cool

Most of the award sites will provide you with their selection criteria. Some award sites look for and base their selection on valuable content; others look for innovative and unique capabilities. Sites vary on what they consider "hot" or "cool," but they are fairly consistent on what doesn't make the grade, as summarized next.

What's Hot	What's Not
Awesome graphics	Single-page sites
Great, original content	Single product promotion
Broad appeal	Offensive language or graphics
Fun features	Lengthy download time

Posting Your Awards on Your Site

If you have managed to collect a few awards for your Web site, you will want to display them somehow. After all, any award is a good award, and the award site that granted you a particular award will expect you to display it in return for the recognition. Posting the awards on your home page might not be the best idea, though. For one thing, the additional graphics that will have to be downloaded will slow the load time for your home page. Second, by posting the awards on your home page, you are placing links leading out of your site on the first page. Thus, you are giving people the opportunity to leave your site before they have even had a chance to explore it. Where should you post your well-deserved awards, then? Simply create an "Awards" section on your Web site. Here, you can list all of your awards without adversely affecting the load time of your home page or losing traffic.

Becoming the Host of Your Own Awards Gala

You can also create your own awards program in order to draw traffic to your site; however, this requires a huge amount of work to maintain. You will need to work at it on a daily or weekly basis, so you must be committed to it. Be sure there is a benefit from a marketing perspective before you design and develop your own awards program. You must also be prepared to conduct your own searches at the outset to find sites to promote if the quality of sites being submitted to you is poor.

- You will first have to develop the criteria you will use in your site selection.

- You will have to develop several Web pages related to the award (information on selection criteria, submission forms, today's or this week's award winner, past award recipients page, etc.) in order to promote the award. (Ensure that you stipulate you are looking for submissions from commercial sites or personal pages and what criteria will be used in judging the submissions.)

- Your award icon must be developed. Have this icon link back to your site. The award distinguishes the winner; thus, the link will probably be displayed prominently on its site. This is a great traffic builder.

- Finally, you have to announce the award and market, market, market.

Internet Resources for Chapter 16

Award Sites
http://www.awardsites.com
Free guide offering . . . Ratings, Recognition, and Resources. Ideal for promoting, marketing, or just browsing some of the best sites on the Internet that just happen to offer a diverse range of information, services, or products . . . including community forums.

Best of the Planet Awards
http://www.2ask.com
Called the People's Choice Award, where you can decide who's best.

Best of the Web Awards
http://botw.org
This award aims to highlight those places that best show the quality, versatility, and power of the World Wide Web.

Jayde.com
http://www.jayde.com/goldlnks.html
Awards the Gold Diamond Award to sites with great style, design, and content. Jayde.com also has an award for commercial sites.

Webby Awards
http://www.webbyawards.com
The Webby Awards have been embraced by the online community as the leading creative honors for digital media. The awards recognize the most creative and innovative Web sites of the year and the talented editorial, technical, and design teams behind them.

WHAT'S NEW

Netscape What's New
http://www.netscape.com/netcenter/new.html
Netscape features a few new Web sites every day and gives them a rating. You can submit your site to Netscape for review.

Yahoo!
http://www.yahoo.com/new
Yahoo!'s "What's New" on the Web.

HOT SITES/COOL SITES

100 Hot Web Sites
http://www.100hot.com
Directory of Web sites based on Web traffic and organized by category.

Cool Site of the Day
http://www.coolsiteoftheday.com
Cool Site of the Day is a wildly popular Internet award site that features interesting, provocative, and irreverent Web sites from around the world.

CoolStop
http://www.coolstop.com
The Best of the Cool Award consistently recognizes truly outstanding sites in terms of design, originality, and content.

JimWorld Way Cool Hot Site Award
http://jimworld.com/hotpg.html
From this site you can visit some of the coolest, most interesting hot sites on the Web. These sites are selected by a blue ribbon panel of one—Jim. The sites here are truly special. Jim receives about 500 submission every week; that's about 2,000 per month. Out of that he usually finds only one winner. Visit a few of these sites. It's worth the time.

USA Today Hot Sites
http://www.usatoday.com/life/cyber/ch.htm
USA Today scours the Web for sites that are hot, new, and notable. Visit their daily list to find some of the best sites the Web has to offer. They look for sites that may stretch the design envelope and show where the Web is headed—sites that offer something unusual or unexpected, or something just plain useful.

Virtual Reference Meta-Index of Award Sites
http://www.refdesk.com//textcool.html
A listing of different sites that host Site of the Day, Hot Sites, and so on.

Web Pages That Suck
http://www.webpagesthatsuck.com
Keep your site from being nominated to this awards site, and you are probably doing well. However, you can learn a lot from Web Pages

That Suck about how to properly design your site from a marketing perspective.

Web Site Awards
http://websiteawards.xe.net
The Web Site Awards Worksheet is a free resource! It helps you apply for Web awards and track your activities. Apply to over 600 award sites around the world!

17

Productive Online Advertising

The world of banner advertising is changing rapidly. Several years ago banner advertising was in vogue, visitors were clicking through, good banner space was hard to find, and prices were rising. What a difference a day makes! The past two years have seen banner advertising prices decline. Quality space is not that difficult to obtain, and click-through rates are on the decline. Banner advertising is being used primarily to meet branding objectives. According to a recent study by AdRelevance, banner advertising used specifically for branding accounts for 54% of impressions. Despite all the doom and gloom and bad press, banner ads can still be an effective advertising medium if the banner ad is properly developed and it is placed on the appropriate site. We are starting to see a shift toward ads using rich media. Advertising online provides visibility—just as offline advertising does. You must develop a banner advertising strategy that works with your product, your marketing objectives, and your budget. In this chapter, we cover

- Your online advertising strategy

- Advertising opportunities on the Web

- Banner ad design and impact on click-throughs

- Banner ad sizes and locations

- Placing classifieds

- Tips to creating dynamite banner ads that work

- The cost of advertising online

- Measuring ad effectiveness

- Banner ad exchange networks

- Using an online advertising agency

- Sources of Internet advertising information

Expanding Your Exposure Through Internet Advertising

Today, Internet advertising is being recognized in the advertising budgets of businesses around the globe. Banner ads are a way to create awareness of your Web site and increase the traffic to it. Your Web site is your online presence. Banners are placed on the sites that your target market is likely to frequent, thus encouraging this market to click-through and visit you!

The Internet offers many different advertising spaces. Banner ads can be placed on search engines, content sites, advertising sites, and online magazines. The choice of where your ad is displayed is based on the objectives you wish to achieve with your online advertising strategy.

There are a number of advantages to online advertising.

- The response from these ads can easily be measured within one day.

- The amount of information that can be delivered, if your Web site is visited, far surpasses that of a traditional advertising campaign.

- The cost of developing and running an online advertising campaign is much less than using traditional media.

Traditionally, advertising used to be handled by a public relations (PR) firm or advertising company that would come up with your marketing concept. As clients, businesses would review and approve (usually after several attempts) the concepts before they were ever released to the public eye. The PR or advertising firms would be responsible for developing TV, radio, and print ads for the businesses. They would come up with the media buy strategy after reviewing appropriate publications, editorial calendars, pricing, and the discounts that they would receive for multiple placements. The ads were then gradually released over the period of the campaign and finally were viewed by the public. At the end of the campaign the PR or advertising company would evaluate the success of the marketing campaign. This is very easy if the objective of the campaign was to achieve x number of sales, but it is much more difficult if the goal of your campaign was to generate brand awareness.

Today, online banner ads are developed in much less time and are placed on Web sites very quickly. Web traffic analysis software can tell you the next day if the banner ad is working or not by tracking the number of visitors who clicked through and visited your site through the ad. This provides you with the opportunity to change the site on which you are advertising or to change the banner ad to see if it will attract a greater audience.

Nielsen Net Ratings (*http://www.nielsen-netratings.com*) (Figure 17.1) offers great up-to-date resources to find out who is doing the most online advertising. You can check this resource to find the top 10 banners displayed on the Internet each week and the top 10 advertisers online. Since everyone is eagerly trying to be number one, these figures change weekly.

Maximize Advertising with Your Objectives in Mind

When developing your advertising strategy, you will need to determine the objectives of your advertising campaign. The most common objectives for an online advertising campaign include

- Building brand awareness

- Increasing Web site traffic

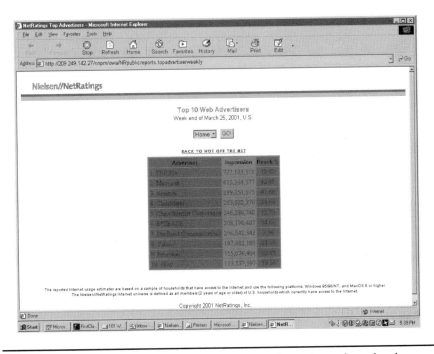

Figure 17.1. Neilsen Net Ratings provides you with continuously updated statistics on who is doing the most advertising on the Internet. The site can also provide you with the top ten most viewed banner ads on a weekly or monthly basis.

- Generating leads and sales

You have a number of choices to make, such as what type of advertising to use and where to advertise. These choices should be made based on your objectives. If your objective is to increase overall brand recognition, a nicely designed banner ad on one of the high-traffic search engines would be effective. If you would like to develop leads and find new clients, then a more targeted approach should be taken, such as placing a banner ad on a high-traffic Web site that is frequented by your target market.

When deciding how to proceed with your advertising strategy, consider how many people you want to reach. Do you want a high-quality response from a small number of very targeted people, or do you want to reach a mass audience of grand proportions?

Think about the people you are targeting. If you sell dentistry supplies to dental practices, then you want to target dentists and hygienists. It would not make much sense to put an ad on Yahoo! when you could advertise on a site about new medical discoveries in dentistry.

Always keep your budget in mind when you are devising your online advertising strategy. There are many ways to stretch your advertising dollar. If you have the time, you can find appropriate sites to trade banners. You can also participate in banner exchange programs.

Online Advertising Terminology

Banner Ads

Banner ads are small advertisements that are placed on a Web site. Companies usually develop their banner ads, find appropriate sites for placement, and then either purchase or trade banner space.

Click-Throughs

When a viewer clicks on a banner ad with the mouse and goes to the site advertised, it is called a "click-through." Sometimes banner advertising prices are determined by the number of click-throughs.

Hits

Hits to a site are the number of times that another computer has accessed that site (or a file in a site). This does not mean that if your site has 1,000 hits, 1,000 people have visited it. If your home page has a number of graphic files on it, this number could be very misleading. A hit is counted when the home page main file is accessed, but a hit is also counted for every graphic file that loads along with the home page. So if a person visits 6 pages on a site and each page has 4 graphics, at least 30 hits would be generated.

Impression or Page Views

When a banner ad is viewed, it is called an impression. Banner advertising prices are often calculated by impressions. If a person visits a page six times, this will generate six impressions.

CPM

Cost per thousand impressions, or CPM, is a standard advertising term. CPM is often used to calculate the cost of banner advertising. If the CPM of banner advertising on a site was US$40 and the number of impressions the ad had was 2,000, then the advertiser would have to pay US$80 for displaying the ad.

Keywords

You can purchase keywords on search engines. This allows your banner ad to appear when someone does a search on the keyword that you purchase. This is very good for zooming in on your target market.

IP Numbers (Geotargeting)

Purchasing IP numbers is one of the latest trends in Internet marketing. Every device that connects to the Internet has its own unique IP number. These are assigned centrally by a designated authority for each country. We are now seeing search engines sell IP numbers to help businesses pinpoint their target demographic group. For example, John Doe is building a new home in Utah and is searching for a company selling lumber in his area. Dooley Building Supplies, a lumber company in Utah, happens to be marketing over the Internet, and as part of Dooley's banner advertising campaign, they have purchased banner ads by keyword and by IP address. Simply stated, they have said they only want their banner ad to appear when the keyword "lumber" is searched on by individuals whose IP address is within a certain range (the range being those existing in Utah). When John Doe does his search on the word "lumber," the Dooley Building Supplies banner ad is displayed at the top of the page holding the search results. Someone in Michigan searching for lumber will see a different banner ad.

Jump on the Banner Wagon

Banner advertising is the most common and most recognized form of online advertising. Banner ads are available in various sizes, but the most common banners are displayed at roughly 468 × 60 pixels. See Figures 17.2a and 17.2b for some of the more popular banner ad sizes. AdRelevance studies have found that a variety of alternative ad dimensions are emerging as mainstream standards alongside full banner ads. They recently polled 115 high traffic sites, and the results showed that the standard banner is truly a standard: 95% of all sites support the format. About 50% of the sites offered a short button (120 x 60 pixels) and about the same percentage offered a micro button (88 x 31 pixels).

Banners usually have an enticing message or call to action that coaxes the viewer to click on it. "What is on the other side?" you ask. The advertiser's Web site, of course. Banner ads can also be static, just displaying the advertiser's logo and slogan, or be animated with graphics and movement.

If you use an advertising or PR company to develop your offline ads, quite often they will provide you with a library of different banner ads that you can use for your online advertising campaign. If you choose not to use an advertising or PR company, you can outsource the banner ad creation activity to another company or create your own.

The banner ad is designed to have a direct impact on the number of click-throughs it will achieve. There are a number of resources online to assist you in developing dynamic banner ads. The Banner Generator at *http://www.coder.com/creations/banner* allows you to create banners online at no charge. The Media Builder at *http://www.3dtextmaker.com* provides you the opportunity to develop animated banner ads directly from its site. Other resources to assist you in designing and building banner ads are identified in the Internet Resources section at the end of this chapter.

There are a wide variety of banner sizes available. You should consult with the owners of the Web sites on which you want to advertise before creating your banner ad or having one created professionally for you.

Figure 17.2a-b. There are many different marketing resource Web sites available online that can provide you with the different size possibilities for your banner ads.

The objective of your banner ad is to have someone click on it. Do not try to include all of your information in your ad. A banner that is too small and cluttered is difficult to read and is not visually appealing. Many banners simply include a logo and a tag line enticing the user to click on it. Free offers or contest giveaways are also quite effective for click-throughs because they tend to appeal to the user's curiosity.

Exploring Your Banner Ad Options

Static banners are what the name suggests. They remain static on the same Web page until they are removed. Your banner ad will be visible on that particular page until your reader moves to another page. *Animated banners* are banners that move on a Web site. Animated banners are usually in GIF format (Graphics Interchange Format) and contain a group of images in one file that are presented in a specific order (see Figures 17.3a–c). When using animated banner ads, you can choose to loop the file so that the banner will continue to move between the images in the files, or you have the option to make it stop after a complete cycle.

Rotating banners are banner ads that rotate among different Web pages on the same site. Some rotating banners rotate every 15 or 30 seconds, so a visitor may see several ads while remaining on the page. Other rotating banner ads rotate every time there is a new visitor to the page. Rotating banners are commonly used in high-traffic Web sites.

Scrolling banners are similar to modern billboards. Here the visitor will see a number of billboard ads, scrolled to show a different advertisement every 10 to 30 seconds.

Banner Ad Tips

Follow these tips to ensure that your banner ad will achieve your marketing objectives:

- Make sure that your banner ad is quick to load. If the Web page loads in its entirety before the banner, then the viewer may click away before ever seeing it. Ideally you should have a very fast banner ad on a relatively slow-loading site. This way your view-

Figure 17.3a. This is the first stage in an animated banner ad. It catches visitors' attention, and makes them think that the banner is doing a search on popular keywords related to skiing.

Figure 17.3b. This is the second stage in an animated banner ad. It acts as though the banner is doing a search on the keywords inputted into the query box.

Figure 17.3c. This is the final stage in an animated banner ad. It acts as though the search was completed, and now takes its opportunity to promote skiing in Canada. This is great because by the time they are ready to promote Canadian skiing, they have the viewer's full attention.

ers have nothing to do but read your banner ad while they are waiting for the site to load. You should always try to keep your banner ad size under 5K.

- To see how big files are when using any version of Internet Explorer, you must follow these steps:

    - Right-click on the banner ad.

    - Select "Properties."

- In the Properties window you will see a "Size" line, which will tell you the banner size.

- To see how big files are when using any version of Netscape Navigator, you must follow these steps:

    - Right-click on the banner ad.

    - Select "View Image," and the banner ad will appear on a page of its own.

    - Right-click on the banner and select "View Info." Another page will pop up and give you the information on the banner ad size.

- Keep it simple! If your banner contains too much text or animation, or too many colors and fonts, this will cause viewers to experience information overload. Viewers will not be encouraged to read or click on your banner.

- Make sure your banner ad is legible. Many banners on the Internet are nicely designed, but difficult to read. Use an easy-to-read font with the appropriate size. Be careful in your choice of color.

- You should always use Alt tags for those visitors who surf the Internet with their graphics turned off or cannot see your banner ad for whatever reason.

- Make sure your banner ad links to the appropriate page in your site. It is not uncommon to click on an interesting banner only to find an error message waiting for you. This is very annoying to Internet users and counterproductive for your marketing effort.

- Check your banner ads on a regular basis to verify that the link remains active and is pointing to the appropriate page on your Web site.

- If you are using animated banner ads, you should limit your ads to two to four frames.

- You should always include a call to action such as "Click here." It is amazing how many people will do what they are told. You still have to make your ad interesting and one that grabs their attention. Don't simply say "Click here"—give your audience a compelling reason to do so.

- Test your banner ads with the different browsers, the different versions of these browsers, and at different screen resolutions to make sure that they look the way you want them to.

- If you know absolutely nothing about advertising and graphic design, do not try to create a banner on your own. Go to a professional. If you do design your own banner, get a second opinion and maybe a third.

Interesting Banner Ads

The following are more technologically advanced forms of banner advertising. They are interesting to viewers because they have attributes that are unique or different in some way. These attributes may be more apt to grab viewers' attention and entice them to click on the banner ad.

Expanding Banner Ads. An expanding banner ad (see Figures 17.4a and 17.4b) is one that looks like a normal banner ad but expands when you click on it, keeping you on the same site rather than transporting you to another site on the Internet. Usually these say "Click to Expand," and the viewer then can learn more about what it is that the banner is promoting. Some of the more advanced expanding banner ads have e-commerce capabilities, which allow you to actually order products from the banner, without actually ever going to the Web site.

Animated Banner Ads. Animated banner ads contain a group of images in one file that rotate in a specific order. These banner ads are more likely to receive a higher click-through than a normal banner ad because with moving images on the Web site, your chances of the viewer's reading the banner are increased. These banners also offer you the chance to deliver more information to the viewer than a normal banner ad, for you can show different files, which contain different data. You should limit your banner ads to two to four frames to keep your load time fast

Figure 17.4a. This expanding advertisement for Investor's Business Daily displays the product, but then prompts the viewer to expand the banner ad.

Figure 17.4b. When the banner expands it explains more about the product, and actually gives the visitor a chance to subscribe directly from the banner ad. This incorporates e-commerce and banner ad technology together.

and to make sure your viewers read your information before they continue to surf the Internet.

Banners Containing Embedded HTML. Lately we are seeing an increase in banner ads containing embedded HTML (see Figure 17.5 and 17.6). This allows viewers to choose commands from a drop-down menu that relates to the Web site the banner ad is promoting. These banners are great because instead of making viewers click-through and then have to navigate through your site, like a conventional banner, these will direct your viewers to the page of interest on your site.

Interstitial Ads. These are advertisements that appear in a separate browser window while you wait for a Web page to load. Interstitial ads are more likely to contain large graphics, streaming presentations, and more applets than a conventional banner ad. Studies have found that more users click on interstitial ads than on banner ads. However, some users have complained that interstitial ads slow access to destination pages.

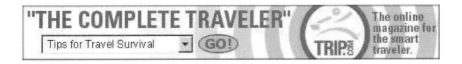

Figure 17.5. Trips.com advertises using banners with embedded HTML which allow the viewer to choose a specific vacation destination from a pull down menu, and then find out what travel opportunities are available. This is great because the viewer can go directly to the page of interest on the Trip.com site, instead of searching through the entire site.

Figure 17.6. Another embedded HTML banner, showing different opportunities for the viewer to choose from.

Java and Flash Banner Ads. These banner ads allow you to use rich media in your advertisements. By using Java and Flash technology, you can incorporate animation and sound into your banner advertisement. Although Java banners are more technologically advanced and offer more features, they also take much longer to download and risk not being viewed. Flash was designed to generate faster-loading Web sites, online animation, and advertising. If you want to incorporate rich media into your banners, you may want to go Flash because you want your visitors to see your banner ads as quickly as possible.

Location, Location, Location

As with all types of advertising, the location of the ad is extremely important. There are any number of targeted sites where you can place your banner ads. Always ensure that your banner advertising location is consistent with your objectives.

Search Engines

If your goal is to reach as many different people as possible, high-traffic search engine sites are where you should be. Cost per thousand impressions is usually US$20 to US$50. If your target market is more selective, then a more targeted buy within the search engine is appropriate. Targeted buys can include tying your banner ad to specific keywords (i.e., every time the keyword is used in a search your banner ad would appear). Targeted ads generally range in CPM from US$40 to US$90 but are quite often worth the extra price because of the correlation to the targeted buyer. If you owned a bed and breakfast and purchased "Bed and Breakfast" as a keyword, whenever someone searched for "Bed and Breakfast," your banner would appear.

Content Sites

If your objectives include bringing interested people from your target market to your site, then advertising on appropriate content sites would be extremely effective. These are sites that concentrate on a specific topic. The CPM of advertising on content sites ranges from US$25 to US$50 depending on the traffic volume they see and the focus of their visitors.

Banner Ad Price Factors

The price of banner ad space varies from site to site. Banner ads are often sold based on the number of impressions or number of click-throughs. As stated earlier, an impression is an ad view, and click-throughs are the actual clicking on the banner. The price per impression should be less than the price per click-through. Banner ad CPM is between US$10 and US$90 depending on the site you are advertising on—how targeted the audience is, and how much traffic it receives. Search engine banner ad CPMs range between US$20 and US$50. Keyword advertising CPMs range between US$40 and US$70. The cost to run a geotracking campaign can be very costly. Before you sign anything, make sure that you understand what you are paying for. Based on industry standards, Ad Resource *(http://www. adresource.com)* shows average CPM advertising rates that are updated quite frequently.

When site owners charge per impression, there is usually a guarantee that your ad will be seen by a certain number of people. The burden is on the seller to generate traffic to its site. When the charges are per click-through, the responsibility is on you, the advertiser, to design an ad that will encourage visitors to click on it. Sites that charge per impression are more common than those that charge per click-through.

There are obvious advantages to the advertiser when paying per click-through. The advertiser doesn't have to pay a cent for the 10,000 people that saw the banner but did not pursue the link. Sites that do not have a large volume of traffic often charge a flat rate for a specified period of time.

Considerations When Purchasing Your Banner Ad

Before you sign on the dotted line to purchase banner advertising, there are a few things you should consider

- How closely aligned is the target market of the site you want to advertise on to yours?

- How many sites are there like the one you are considering advertising on? Are there a lot of sites you can use to reach the same audience?

- What banner sizes are allowed? Generally, the larger the banner size, the more it will cost.

- How many ads are on each page? The more ads on a page, the lower the click-through rate for any particular ad on that page. Generally, the more ads on a page, the lower the price per ad.

- What banner rotation system is being used? Is there a comprehensive program that automatically profiles the visitors and provides the appropriate banner? The more targeted the audience, the more expensive the ad; these profiling systems can provide ads to a very targeted audience.

- What are the site's competitors charging?

- Does the site have a sliding-scale ad rate?

Make Sure Visitors Can See Your Banner

A major thing that is often overlooked is the fact that some people surf the Internet with their graphics turned off. Not a big deal, right? What if you purchased a banner ad? They are not going to see it, so why will they click through? A easy way to make sure that the viewer still knows that your banner is there is to attach an Alt tag to your banner. An Alt tag is a small piece of HTML code that is added to a Web site. It tells the browser what is supposed to be displayed if the graphic cannot be viewed. It is here that you should develop a clever tag line that will still entice the viewer to click through to your Web site. Remember that it is important to include an Alt tag on all of the graphics on your Web site.

Banner Ad Placement: Where Should Your Ad Be?

As it is for an advertisement in a newspaper or in a magazine, the location of your banner ad on a Web site is very important. A past study by graduate students at the University of Michigan has shown us that by placing a banner ad on the lower right-hand corner, next to the scroll bar, you receive a higher click-through rate. This is because when people scroll down the page, their eyes are in the bottom corner, so they see your ad. The study also showed us that placing a banner ad a third of the way down the page received a 77% higher click-through rate than those placed at the top. It is very common for the search engines to place their banners a third of the way down the page for prime advertising exposure.

When placing a banner ad, you must always remember your objective, which is to increase the traffic to your site. You should always do research on a Web site before you place an ad on it. You want to find out if it receives high traffic; you don't want to pay for an ad that will not be seen by anyone. You should try to place an ad on a site that is aimed to your target audience. You want to make sure that your banner is as appealing as possible and includes a call to action that will entice visitors to click-through.

Making It Easy with Online Advertising Networks

If your objective is to reach a large number of users through a wide variety of sites, Internet ad networks may be appropriate. Ad networks have a wide range of different Web sites that people look at every day. If you are going to join an ad network, you are known as an advertiser. You have to supply your banners to the ad network and determine how you want them to promote you. ValueClick (*http://www.valueclick.com*) is an example of a very popular ad network (see Figure 17.7). ValueClick has 20,000 different Web sites in its network and is emerging as an ad network leader. It can target a specific industry of your choice or advertise your banner to a mass audience. For a more targeted audience, your CPM will be higher. Even though you have to pay a little more initially, it will save you in the long run.

The benefit of joining an ad network is that the network will not only target your audience, it also will provide you with real-time reports that indicate the success of your banner ads. This allows you to evaluate the success of your current banner ad campaign and offers you the chance to change your marketing strategy if you are not happy with your results. Maybe you want to take a different approach, or maybe a different banner design might work better for you. Whatever it may be, the data that the ad network can provide you with is very beneficial to determining the strength of your banner ad campaign.

You can also join an ad network as a publisher. Publishers are the Web sites that banners are placed on. If you have a Web site and would

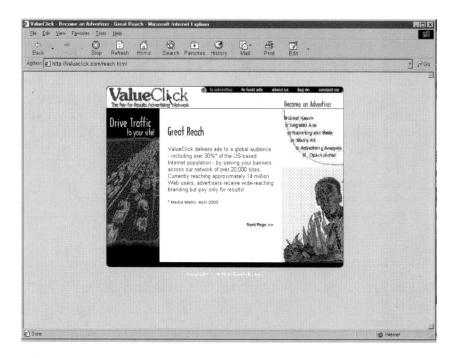

Figure 17.7. ValueClick is one of the world's largest ad networks offering its advertisers the opportunity to target their audience using ValueClick's Web site network.

like to make some additional online revenue from your site, you can join an ad network, which will place banner ads on your site and pay you for the usage of this space. Very similar to an affiliate program, or banner exchange, by joining an ad network you can dramatically increase your online revenue. A detailed list of ad networks is listed in the Internet Resources section at the end of this chapter.

Saving Money with Banner Exchange Programs

Banner exchanges work much as you would expect (i.e., your ad is placed on other sites in exchange for someone else's banner ad being placed on your Web site).

To register with a banner exchange, you often have to go through a qualifying process. What this means is that your site has to meet certain minimum standards. Once you have passed the test, the banner exchange will provide you with HTML code to insert into pages of your site where the banner ads will appear. Every time this HTML is accessed, a random banner ad appears for the viewer to see.

This process is monitored and tracked. Each banner that is accessed from the exchange and is displayed to a visitor earns you some sort of credit or token. These credits or tokens are used within the banner exchange like a bartering system. The credits you earn are exchanged for having your banner displayed on another site.

Sometimes some of the credits you earn go to the banner exchange itself, as a fee for managing the process. The banner exchange will sell the credits to paying advertisers or use them to promote the exchange. Some banner exchanges will allow you to focus your exposure on your target market.

When determining which banner exchanges to belong to, look for restrictions. When banner exchanges have no restrictions, you never know what could be loading to your pages. Don't join banner exchanges without size specifications for the banners. Your site could be displaying huge 150 × 600 pixel banners that make your visitors wait while they load. Ensure that the load time of every banner displayed on your site will be reasonable.

Applying to join a banner exchange is very easy. As an example, we will use MSN's LinkExchange (*http://www.adnetwork.bcentral.com*). To apply to join the LinkExchange program, you have to follow a few short steps (Figures 17.8, 17.9, and 17.10). First you have to agree to their terms and agreement of participating in the program. Next you have to fill out a few forms containing your personal and Web site information. Then simply submit this information to LinkExchange for review. If you are accepted, someone will contact you and give you the appropriate HTML code that you will need to place on your Web site to be able to start the program.

LinkExchange offers you the chance to promote your banner ad on over 400,000 different Web sites across the world. In exchange, you must agree to display the LinkExchange HTML on your site. This HTML will enable LinkExchange to display different banner advertisements for LinkExchange sponsors and LinkExchange members on your site in return for the free service that you are receiving. Your banner ad will be

Figure 17.8. The first step to signing up for the LinkExchange program is accepting the terms and conditions of the program. By doing so you fully understand not only what is involved in the program, but also what you cannot do.

displayed once for every two banners you display on your Web site. This can generate a lot of exposure for your site.

Here are some of the other popular online banner exchange programs. A more complete list can be found through searching on "banner ad network" on your favorite search engine.

- BannerSwap: *http://www.bannerswap.com*

- Cool Banners Banner Exchange Network: *http://www.coolbanners .com/bp/*

- Net4Banners: *http://www.net4banners.com*

- SmartClicks: *http://www.smartage.com/promote/smartclicks/*

Figure 17.9. The second step in the LinkExchange program is very easy. You simply fill out some personal information about yourself and your Web site.

Bartering for Mutual Benefits with Banner Trading

Using this technique requires you to barter with other Web sites to trade banners with their sites. If you are browsing the Internet and find a site that you think appeals to your target market, then ask for a trade. Send the Web master an e-mail outlining your proposition. Include the reason you think it would be mutually beneficial, a description of your site, where you would place that site's banner on your site, and where you think your banner might go on its site.

When you make arrangements like this, be sure to monitor the results. If the other site has low traffic, then more visitors may be leaving your site through their banner than are being attracted. Also, check the other site regularly to make sure that your banners are still being displayed for the duration agreed upon.

Figure 17.10. The third step is simply to review your information to make sure that it is correct, and then submit the information for review. If you get accepted to the program you will be contacted by MSN and they will tell you all the information that you will need to immediately setup your exchange program. This is a very easy way to promote your Web site. You can apply in a matter of minutes.

Tips for Succeeding with Classified Ads

Classified ads are also displayed on various Web sites. Some sites offer to display classified ads for free; others will charge a small fee. Here are some great tips for creating effective classified ads:

- *Headlines.* The headline of your ad is very important. The subject line determines how many people will read the rest of your ad. Look at the subject lines of other ads and see what attracts your eye.

- *Entice.* Use your classified ad to get people to request more information, not to make immediate reservations. You can then send them a personalized letter outlining all of the information and make a great pitch to attract an order.

- *Be Friendly.* Your classified ad shouldn't be formal and businesslike. Make your ad light and friendly.

- *Call for Action.* Do not only offer information about what you are selling. Call the reader for action—for instance, to order now!

- *Do Some Tests.* Run a number of different ads and use a different e-mail address for each one. This way you can determine which ad receives the most responses. You can then run the best ad in a number of different places to find out which place gets the biggest response.

- *Keep a Record.* Keep records of your responses so that you will know which ads were the most successful.

Form Lasting Advertising with Sponsorships

Sponsorships are another form of advertising that usually involve strong, long-lasting relationships between the sponsors and the owners of the sites. Sponsors may donate money, Web development, Web hosting, Web site maintenance, or other products and services to Web site owners in this mutually beneficial relationship. By sponsoring Web sites on the Internet, you can achieve great exposure for your site. People appreciate sponsorships and will look at banner ads that are from a sponsor. The benefits of sponsorships on the Internet are that you can target a specific audience, you usually get first call on banner ad placement, and you show your target market that you care about their interest. Overall, by sponsoring sites on the Internet, you have the opportunity to get directly in the face of your target market.

There are a number of different ways in which you can advertise online through sponsorships. The following is a list of the more common forms of online sponsorship:

- *E-Zines and Newsletters.* An example of this would be Nike sponsoring a Golf Digest e-zine.

- *Content Sites.*   An example would be DuPont sponsoring a Nascar racing Web site.

- *Online Chat Sessions.*   An example would be CDNow sponsoring a chat on the Ultimate Band List.

- *Events.*   An example would be a search engine such as AltaVista or Google sponsoring a seminar on search engine strategy.

Commercial Links

Another form of online advertising is commercial links. A number of targeted sites provide a lengthy list of URLs related to a specific topic. These sites will often provide your listing for free but charge a fee to have a hypertext link activated from their site to yours. There are also Web sites where you can be listed if you don't have a Web site and would prefer to have only your business name and phone number or e-mail address listed. These are great sites, especially because they are targeted toward your demographic group. An example of this would be Franchise Solutions (*http://www.franchisesolutions.com*). This site (Figure 17.11) has a database of franchise and business opportunities targeted toward entrepreneurs wanting to open their own business. If you are a franchiser and are interesting in expanding your business, you would want to have a link on this Web site because your target market will visit a site like this.

Sponsoring a Mailing List

Another online advertising opportunity is presented by mailing lists. Mailing lists provide a very targeted advertising vehicle. Mailing list subscribers are all interested in the list topic and are therefore potential clients, if you select the mailing list appropriately. The rates for sponsoring lists are quite low. The cost would be determined on a price-per-reader basis and is usually between 1 and 10 cents per reader. Subscribe to the lists that have appeal to your target market and read the FAQ files to determine whether advertising or sponsorship opportunities exist for each mailing list. If the mailing list allows sponsorship, contact the mailing list administrator to inquire about the cost of sponsoring and, if it is reason-

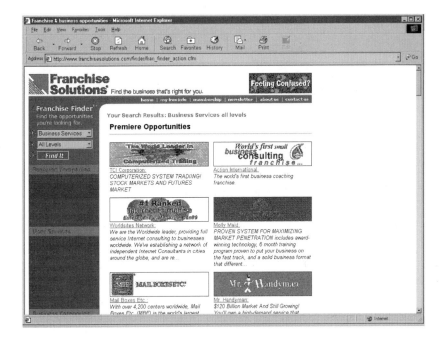

Figure 17.11. Franchise Solutions is a fine example of a commercial Web site that offers companies the opportunity to purchase links on its site. If you are a franchiser, you would want to be on sites like this because they share the same target audience.

able, check availability and sponsors. All of the members of the mailing list have subscribed and want to be on the list; therefore, it is likely that they will read your e-mail. This is an excellent opportunity for you to expose your products and services to these potential consumers. A good example of this would be Trip.com's sponsoring a mailing list about different vacation destinations around the world. Readers are interested in the topic, so they may be encouraged to click-through and book a trip.

Online and Offline Promotion

Your advertising strategy shouldn't be limited to online activities. It is important to integrate your offline advertising strategy to include promotion of your Web site. For more information on offline promotion, see Chapter 24.

Internet Resources for Chapter 17

BANNER AD TOOLS

Animation Online
www.animationonline.com
Create your own animated banner in minutes for free from this site.

Animated Communications
http://www.animation.com
Another online resource to build your own animated banners in minutes.

The Banner Generator
http://www.coder.com/creations/banner
The Banner Generator is a free service to let you create graphical banners for your Web pages.

Creative Connectivity
http://www.crecon.com
Home of the Instant Online Banner Creator.

ONLINE ADVERTISING AGENCIES

MMG: The Online Agency
http://www.mmgco.com/index.html
MMG specializes exclusively in online media planning, buying, tracking, and reporting. They combine state-of-the-art technology with expert knowledge to place advertising for clients in the right place, before the right audience, at the right time, and for the right price. For companies with quarterly online advertising budgets of $100,000 or more.

Thielen Online
http://www.thielenonline.com/index.htm
Full-service advertising agency, located in Fresno and Sacramento, California, with strategic online marketing and complete Web site development capabilities.

AD NETWORKS

24/7 Media
http://www.247media.com

24/7 Media is a top-reach network of branded sites in a vast variety of categories. This allows advertisers to zone in on their target market and get the results that they want from their online marketing efforts.

B2B Works
http://www.b2bworks.com
B2B Works has well over 70 different industries in its network and is emerging as an ad network leader. It can target a specific industry of your choice or advertise your banner to a mass audience.

DoubleClick
http://www.doubleclick.com
The DoubleClick ad network's goal is to provide solutions to make advertising work for companies on the Internet. Five different types of services are offered to help advertisers prosper on the Internet. The site will enable you to market globally and locally. It can help you to build brand awareness, or to close the loop on your target market. DoubleClick also offers its clients the opportunity to participate in the e-commerce world by offering online sales technology to advertisers that would like to sell products online.

ValueClick
http://www.valueclick.com
ValueClick is the Internet's largest results-based advertising network. It uses a cost-per-click model, which enables participants to pay only for the viewers who click through to their Web site.

Banner Exchanges

The Banner Exchange
http://www.bannerexchange.com
When you register, you agree to show banners on your site. Each time a banner is displayed on your site, you receive half a credit. For every full credit you accumulate, your banner will be shown on the Banner Exchange network of Web pages.

GSAnet
http://bs.gsanet.com
GSAnet Banner Swap is unique in that it offers up to a 1:1 display ratio to members depending on where you locate the banner on your Web page(s). In addition, small sites (sites with few visitors) see an even greater ratio due to what are called "charity banners."

LinkExchange
http://www.linkexchange.com
Free banner advertising on over 450,000 Web sites. Support for over 3,000 geographic regions and subject categories, and over 30 languages. You are provided with reports and statistics about the people who visit your site.

LinkMedia
http://www.linkmedia.com/network
LinkMedia Free Exchange is a free service for the Internet community. As a member of the LinkMedia Free Exchange, you will receive free banner advertising on other member sites. In return, you will display banner ads on your site.

Smart Clicks
http://www.smartclicks.com
Free banner exchange with automatic or manual targeting, animation allowed, real-time reporting, and much more!

BANNER ADVERTISING PRICE INFORMATION

Ad Resource
http://www.adres.internet.com
Web advertising, marketing resources, and secrets. Ad Resource offers an extensive price guide about Internet advertising, including what the Top 100 sites are charging. This site also has a large number of Web advertising-related links.

ONLINE ADVERTISING EDUCATION

Adbility
http://www.adbility.com
A great site about ad networks, brokers, exchanges, pay-per-click and pay-per-sale (commission) ads, counters, trackers, software, and much more.

Advertising Age Magazine
http://adage.com/news_and_features/deadline
This advertising industry publication always has interesting articles on advertising online.

Four Corners Effective Banners

http://www.bannertips.com

This site is dedicated to the study of all things banner-like, including banners, click-through ratios, banner advertising, banner link exchanging, and so on. You'll learn how to improve your banners and increase your site traffic. The best part is that this entire site is free!

Internet Advertising Bureau—Online Advertising Effectiveness Study

http://www.mbinteractive.com/site/iab/study.html

The IAB Online Advertising Effectiveness Study is the most comprehensive and projectable test of online advertising effectiveness to date. With 12 major Web sites and over 16,000 individual users taking part in the test, the study ranks as the largest, most rigorous test of advertising effectiveness conducted to date in any medium.

Nielsen Net Ratings

http://www.netratings.com

Nielsen Net Ratings provides you with continuously updated statistics on the top advertisers on the Internet, and which banner advertisements are the most commonly viewed on the Internet. The site also offers a wide range of other Internet-related statistics that may prove important to your marketing needs.

Website Promoters Resource Center

http://www.wprc.com

The focus of the Website Promoters Resource Center is to stay on the cutting edge of the developing Web site promotion industry. If you are looking for resources to help conduct your own promotional campaign, or seek to hire a professional staff to conduct it for you, this is a good place to start.

18

The Cybermall Advantage

Cybermalls
Internet shopping centers.

Cybermalls are Internet shopping centers that contain "stores" related to a specific topic. Some of the more successful malls are those that concentrate on a specific type of product or service category; others focus on a specific geographic area, and still others focus on a specific demographic group. With more and more sites becoming e-commerce enabled, we are seeing a real growth in cybermall participation. These cybermalls bring in targeted, interested people who are looking for a specific type of product or service. The Hall of Malls *(http://www.nsns.com/MouseTracks/HallofMalls.html)* is one site that provides a list of cybermalls you can search to determine if there are any that are appropriate for your company. In this chapter, we cover

- Can your site benefit from being linked in cybermalls?

- Cybermall features

- Types of cybermalls—which is best suited to your business?

- Where to look for cybermalls

- Discounts and coupons to lure customers

- Selecting the appropriate cybermall

- What will it cost?

- Checking visitor statistics

The Advantages of Internet Shopping Centers

Cybermalls are collections of commercial Web sites on the Internet. There are literally thousands of cybermalls, and they are growing in popularity. Cybermalls provide an arena where people can shop online via the Internet. As in traditional malls, cybermall merchants benefit by receiving more traffic due to the promotional power of, and services offered by, the mall owner. These malls are accessed by the consumer through a common Internet address.

Some cybermalls will design, build, and host your Web site, and offer ongoing maintenance of your site for a fee that is comparable to that charged by other Web developers and service providers. Other malls simply provide a link to your site on another server. If you already have a Web site and choose this option, the charges are generally a lot less.

When Are Cybermalls Appropriate?

There are many different reasons that businesses choose the cybermall route. Some businesses choose to participate in a cybermall and also offer their products or services from their own site. Some businesses choose to participate in a number of different cybermalls. Any one of the following may provide sound reasoning for their business decision:

- *You want to increase targeted traffic to your site.* The cybermall has significant traffic from your target market, and by participating in the cybermall you will increase traffic to your site.

- *You don't have a credit card merchant account.* Some financial institutions charge a premium for small-business merchant accounts if the business is going to be selling online, or they may even refuse to provide a merchant account for online vendors. The cybermall may provide merchant accounts or merchant account services to its tenants.

- *You don't know how or don't have the time to work on building traffic to your site.* In a cybermall, the onus is on the mall to perform online and offline marketing activities to increase the traffic to its site. Your site will benefit from the general traffic that comes through the mall doors as long as your product is of interest to the incoming mall visitors.

- *You don't have a secure server.* The fact that a cybermall has a **secure server** may be reason enough to locate your online business there. If you are going to be selling online, you need a secure server, and the volume of business you are going to do may not warrant the purchase price and expertise required to set up your own secure server.

Secure server
A server that allows secure credit card transactions.

- *You can locate your online storefront in a niche mall that caters to your target market.*

- *You don't have credit card validation.* Many malls provide electronic commerce or e-commerce solutions for their tenants. Credit card validation online means that once the purchaser provides the credit card number as payment, the transaction is then authorized and approved by the financial institution. The transaction amount is automatically deposited into the bank account of the vendor, minus, of course, the credit card commission and usually the credit card validation charge.

- *You don't have shopping cart capability.* Shopping carts online allow mall visitors to drop items into their shopping cart as they travel through an online store or cybermall with the click of their mouse. When they have finished their shopping, they can review and edit their invoice online. They may decide they wanted two copies of that CD rather than one, and can make the change with one keystroke. Or they may delete a few items when they see that the total of the invoice is more than they were planning to spend. When the online invoice reflects exactly what they want, they complete the transaction by providing their credit card for payment. When a business does not have the technical or financial resources to put shopping carts on its site, a cybermall might provide this valuable service.

Cybermall Categories

Cybermalls can be organized in a number of ways. Some cybermalls are product-specific, some are industry-specific, some are demographic-specific, and still others are geographic-specific.

Product- or Service-Specific Cybermalls

All of the tenants in a product-specific cybermall provide similar types of products. These types of cybermalls are of interest to the same target market. A model airplane cybermall would consist of a number of merchants that all provide products or services related to model airplanes. Other cybermalls that would fit into this category would be computer software cybermalls, electronics cybermalls, environmentally friendly products cybermalls, and vacation malls. Figures 18.1, 18.2, and 18.3 illustrate some of these types of cybermalls.

Industry-Specific Cybermalls

All of the tenants in this situation would be in the same industry. A financial services industry cybermall would provide a wide range of different products and services such as insurance, banking, investment, and accounting services and products.

Demographic-Specific Cybermalls

There are many cybermalls that target a specific demographic group. These cybermalls provide a variety of products and services that are of interest to a particular group. There should always be some common

Figure 18.1. Online Vacation Mall allows you to order airline tickets, make hotel reservations, book your car rental, and order attraction tickets from one location.

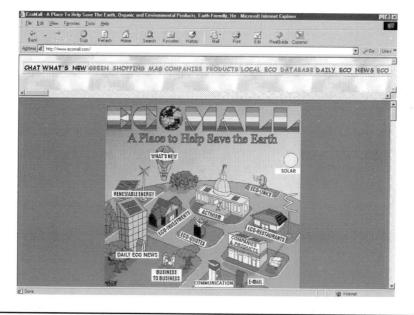

Figure 18.2. EcoMall provides you with everything green.

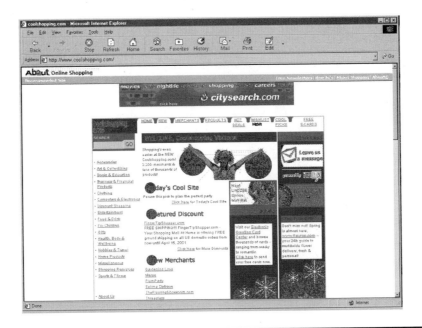

Figure 18.3. *Coolshopping.com* is a general mall offering everything from candy to cars.

theme that ties the visitors together for target marketing purposes. A children's cybermall that has vendors providing everything from clothing to books to gifts to toys would be a good example of this type of cybermall. A seniors' cybermall would offer a wide range of very different products and services, from senior travel to insurance to healthcare to estate planning services, that are of interest to that demographic group.

Geographic-Specific Cybermalls

In geographic-specific cybermalls, all of the tenants are located in the same geographic region. Many of these cybermalls are provided by an ISP for its clients. In many cases participation in these types of malls is done to provide easy access through a variety of means for the customer, to build name recognition with the local customer base, and as a means of advertising and cross-promotion.

Typical Cybermall Products and Services

Most of the items you would find in your local shopping malls are appropriate for a cybermall. Some businesses that are not typically found in retail shopping centers because of the space requirements, such as car dealerships, are also appropriate for cybermalls. Products and services that are popular in cybermalls today include

- Software

- Books

- Computers

- Electronics

- Gifts

- Games

- Clothing

- Travel

- Arts and collectibles

- Automotive

- Food

- Health and fitness

- Housewares

- Financial products and services

- Professional services

- Sports and recreation

- Specialty shops

Some malls choose to concentrate on a specific niche, such as the one shown in Figure 18.4. The niche can be a type of product or a service category. These malls bring in very targeted, interested people looking for a specific type of product or service. A number of cybermalls focus on niche categories such as new automobiles, used automobiles, antique or collector automobiles, environmentally friendly products, tourist resorts, electronics, magazines, coins, stamps, and software.

Selecting the Right Cybermall

Before you commit to a cybermall that is going to host your site, you should check out a number of things in your evaluation process. Choos-

Figure 18.4. The Factory T-Shirt Outlet is a storefront that focuses on one product but provides a range of services such as gift wrap, delivery, and a "dressing room" (where shoppers select sizes and colors).

ing a successful mall is tricky, but if you use the following guidelines you will be better equipped to make the right decision.

Traffic

Obtain details on mall traffic and the number of unique visitors to the home page of the mall, if possible. Any other count of hits may include hits to the pages of merchants in the mall, which would be misleading. Talk with other merchants residing in the mall about their traffic, as well as their experience with the mall itself (fee increases, hidden costs, server downtime, etc.). Many progressive malls now provide their tenants with access to their Web traffic analysis.

High-Speed Access

The cybermall merchant should have a high-speed connection. If access is slow, the visitors will not wait. This is very similar to traditional retail outlets. If the line at the cash register is too long, customers will not wait and will shop elsewhere.

Home Page and Interface

A good cybermall should have a good-quality, attractive home page with consistent navigation throughout the site. It is great if there is space for specials, coupons, or other advertising that you can participate in.

Domain Name

The mall you choose should have a logical and easy-to-remember domain name.

Hardware

The cybermall's server should be reliable, state-of-the-art, and fast, and have lots of capacity to handle the anticipated volume. There should be technicians available to provide technical support and quickly resolve any problems that occur.

Categories

Before choosing a mall, make sure that your business fits within one of the categories in the mall. Don't join a mall that is targeting a different demographic group from yours.

Online and Offline Promotion

Make sure that the mall you choose is promoted both online and offline. Many of the malls promote online only. The cybermall owner should be able to provide you with details of their Internet marketing strategy to increase the traffic of the targeted market to their site.

Site Maintenance Activities

Successful Web sites must be updated on a continual basis. Ensure that the mall provides software tools to make it easy for you to maintain your own site or, if the mall provides the updates, that the fees regarding changes are not too expensive.

Secure Server

Ensure that the mall has a secure server that allows you to offer secure credit card sales transactions. Most consumers will not purchase online without it.

Credit Card Merchant Account

Merchant accounts for the popular credit cards are usually difficult to obtain for businesses with only a virtual presence. If you don't have a merchant account, you will want to choose a mall that offers this service.

Promotions

Find out what type of promotional efforts the mall is involved in. Many malls indicate that they promote extensively, but be sure they are actually targeting shoppers, *not merchants.*

Commission Fees

Some malls charge a commission on every sale. Check the details on all commissions, transaction fees, and other charges. If the mall is responsible for all the traffic to your site, it should be compensated for this activity either through your monthly rental charge or by a commission on sales. If you are making an effort to promote your site yourself and the traffic to your site is a result of your marketing efforts, it is unreasonable for the mall to expect to be compensated for each transaction on your site.

Cybermall History and Reputation

Find out how long the mall has been in existence. Talk to existing tenants and past tenants about their experience.

Other Features and Services Provided by the Cybermall

Cybermalls may include a variety of other products and services to their tenants. When comparing cybermalls, make sure you are comparing apples with apples. Some additional features and services provided by cybermalls might include supplying mailing lists and autoresponders, or providing chat rooms and bulletin boards.

Cybermall Features

Cybermalls may provide a number of features to their tenants as well as to the tenants' customers.

Electronic Shopping Carts

Shopping carts like the one shown in Figure 18.5 are commonplace on the Internet. They enable users to click on items they would like to purchase from various mall vendors and put them in their shopping cart. At the end of their online shopping trip, they have an opportunity to review the contents of their cart as well as the invoice. Purchases can be edited before an order is placed.

Secure Ordering

Most cybermalls offer a secure server and encrypted transactions for their tenants' online transactions. Technology is advancing rapidly in

Figure 18.5. Omaha Steaks provides a shopping cart to facilitate visitors' purchases.

the area of e-commerce, and the cybermalls are among the first Web sites on the Internet to make use of the latest capabilities. Some malls now offer online charge card authorization and automatic deposit for their tenants.

Search Capabilities

Many cybermalls will provide a site search capability to assist shoppers with finding the items they are looking for.

More Than One Cybermall?

It may be appropriate to join more than one cybermall, especially if you have your own site and are just paying a monthly fee for the link from your storefront in the mall to your site. If you decide that this is appropriate for your business, you should have some mechanism in place to track the traffic to your site to determine which malls are effective. This can be accomplished quite easily these days with all the Web traffic analysis tools that are available. See Chapter 25 for a full discussion of Web traffic analysis.

Cybermall Pricing

Malls charge their tenants in a variety of ways. If you choose a mall that hosts one page as a storefront and a link from that storefront to your site on a different server from the cybermall, the charge is generally a flat fee per month. If your Web site is hosted by the cybermall, you may be charged on a flat-fee basis, your charge may be a basic fee with add-ons, or you may be charged on a commission-on-sales basis. The variable charges are generally either on a commission or a set-fee-per-transaction basis.

Cybermall charges to be linked to their storefront can be anywhere from $25 a month to over $1,000 a month, which includes services and a number of features provided by the host.

Where to Look for Cybermalls

To find cybermalls, you can use the search engines. A number of meta-indexes of cybermalls can be found online. There are cybermall Web rings that can be researched and also cybermalls of cybermalls. There are all kinds of locations and sites listed in the Internet Resources at the end of this chapter to assist you in finding the appropriate cybermall for your business.

Enticing Customers with Coupons and Discounts

To increase the traffic to your cybermall site, you can post coupons either as banner ads or as links from other sites. The sites you choose to host these banner ads or links should be those that appeal to your target market, or you might consider purchasing a keyword from a search engine. See Chapter 17 for advice on appropriate banner advertising.

You can also use online coupons, which can be printed from your site, to increase the traffic to your offline locations. If your customers know they can check your weekly coupons or sales, it will encourage repeat visits from them. You might also consider trading coupons with other online vendors who offer noncompeting products to the same target market.

Internet Resources for Chapter 18

Access Market Square
http://www.icw.com/mall.html
Access Market Square has an occasion (birthday, anniversary, etc.) reminder service that also provides personalized gift ideas. The site also has a great search engine that allows you to enter names of items, brand names, product types, or store names. They provide a wide variety of products by category, including art, audio/video, automotive, books, clothes, computers, electronics, flowers, food, health, jewelry, music, sports, travel, and others. Access Market Square uses VeriSign for secure ordering capabilities.

American Shopping Mall

http://www.greenearth.com

The American Shopping Mall has been rated among the top most visited sites on the Internet by *PC Magazine*. It professes to be one of the busiest virtual shopping malls on the World Wide Web, with over 32 million visitors last year and over 50 million visitors since its opening in 1995.

The Cybermall.com Directory

http://www.cybermall.com

Evaluation of hundreds of online malls and selection of only what they determine are the very best. Malls cannot purchase a listing on this site (unlike other directories) and are selected exclusively because they provide you with a positive home-shopping experience. You get access to the better shopping malls without fighting through hundreds of them. The categorical listings include brief site reviews to help you find the quality shopping sites you want without all the work.

eMall

http://www.emall.com

This is a great location for organic and natural foods. They have a Complete Health Online Store, a Spice Merchant section with the flavors of Asia, fine teas, and sun-roasted Mexican coffees.

Excite Stores

http://www.excitestores.com

This is an electronic commerce enabler of small and medium-sized businesses that allows them to cost-effectively engage in electronic commerce through the use of Excite Stores' proprietary e-commerce tools and services. Excite Stores offers its electronic commerce services directly to merchants, as well as through partnerships with leading ISPs, Web-hosting firms, and financial service companies with an Internet focus.

The Hall of Malls

http://nsns.com/MouseTracks/HallofMalls.html

The most comprehensive list of all known online malls located on the Net.

MallPark

http://www2.mallpark.com

Thousands of online merchants by shopping category! Instant searching. Secure order forms, shopping carts, merchant accounts to accept credit cards, and merchants can link for free.

Malls.com
http://malls.com
Besides providing a range of products and services from this mall, Malls.com provides a huge meta-index of all the malls on the Net at *http://malls.com/metalist.html*. This list is a great starting point when doing your cybermall research.

ShopNow Market
http://www.internet-mall.com
ShopNow Market's Merchandising Program gives you two key components to successful online marketing: strategic positioning and targeted, focused traffic-generation programs. You'll benefit from their partnerships with high-traffic sites such as Yahoo! and PC World as well as from an aggressive advertising and marketing campaign designed to drive hordes of shoppers to this portal—and to your business. They provide Merchant Listings with options ranging anywhere from an Entry Tenant position with a listing on the department level for just $25 a year to virtually owning the category with top-level placement and other "spotlight" positioning as a $995 per-month Anchor Tenant. They provide à la carte programs for banner, sponsorship, and e-mail advertising. They also offer sponsorship and promotional packages.

19

Maximizing Media Relations

Your online media strategy can be extremely effective in building traffic to your site. Press release distribution can be done easily. Build the right list of e-mail addresses or make use of one of the online press distribution services. Most reporters and writers have e-mail addresses. Some do not like to receive e-mailed press releases; others prefer the e-mail versions. When e-mail press releases are sent out, reporters will reply by e-mail; they will expect your response within 24 hours. Develop a media kit that you can e-mail out to editors. In this chapter, we cover

- Developing your online media strategy

- Public relations versus advertising

- Online public relations versus traditional public relations

- Effective press releases

- Press release and distribution services online

- How to distribute press releases online

- Providing an area for media on your site

- How to find reporters online

- How reporters want to receive your information

- Encouraging republication of your article with a direct link to your site or article

- Providing press kits online

- Electronic newsletters

- Resources

Managing Effective Public Relations

Media relations are very important to your marketing efforts. The best results are achieved when you integrate both online and offline publicity campaigns. Press release distribution can be accomplished easily if you have an established list of reporters and editors, or if you make use of a press distribution service.

Maintaining effective public relations will deliver a number of benefits to your company. Your company and products can be given exposure through press releases, and a positive image for your company will be portrayed. Your relationship with current customers will be reinforced, and new relationships will be formed.

Benefits of Publicity versus Advertising

Media coverage, or publicity, has a major advantage over paid advertisements. Articles written by a reporter carry more weight with the public than ads do because the media and reporters are seen as unbiased third parties. The public gives articles printed in media publications more credibility than they do paid advertisements. Another advantage of distributing press releases is that it is more cost-effective than advertising. You have to pay for advertising space on a Web site or time on the radio, but the costs of writing and distributing press releases are minimal.

One of the disadvantages of press releases compared to advertising is that you don't have control over what is published. If the editor decides to cast your company in a negative light, then there is nothing you can do to stop him or her. If the writer of the piece does not like your company, for whatever reason, this may come across in the article. Basically, after your press release is distributed, you have no control over what will be written about your company.

It is important to note that when generating publicity, you may lose control over the timing of your release as well. For example, you may want an article released the day before your big sale, but the editor may relegate it to a date the following week. There is nothing you can do about this. It is not a good idea to rely exclusively on publicity for important or newsworthy events, because if the release is not reviewed or is not considered newsworthy, you may be stuck with no promotion at all.

What Is a Press Release?

Before you begin your media campaign, you should know what press releases are and how to write them. Press releases are designed to inform reporters of events concerning your company that the public may consider newsworthy. Press releases can get your company free public attention. A press release is a standard form of communication with the media. Press releases must contain newsworthy information. Companies that continually send worthless information in a blatant attempt to get their name in the press will not establish a good relationship with the media.

Writing a Press Release

Journalists are being bombarded with volumes of press releases. To improve the chances of having your story interest the journalist enough to publish it, you must make the journalist's job easier by presenting your press release in an appealing format and style. Your press release should be written as if it was prepared by an unbiased third party. The press release should follow a standard format, which is described in the following paragraphs.

Notice of Release
The first thing the reader sees should be:

FOR IMMEDIATE RELEASE

unless you have sent the information in advance of the time you would like it published. In that case, state it as follows:

FOR RELEASE: Wednesday, April 14, 2002 [using the date you want it released].

Remember that no matter what date you put here, the publication can release the information before or after the specified date. If the news is really big, it is not likely that the publication will hold it until the date you have specified.

Header
The header should be in the upper-left corner. It should contain all of the contact information for one or two key people. These contacts should be able to answer any questions regarding the press release. If reporters cannot get in touch with someone to answer their questions, they may print incorrect information or even drop the article all together.

Connex Network Incorporated
75 Brentwood Drive
Bedford, Nova Scotia
Canada B4A 3S2
Tel 902-468-2578; Fax 902-468-0380
Contact: Susan Sweeney
email: susan@connexnetwork.com
http://www.connexnetwork.com

Headline
Your headline should be powerful, summarizing your message and making the reader want to continue reading. Your headline is critically important; if you get it right, it will attract the attention you are looking for. Keep the headline short—less than ten words.

City and Date
Name the city you are reporting from and the date you wrote the press release.

The Body
Your first sentence within the body of the press release should sum up your headline and immediately inform the reader why this is newsworthy. With the number of press releases reporters receive, if you don't grab their attention immediately they won't read your release. Begin by listing all of the most relevant information first, leaving the supporting information last.

Ask yourself the five W's (who, what, where, when, and why) and answer them up front. Write the press release just as if you were writing a newspaper article for publication. Include some quotes from key individuals in your company and any other relevant outside sources that are credible. If there are any statistics that support your main message, include them as well, providing references.

Your last paragraph should be a short company description.

The Close
If your release is two pages long, center the word "-more-" at the bottom of the first page. To end your release, there are three ways of standard notation to do this: center the symbol "#," the word "end," or the number "-30-" at the end of your message. A sample press release is shown in Figure 19.1.

Advantages of Interactive Press Releases

Online press releases take the same standard format as offline press releases, but the online press release can be interactive, with links to a variety of interesting information that supports your message. Reporters can easily find out other facts by following your links. Additional items included in your interactive press releases are

- A link to the e-mail address of the media contact person in your organization so that with the click of the mouse a journalist can ask a question of the contact via e-mail.

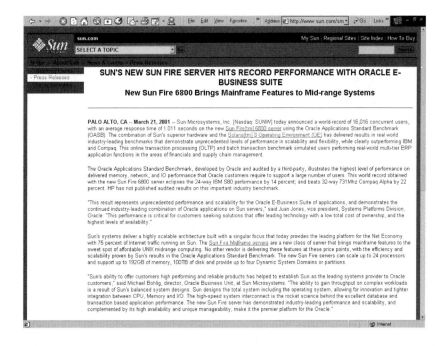

Figure 19.1. A press release from Sun Microsystems. This press release contains several hypertext links, enabling a journalist to quickly access additional information and perform due diligence.

- A link to the company Web page so that the journalist can quickly and easily access additional information as part of his or her due diligence or find required information.

- Links to articles that have been written about the company and related issues, both on the corporate Web site and on other sites.

- Links to graphics and pictures for illustration. If your story relates to a product, have a link to a graphic that can be used. The reporter or individual can simply right-click, "Save picture as . . . ," and incorporate the images in the story.

- Links to key corporate players, their biographies, their photos, and possibly some quotes. Journalists usually include quotes in their stories.

- A link to a FAQ section where you can have frequently asked questions and a few that you wish were frequently asked.

Figures 19.2 through 19.6 are examples of online press releases.

Sending Press Releases on Your Own versus Using a Distribution Service

When distributing press releases on your own, you save the money it would cost to have a service do it. You can also be more targeted in your efforts than a service would be. Some services' lists may be out-dated or incomplete. Their lists of reporters and editors may not be comprehensive and may not have been updated. On the other hand, some services may get your press release taken more seriously. A reporter who recognizes the name of the service may be more receptive than if it were to come from an unknown company. Using a service is bound to save you a lot of time.

Figure 19.2.   This press release contains textual URLs within the release that can easily be used later if the document is printed for later reference.

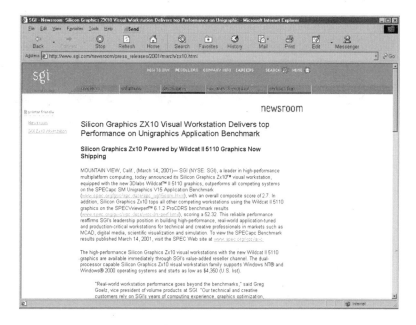

Figure 19.3. SGI provides a press release that contains a textual URL as a hypertext link, covering all the bases.

Figure 19.4. VA Pepsi press release about premiering Pepsi's Britney Spears commercial on Yahoo!.

Figure 19.5. Pepsi's site with a chronology of past press releases.

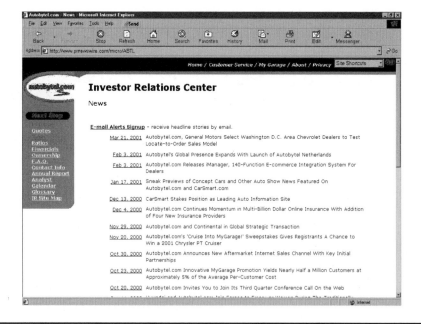

Figure 19.6. AutoBytel's chronology of past press releases. Note the option to sign up to receive e-mail alerts.

If you decide to send your press releases on your own, you will have to build a list of journalists. When reading publications, look for the names of reporters and find out their contact information. If you don't know whom to send a press release to at any publication, you can always call and ask for the name of the appropriate editor. Subscribe to a personalized news service to receive articles about your industry. This is a great way to find the names of journalists who might be interested in what you have to say.

There are a number of online resources to assist you in building your press-distribution list, such as the one shown in Figure 19.7. Mediafinder (*http://www.mediafinder.com*) is a Web site that may be useful. It provides access to a database of thousands of media outlets including magazines, journals, newspapers, newsletters, and catalogs. Press Access *(http://www.pressaccess.com)* has a large database of journalists and industry analysts (Figure 19.8). Their press access editorial database is available online, 24 hours a day, and contains in-depth in-

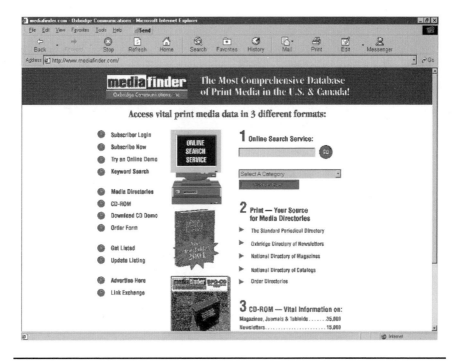

Figure 19.7. Use Mediafinder to locate appropriate magazines, journals, newspapers, newsletters, and catalogs.

Figure 19.8. Press Access Online provides information on editorial calendars, editors, and their preferences.

formation on journalists, publications, calendars, and so on. MediaMap (*http://www.mediamap.com*) is another public relations resource and has detailed profiles on more than 20,000 media contacts, including their phone numbers, fax numbers, e-mail addresses, and work preferences (Figure 19.9). They also have editorial calendars that tell you who will be writing a scheduled story, what the topic of the story is, and when it will be written.

There are a number of press release distribution services online (Figure 19.10 and 19.11). You will find a number of them in the Internet Resources at the end of this chapter.

Golden Tips for Press Release Distribution

When distributing your press releases, don't send them to the news desk unaddressed. Know which editor handles the type of news in your release, and address the press release to that person. Don't send the press

Figure 19.9.   MediaMap is a software and media information company.

Figure 19.10.   INB is an e-mail press release service company, including the distribution and writing of e-mail press releases.

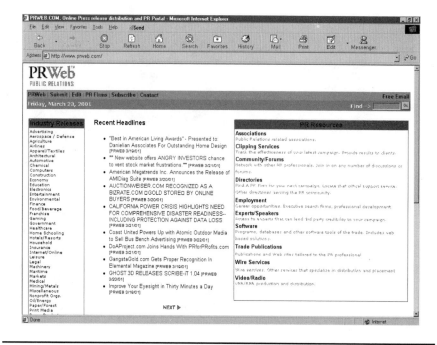

Figure 19.11. You can submit your press release to PRWeb.

release to more than one editor in any organization unless there is more than one angle to the information in the press release. Call ahead, if possible, to discuss and solicit the editor's interest in your press release before sending it. Also, follow up with a phone call a few days later to ensure that it was received and to answer any questions. Be sure to review editorial calendars of publications in your industry to see if there are upcoming articles where your story may make a contribution.

Press Release Timing and Deadlines

One of the most important things to remember when sending a press release or advisory is the deadline. Know how far in advance you should send your information for each of the different media. Here are some time guidelines for your press release distribution.

Monthly Magazines

For monthly magazines, you should submit your press releases at least two to three months before the issue you want it to appear in. Magazines are planned far in advance, because it often takes a number of weeks to have the magazine printed and in subscribers' mailboxes.

Daily Newspapers

It is a good idea to have your press release arrive on the editor's desk at least several weeks in advance. If it concerns a special holiday, you should send it even earlier.

TV and Radio

When submitting press releases to TV and radio, remember that you may be asked to appear on a show as a guest. Be prepared for this before you submit the release. TV and radio move very quickly; a story that has been given to the news director in the morning may appear on that evening's news.

Formatting Your E-mail Press Release

Your press releases can be e-mailed. Some reporters prefer e-mailed releases; others say they prefer mailed or faxed releases. Check the reporter's preference before you send your press release. If you e-mail your press releases, make sure that your e-mails are formatted properly. Refer to Chapter 9 for guidelines on how to create effective e-mail messages.

Keep your e-mailed press releases to one or two pages with short paragraphs. It is best to insert the press release in the e-mail. Do not send your press release as an attachment. You don't know which platform or word-processing program the reporter is using. You might be using Microsoft Word 2000 on a PC, but the reporter could be using an incompatible program on a Mac and will not be able to open the file. There may also be problems downloading, which may prevent your release from being read. The person on the receiving end of your e-mail may be using an old computer with a slow dialup connection, so that what may take you 2 minutes to transfer might take the recipient 20 minutes to download. In addition, you may be using a PC platform but the reporter may be using a MacOS-based computer. Someone who spends 20 minutes downloading your e-mail only to find that it's useless won't be impressed—great start to getting the journalist to do a positive story on you!

Make sure the subject line of your e-mail is compelling. Journalists can easily delete e-mailed releases, unopened, and quite often they do, because journalists receive large volumes of these daily. Make sure your e-mail is clear and concise. Get to the point with the first sentence. If you don't grab the reader's attention at the beginning of the release, the recipient may not keep reading to find out what your news is.

It's very important to be able to send press release information in digital format (as a file rather than hard copy). The journalist, with a quick copy and paste, will then have the "first draft" of the story (Figure 19.12). You have made it very easy for him or her to then edit the draft and have a story very quickly. Everybody loves to save time, and a lot of these journalists are under tight deadlines.

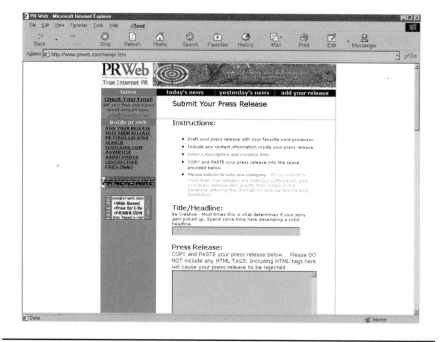

Figure 19.12.   When a press release is provided in digital format, it can easily be copied and pasted into another document.

What Is Considered Newsworthy

Your press release has to contain newsworthy information for it to be published. One of the main concerns for public relations representatives is figuring out what is considered newsworthy and what isn't. You have to have a catch, and, if possible, it should appeal to some sort of emotion. Here is a list of newsworthy items:

- A merger or partnership between your company and another

- A free service or resource offered by your company to the general public

- A survey or forum that your company is holding to discuss an already hot news topic

- The appearance of a celebrity at a company event or upcoming online promotions

- Your participation in a trade show

- The findings of a report your company has conducted

- A breakthrough in technology resulting in a significant new consumer product

- The development of new strategic alliances or partnerships

- A charitable contribution by your company

- A milestone anniversary that your company is celebrating

- An award presented by your company

What Isn't Considered Newsworthy

Some things that aren't news to the general public may be news to targeted trade magazines and journals. Use your own judgment when trying to determine if your press release is news or just an excuse to get your company's name in the press. If your release focuses on any of the following, it is probably not newsworthy enough to publish.

The launch of a new Web site has not been news for a number of years now. Unless the site is based on a breakthrough in Internet technology or serves the public interest in an innovative way, you won't get a mention in the news. Nor is a new feature or change to your Web site newsworthy information. Even if your site has undergone a major overhaul, this is not news to the general public.

Launching a new product is not newsworthy unless the product represents a significant breakthrough in some area. The upgrade of an old product simply won't cut it.

Preparing Your Press Kits/Media Kits

Your press kit is an essential item at press conferences and interviews. This kit can also be sent to reporters when they request more information about a press release you have sent to them. Your press kit should start with a folder displaying your company logo and basic contact information. The folder should have pockets inside so that different sheets of information can be inserted. The following items should be included in your press kit:

- A press release outlining the newsworthy event

- A company history

- Brochures

- Other articles written about your company

- Pictures

- Background information on key players

- FAQs and answers to anticipated questions

- Quotes from key individuals

- Contact information

- Business card

Developing an Online Media Center for Public Relations

If publicity is a significant part of your public relations strategy, you should consider developing an online media center as part of your site (see Figures 19.13 and 19.14). The media center should easily be accessible from your navigation bar. It would include all the components a journalist will need when doing a story on your company. Journalists should be able to find pictures to include in the story and all the information necessary to do their due diligence. They should be able to send a question to the appropriate media contact within the organization with one click. The media center should include

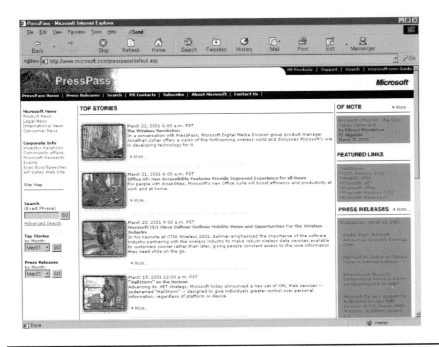

Figure 19.13. Microsoft's media center. PressPass makes information readily available to the press.

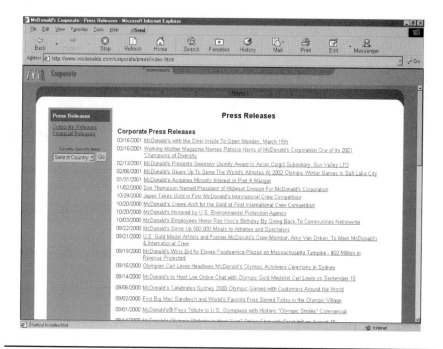

Figure 19.14. McDonald's provides an archive of its press releases online.

- A chronology of press releases distributed by the company

- The company's history and background information

- An electronic brochure

- Links to other articles written about your company

- Links to pictures of a related product or products. Perhaps have a gallery where journalists can choose the pictures they want to include in their story with a right mouse click and "Save image as . . ."

- Background information on key company personnel, along with their pics, bios, and quotes.

- A link to your company's media contact and contact information

- FAQs and answers to anticipated questions

By having a media center on your site, you are sending a clear message to the journalist. You are saying, "You're very important to me! I want to provide you with everything you need to quickly and easily complete your story on our company." With the media center you are providing all the information, in a format journalists can use, to enable them to do the story no matter what time they choose to do it.

Internet Resources for Chapter 19

PRESS RELEASES

Care & Feeding of the Press
http://www.netpress.org/careandfeeding.html
Journalists' manifesto for how PR people should work with the media.

Press Release Tips for PR People
http://marketing.tenagra.com/releases.html
Talks about what a journalist expects to receive and how you should write releases.

A Template for a Killer Press Release
http://www.netrageousresults.com/pr/prtemplate.html
Example format for a successful press release to get yours noticed.

Xpress Press—E-mail Press Release Information
http://www.xpresspress.com/PRnotes.html
Information on how to write and format a press release to be distributed by e-mail.

WHERE TO SUBMIT YOUR PRESS RELEASES

Businesswire
http://www.businesswire.com
Press release distribution service. This site provides a wide range of services and has several showcases.

Click Place Direct

http://www.ideasiteforbusiness.com/direct.htm

Press release contact list of 1,800 of the nation's top business-related newspapers and magazines.

Internet Media Fax

http://www.imediafax.com

Custom online news-distribution service that creates targeted media lists "on the fly."

Internet News Bureau Press Release Service

http://www.newsbureau.com

For a fee you can distribute your press release to thousands of online media outlets here. Also links to a number of good PR resources.

Internet Wire

http://www1.internetwire.com

The Internet Wire offers online press release distribution via e-mail (Figure 19.15).

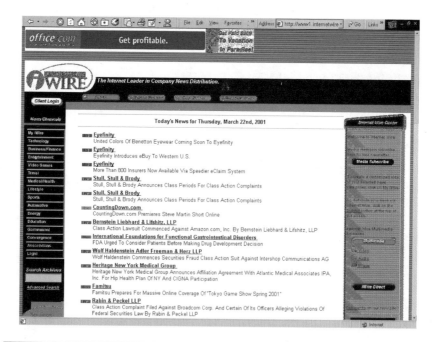

Figure 19.15. Internet Wire is an online press release distribution company.

Partyline
http://www.partylinepublishing.com
The standard media placement newsletter for the public relations trade.

PR Newswire Home Page
http://www.prnewswire.com
A leading source for worldwide corporate media, business, the financial community, and the individual investor.

PR Web
http://www.prweb.com
A dynamite site that distributes press releases but also provides an extensive list of PR resources as well.

Xpress Press News Release Distribution Service
http://www.xpresspress.com
Press releases delivered electronically by e-mail to 4,000 journalists and media members in the United States and internationally.

PRESS RELEASE DISTRIBUTION SOFTWARE

Press Blaster
http://www.pressblaster.com
Press Blaster is software for Windows that turns your PC into your own in-house press release distribution center! You can select your contacts, send e-mail, and print mailing labels, all from one easy interface. You'll also get the coveted database that all the major players use to get their free press.

PRWizard
http://www.prwizard.com
PRWizard is a powerful, automated press release submission software that lets you effortlessly broadcast your press release to almost 11,000 targeted media contacts.

20

Increasing Traffic Through Online Publications

E-zines
Electronic magazines.

More than 60% of Internet users frequently read online publications, or **e-zines**. You can identify appropriate marketing opportunities by searching for and reading e-zines that are relevant to your business. In this chapter, we will cover

- What are electronic magazines?

- Finding online sites to advertise or arrange links

- How to find appropriate e-zines for marketing purposes

- Submitting articles to appropriate e-zines

- Advertising in appropriate e-zines

- E-zine resources online

Appealing to Magazine Subscribers on the Net

Many Web users frequently read e-zines. This is one of the reasons they are among the most popular marketing tools on the Internet. Five years ago there were a few hundred e-zines in publication. Now there are thousands of e-zines dedicated to a wide variety of topics such as travel, business opportunities, food, childcare—you name it. For any topic you are interested in, there quite likely are several e-zines dedicated to it.

What Exactly Are E-Zines?

E-zines, or electronic magazines, are the online version of magazines. They are content-rich and contain information regarding a certain topic in the form of magazine articles and features. Many e-zines display ads as well. Some e-zines are Web site based and others are e-mail based.

Many offline magazines provide a version online as well (Figure 20.1). *Time, People,* and *Sports Illustrated* are all accessible via the Internet. Some of these provide the full version of their traditional magazine; others are selective about the articles they provide, and still others provide the previous month's edition.

Web-Based E-Zines

There are Web-based e-zines that have only an online presence (Figure 20.2). These e-zines are accessed through their Web sites by browsing from page to page. They have the look and feel of a traditional magazine. They include lots of glossy pictures and advertisements. Usually there is no charge to view the Web based e-zines, but some do charge a subscription fee. These Web-based e-zines tend to be as graphically pleasing as offline magazines.

E-mail E-Zines

E-mail e-zines are not nearly as pretty as the Web-based e-zines. They tend to be more content-oriented (see Figure 20.3) and, as such, tend to be more of a target-marketing mechanism. E-mail e-zines tend to be several pages in length with several articles and often have classified advertising. Circulation of these e-zines is often in the thousands. Most of these e-zines run weekly or biweekly editions. Most e-zines are free to subscribers.

Figure 20.1.   *People* magazine is an example of an offline magazine that has an online version.

Figure 20.2.   *Vermont Living* is a Web-based e-zine.

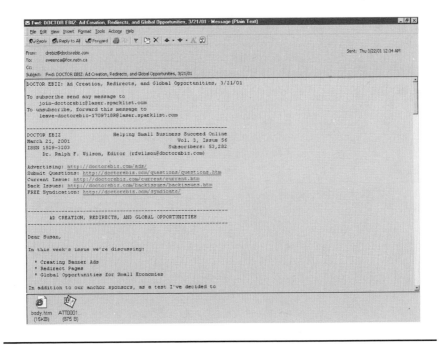

Figure 20.3. Dr. Ralph Wilson produces a dynamite e-mail based e-zine called Dr. E-Biz.

Those individuals who are interested in the subject have taken the time to subscribe and ask to receive the information directly in their e-mail box. Once you have found an e-zine that caters to your target market, the e-zine may be a very valuable marketing vehicle.

Every subscriber to an e-mail based e-zine has access to the Internet. These people regularly receive and send e-mail and quite likely surf the Net. If you advertise in this type of medium and place your Internet address in the ad, your prospective customer is not more than a couple of clicks away from your site.

People subscribe because they are interested. Even if they don't read it immediately when it is received, they usually read it eventually. Otherwise, they would not have subscribed. Subscribers will see your URL and product advertisements. For this reason, e-mail e-zines are a great marketing tool.

Using E-Zines as Marketing Tools

Online publications are superior marketing tools for a number of reasons. They can be used in a number of different ways to increase the traffic to your Web site. You can

- Advertise directly

- Be a sponsor

- Submit articles

- Send press releases

- Start your own

Finding Appropriate E-Zines for Your Marketing Effort

There are many locations online to find lists and links to both Web-based and e-mail e-zines. A number of these resources are listed in the Internet Resources at the end of this chapter.

You evaluate the appropriateness of an e-zine's marketing potential by the audience, the reach, and the effectiveness. The most important element of choosing an e-zine is to choose one that reaches your target market. The reason e-zine ads are effective is that there is a high correlation between the target customer and the magazine's subscribers. If you advertise in an e-zine simply because it has the largest subscriber rate, you will probably be disappointed unless your products or services have mass market appeal.

You should review a number of the e-zine-listing sites, such as the one shown in Figure 20.4. Some of these sites have search capabilities on appropriate keywords. Others have their e-zines listed by category. Once you have a list of e-zines you feel fits well with your marketing objectives, you should subscribe and begin receiving and reviewing these e-zines.

The Multiple Advantages of E-Zine Advertising

One of the major advantages of e-zine advertising is the lifespan of your ads. E-zines that are delivered to e-mail addresses will be read by the

Figure 20.4. E-zine Search *(http://www.ezinesearch.com)* provides a searchable directory of e-zines.

recipient and sometimes saved for future reference. Many e-zines archive their issues with the ads intact. Advertisers have received responses to ads that are several months old!

When you place an ad in an e-zine, you will see it in a relatively short period of time, perhaps the next day or the next week depending on how often the e-zine is published. Most traditional magazines close out their ad space months before the issue is available on the newsstand.

Your ad in an e-zine is also much more likely to be noticed because there are so few of them. In a traditional magazine every second page is an ad, whereas e-zines have a much greater focus on content and far fewer ads.

When your ad appears in an e-zine, your customer is just a click away because your ad is usually hypertext-linked to your Web site. This brings your customer that much closer to being able to purchase your products or services.

Another advantage of e-zine advertising is that e-zines are often shared with friends and associates. Your ad may be passed around a number of times after it first enters the mailbox of the subscriber. You are being charged for the ad based on the number of e-mail subscribers. Therefore, the extra viewers of your ad will be at no cost to you.

One of the most tangible advantages of e-zine advertising is the relatively low cost due, in part, to the low overhead for development, production, and delivery. E-zines need to fill all of their available space. If an e-zine advertising section has empty spaces, they are often willing to negotiate. Some will even barter with you—advertising space at a discounted price in exchange for their e-zine promotion on your Web site.

E-zines provide a very targeted advertising medium. People subscribe to various e-zines because they have a genuine interest in the topics covered. This provides a major advantage over other advertising mediums. E-zine ads have been shown to have very high response rates due to their targeted nature.

Because they are distributed via the Internet, e-zines reach a far wider audience geographically than most traditional magazines. It is not uncommon for an e-zine to have subscribers from all around the world.

There are thousands of e-zines out there related to every topic imaginable. Most e-zines have thousands of subscribers. When you couple the low cost to advertise in these e-zines and the many e-zines that may reach your target market, it is no wonder many companies are allocating more and more of their advertising budgets to online activities.

Guidelines for Your Advertising

Once you have found e-zines that reach your target market, you should consider a number of other factors before you make a final decision on placing your ad.

- Check the ads displayed in the e-zine for repetition. If advertisers have not advertised more than once, then they probably did not see very positive results.

- Respond to some of the ads and ask the advertisers what their experiences were with advertising in that particular e-zine. Be sure to tell them who you are and why you are contacting them. If you are up front, they will probably be receptive to your inquiry.

- Talk to the e-zine publisher and ask questions (e.g., how many subscribers there are). Ask what other advertisers have had to say about their results. Find out what types of ads they accept and if there are any restrictions. Check to see if the publisher has a policy of never running competing ads. Maybe the e-zine has a set of advertising policies that you can receive via e-mail.

- Find out if your ad can have a hypertext link to your Web site. If the e-zine allows hypertext links, make sure you link to an appropriate page—one that is a continuation of the advertisement or a page that provides details on the item you were advertising. Provide a link to the order form from this page to assist the transaction.

- In some cases the e-zine will have an editorial calendar available to assist you with the timing of your ad. The editorial calendar will tell you what articles will be included in upcoming issues. If an upcoming issue will have an article relating to your type of products or services, you may choose to advertise in that issue. You might contact the editor regarding a product review or submit an article relevant to the issue topics.

- Make sure that the advertising rates are reasonable based on the number of subscribers, and ask yourself if you can afford it. Find out the "open" rate or the rate charged for advertising once in the e-zine. Ask what the rate is for multiple placements. If you are not in a position to pay for the advertising now, ask if there are any other arrangements that could be made. For example, the publisher may accept a link on your Web site in exchange for the ad.

- You should develop your ads with your target customer in mind. They should attract your best prospects. Wherever possible, you should link to your site or provide an e-mail link to the appropriate individual within your organization.

- You should develop a mechanism to track advertising responses. You could use different e-mail accounts for different ads to determine which ads are bringing you the responses. You can also use different URLs to point viewers to different pages within your site. If you have a good traffic-analysis package, you will be able to track the increase in visitors as a result of your ad.

- Make sure you are versed in the publication's advertising deadlines and ad format preferences.

Providing Articles and Press Releases to E-Zines

Besides advertising, a number of other marketing opportunities can be explored with e-zines. Once you have found the e-zines that cater to your target market, these e-zines may be appropriate recipients for your press releases. Refer to Chapter 19 for recommendations on press release development and distribution. The editors may also accept articles of interest to their readership. You might be able to incorporate information on your products and services in an interesting article that would fit the editor's guidelines.

There are many e-zines looking for great content. If you can write articles for them that provide great content for their readers and at the same time provide a little exposure for you, it's a real win–win situation. You'll want to target those e-zines that have the same target market you do and have a broad subscriber base. You'll want to make sure the e-zine includes a resource box at the end of the article crediting you as the author and providing a hypertext link to your Web site or your e-mail address. Having articles published enhances your reputation as an expert, and people like to buy products and services from people who are experts in their field.

Besides sending your articles directly to targeted e-zines, you can also submit them to "article banks" online. Article banks are online resource sites for e-zine publishers. E-zine publishers search through these article banks for appropriate articles for their e-zine and, if they use one, they include the resource box of the author.

Reasons You Might Start Your Own E-Zine

You can start your own e-zine. There are lots of resources online regarding e-zine development and administration. Don't make this decision without lots of thought, though, as you can damage your reputation if you don't deliver consistent, valuable content.

There are a multitude of reasons why you should consider developing and distributing your own e-zine. E-zines can be an extremely effective online marketing tool for the following reasons:

- You become established as an "expert." By providing your readers with valuable articles related to your area of expertise, you become, in their eyes, a valued and trusted expert.

- You establish trust. The first time someone visits your Web site, he or she has no idea who you are, how capable you are, or how professional you are. Sure, visitors get an impression from the look and feel and content of your site, but are they ready to do business with you? By providing them with free, valuable content over a period of time, you earn your visitors' trust, and they are more likely to turn to you when they need the type of product or service you provide.

- You generate significant traffic to your Web site. Your e-zine should always reference and provide a hypertext link to something available from your Web site. Once your visitor links through, there should be elements to create stickiness that encourage him or her to stay awhile and visit a number of pages on your site. The more often people visit your site, the more likely they are to do business with you.

- You build loyalty. Relationship marketing is what it's all about on the Web. You build relationships over time, and your e-zine will help you do just that. Your subscribers receive something free from you every month. Whom are they going to do business with when they have a need for your product or service? People prefer to spend their money with businesses they know and trust.

- You stay current with your customers and potential customers. When you are in front of your subscribers every month, you're not too easy to forget. You can keep them up to date on what's new with your company and your products and services, or what's new in your area of expertise.

Developing Your Own E-Zine

If you do start your own e-zine, you should spend sufficient time planning and testing before you publish to ensure that you do it right. You don't get a second chance to make a first impression, and you want your readers to subscribe and tell others about the great e-zine they found. You want them to be excited to read your e-zine every time it is delivered to their e-mail box. The following tips will help you in your e-mail based e-zine planning and preparation:

- Provide great content. This goes without saying. If you have content that people want to read, they will remain subscribers. Don't think that shameless self-promotion is great content; your target audience certainly won't. As a rough guide, make sure your e-zine is 80% rich content and no more than 20% promotion and ads. Your e-zine should be full of what your target market considers useful information.

- You should keep length a consideration because you want your e-zine to be read and not put aside for later because it is always too long to read quickly. In this case, less is more. Subscribers should be able to read your e-zine in 5 minutes or less. If you do have a lengthy article, you might give a synopsis in the e-zine with a hypertext link to more detail on your Web site.

- Limit your content to four or five dynamite articles. Provide a brief table of contents at the beginning of the e-zine. Keep the copy short and to the point.

- Keep your line length under 60 characters including spaces to avoid word-wrap issues.

- Encourage your readers to send a copy to others they feel might be interested in your great content. Make sure you provide subscribing instructions as well for those who receive these forwarded copies. You should also provide instructions on how to opt out, or unsubscribe.

- Test your e-zine with different e-mail programs to ensure that your e-zine looks the way you designed it no matter which e-mail program your reader chooses to use. Send test copies to friends with different e-mail readers like Outlook Express, Netscape Mail, Pegasus Mail, and Eudora. See how it looks, ensure that word wrap is not an issue, and make sure the hypertext links work.

- Keep your subscriber addresses private and let them know your privacy policy.

As the word about your e-zine spreads, you will have a large community of people who fit your target market reading it.

Once you have your own e-zine, you'll have to

- Promote it to your target market through newsgroups, mail lists, your Web site, and your e-mail signature file. If you do promote your e-zine in newsgroups and mail lists, be sure it is appropriate to advertise your e-zine in a given newsgroup or mail list before you post. You do not want to be accused of spamming. However, promote your e-zine shamelessly on your site (let people subscribe to the e-zine on your site) and in your signature file.

- Provide an opportunity for subscribers to let others know. In your online e-zine, have a form that allows subscribers to e-mail a copy of the e-zine to their friends and colleagues. Use a call to action statement such as "Do you know someone who might be interested in this e-zine? Click here to send them a copy." This is a great way to pick up additional subscribers because some of the nonsubscribers who read your e-zine might then become subscribers if your content is interesting to them.

- Make it easy for people to subscribe to your e-zine. Provide clear subscription instructions in each e-mail version of your e-zine and on the online version. Have a form handy on your site to collect e-mail addresses from people who wish to subscribe.

- Provide an archive of past issues on your Web site so that visitors can sample your wares before subscribing. Make sure you provide an option for visitors to subscribe from that page as well.

- Don't provide your list of subscribers to anyone. This will protect your subscribers' privacy and keep your list spam-free. Thus, when you mail your e-zine, use the BCC feature or use a specialized e-mail program that hides all the recipients' addresses so the entire list is not compromised. People will not be happy if they start receiving spam as the result of your e-zine.

Internet Resources for Chapter 20

BestEzines
http://www.bestezines.com/ezines/master.shtml
Directory of e-zines organized by category. A great site to find appropriate e-zines to reach your target market.

The Book of Zines
http://www.zinebook.com/main.html
Dynamite site with tons of links to e-zines, advice on developing your e-zine, reviews, interviews, how-to section, newly noted, and zine tips.

Ecola Newsstand
http://www.ecola.com
Ecola Newsstand has over 6,800 magazines, newspapers, and publications. There are over 100 categories of magazines to choose from.

Electronic Newsstand
http://www.enews.com
Founded in 1993, this was one of the first content-based sites on the Internet. Since then, the site has grown to become the largest and most diverse magazine-related resource anywhere on the Web.

The Etext Archives
http://www.etext.org/Zines
Complete with a search engine, this site offers places to find all of your online publication resources.

eZINE Search
http://www.ezinesearch.com/search-it/ezine
Billed as the world's ultimate e-magazine database. Searchable by category.

Ezine-Universe

http://ezine-universe.com

Ezine-Universe is a great directory of e-mail based e-zines.

InfoJump

http://www.infojump.com

Browse a huge directory of e-zines by category.

The Magazine Rack

http://magazine-rack.com

Provides a searchable directory of online magazines, newspapers, journals, and e-zines.

MediaFinder

http://www.mediafinder.com

A national directory of magazines with details on target audience, publisher, contact, telephone numbers, Web addresses, e-mail addresses, editorial descriptions, issue frequency, and subscription price. In a lot of cases there is an information request form attached should you want further details. Great resource!

21

Web Rings as a Promotion Tool

Web rings provide a different way to organize sites. They are a free service offered to the Internet community. Web rings arrange sites with similar content by linking them together in a circle, or a ring. Each link in the ring is directed to a CGI script on the Web ring's server that sends the viewer on to the next site in the ring. There are literally thousands of rings with subjects such as communications, games, art, real estate, and so on. If there isn't a ring suitable for your site, you can create your own. The types of visitors you will receive from participating in the Web ring will be potential customers who are responsive to the content of your site and curious about your products or services. In this chapter, we cover

- What are Web rings and how do they work?

- What promotion possibilities are available with Web rings?

- How do I participate and what will it cost?

- Where will I find Web rings that work for my company?

- What Web ring resources are available on the Net?

An Effective Alternative to Search Engines and Directories

Web rings are a fast-growing service on the Internet, providing one of the easiest ways for visitors to navigate the Internet. In each of its tens of thousands of topic-specific rings, member Web sites have linked their sites together, thus permitting more targeted visitors to reach the joined sites quickly and easily.

People are increasingly becoming dissatisfied with search engines and directories as tools to identify specific topic-related sites. Searches on a specific keyword have yielded results that often include totally unrelated sites. For instance, if you were planning a vacation to Mexico and you wanted to search for resorts in Mexico, the search engine results would likely include sites somewhat related but not exactly what you were looking for. The results would include book titles at Amazon.com related to Mexican travel, personal pages with other people's experiences traveling in Mexico complete with pictures from their family vacation, travel agencies, and tour company sites. The Web ring provides an alternative to these tools.

Site owners typically trade links with other Web sites to help advertise each other's sites. The Web ring was developed to enlarge the scope of link trading. A Web ring joins together many sites with a common topic.

Two of the major Web ring sites are

- Yahoo!WebRing at *http://dir.webring.yahoo.com/rw*

- RingSurf at *http://www.ringsurf.com*

What Are Web Rings?

A Web ring is made up of a number of topic-specific sites that are grouped together. There are country inn Web rings, Star Trek Web rings, prenatal-care Web rings, BMW Web rings, and remote-sensing Web rings in the huge list of Web rings that exists today. At Yahoo!WebRing there are several major categories.

- Business and Finance

- Computers and Internet

- Cultures and Community

- Entertainment and Arts

- Family and Home

- Games

- Government and Politics

- Health and Wellness

- Hobbies and Crafts

- Music

- Recreation and Sports

- Regional

- Religion and Beliefs

- Schools and Education

- Science

- Sex and Romance

Ringsurf.com also has many categories:

- Arts and Humanities

- Business and Economy

- Computers

- Entertainment

- Games

- Health

- Internet

- Miscellaneous

- Society and Culture

- Sports and Recreation

Each of these major categories has a number of subcategories, and each of the subcategories has a number of individual rings.

Rings can contain any number of sites. There must be at least five before the ring will be listed in the directories. Generally, the rings will contain somewhere between 20 and 200 sites. Some rings are smaller, and some rings are substantially higher, with close to a thousand sites included.

Each ring was started and is maintained by an individual Web site owner. Through navigation links found most often at the bottom of member pages, visitors can travel to all or any of the sites in a ring. They can move through a ring in either direction, going to the next or previous site, or listing the next five sites in the ring. Visitors can also jump to a random site in the ring or survey all the sites that make up the ring.

An extraordinary system, Web rings are entirely open and free of charge to both visitors and members. As more and more people discover Web rings, we will see phenomenal growth in this as a preferred method to surf the net. At the time this edition was written, RingSurf had 12,223 Web rings with 119,314 member sites.

How Do Web Rings Work?

To surf a ring, all you have to do is use the links at the bottom of the page in the Web ring block. At the bottom of a Web ring participant's pages, you will find the Web ring navigation aid. A common Web ring graphic will include links to the "Next" site in the ring, the "Previous" site in the ring, or a "Random" site in the ring. You also have the option, in many cases, to see a list of the "Next 5" sites in the ring or to view the entire "Index" of the ring's sites. Once you begin surfing a ring, there is no clear beginning or ending, just a circle of related material. The Web ring program compensates for sites that are unreachable because they no longer exist or have server problems. You will always be able to navigate the ring.

When using a search engine, you are provided with a list of resulting sites, only some of which are appropriate. You visit the sites listed and then, depending on which browser you are using, you may use your "Back" button to return to the results page to make another selection. With a Web ring this backing out is unnecessary. Once you're finished reviewing a site in the ring, you proceed to the next site that is of interest or simply surf through the connected sites one by one.

How to Participate in Web Rings

The first thing to do is find Web rings that are appropriate for your product or service—those that cater to your target market. You can review the directories at the Yahoo!WebRing site *http://dir.webring.yahoo.com/rw* and also at the RingSurf site *http://www.ringsurf.com*.

Once you have found an appropriate Web ring, you contact the owner to ask permission to join. See Figure 21.1 for an example of this. The owner will review your site to determine your "fit" with the theme. Once you are accepted, the owner will provide you with the required code and accompanying graphics, which you will insert on your page. The ring owner provides all the required material; you slip it into your HTML file, and that's that.

Once the code is on your site, Yahoo!Webring or RingSurf monitors the traffic and collects the statistics for your site as they do for all Web ring sites. This is very beneficial to you because you can see how much traffic you are getting through the Web ring.

Any Web site owner who feels no existing ring is suitable can apply to create a new ring. If the application is approved, Yahoo! Webring or RingSurf will provide all the necessary code and instructions. New Web rings are listed in the directory once they contain at least five sites.

Figure 21.1. This inclusion request was taken from The Lady Bug Lovers Web ring to show how easy it is to join a Web ring.

Web Ring Participation Costs

The cost to participate in these Web rings is absolutely nil. No application fees, no charge for the approval, no charge for the code to be inserted on your pages, no charge for the increased traffic a Web ring brings.

The Benefits of Web Rings

There are many benefits to both the users of Web rings and the participating Web sites. Benefits to the user include

- Web rings provide a great navigation tool when looking for more information on a specific topic.

- Web rings are easy to use. They provide one of the most efficient ways to find specific content on the Internet.

- Web rings avoid the duplication found in search engines, where a site may appear several times in one search. Each site is linked only once in each Web ring.

- Web rings speed up search time.

- Web rings eliminate sifting through mounds of search engine results for appropriate sites.

Benefits to participating Web sites include:

- Web ring participation increases the number of targeted visitors to your Web site.

- The organizers of the Web rings make it easy to monitor how successful your ring is. Traffic reports and "top" rings statistics are made available to participants.

- Web rings drive traffic to your site.

Business Reluctance to Participate in Web Rings

One of the biggest hurdles Web rings face in being adopted by the business sector is that when you join a ring, you are linking to the competition, as shown in Figure 21.2. It is likely that this mentality explains why Web rings have been so popular for personal sites and special-interest groups, but have failed to catch on in today's business community. But, again, small businesses and retail-oriented sites have not shied away from rings. For example, rings and banner programs are hot marketing strategies for stores that sell collectibles. This is particularly true for hard-to-find collectibles. Take the Pez phenomenon: *Not* being on a Pez Web ring could be a crucial mistake for vendors. After all, if a customer hits a site and it doesn't have a specific Pez, the quest isn't over—it's on to the next site. What better way to get there than via a ring? Your site might just be the next one.

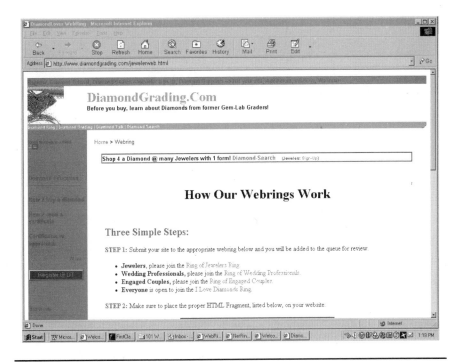

Figure 21.2. The Ring of Jewelers Web ring is an example of a ring that contains many competing businesses.

Lately we have seen a growth in commercial application of Web rings. There are a few reasons for this.

- A number of articles have appeared in Internet marketing magazines related to the high volume of traffic through these Web rings. Businesses have sometimes found that the bulk of the traffic to their site is coming through the Web ring.

- Other articles talk about the benefits of being conveniently located near your competition, bringing more traffic for everyone. Several have likened it to what happens in the real world in the fast-food industry. When a McDonald's opens, you quickly see a Burger King, Wendy's, Pizza Hut, KFC, and Taco Bell all open up close by. This means more business for everyone.

Other Marketing Opportunities Provided by Web Rings

When you have found a Web ring that attracts your target market, you can participate and enjoy the increase in visitors to your site. The International Aquaculture Web ring shown in Figure 21.3 is an example of a professional type of Web ring. It is a Web ring devoted to aquaculture suppliers and aquaria traders. Web rings provide an array of other opportunities as well.

You can search through the list of participants in a Web ring to arrange reciprocal links. You can also search a Web ring for banner-advertising purposes. You can either exchange banners or purchase advertising on these sites. You can find sites that may be appropriate for cooperative advertising purposes. You can exchange coupons with another site you are linked to, which works especially well when you sell noncompeting products to the same target market.

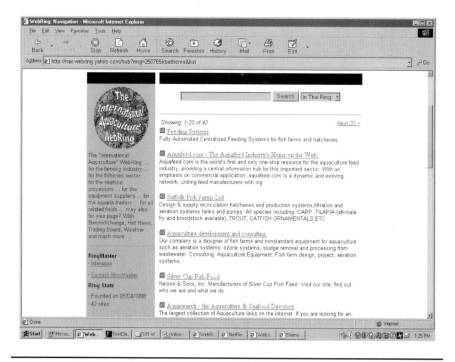

Figure 21.3. The International Aquaculture Web ring is an example of a professional Web ring; it is exclusively for suppliers to and traders within the aquaculture industry.

Internet Resources for Chapter 21

RingSurf

http://www.ringsurf.com

Sites of a particular subject together in a ring. A visitor to any site in the ring can easily move forward or backward through the ring and visit other sites in the ring within that subject area. This drives targeted qualified traffic to all the ring sites. Surfers don't want to deal with mounds of irrelevant search engine results. They want to visit sites on topics they love. It's so simple, and everybody's a winner. RingSurf is a completely free service that lets user quickly, easily, and reliably navigate thousands of related Web sites organized by areas of interest. Joining a Web ring is great way to increase traffic to your site.

Yahoo!WebRing

http://dir.webring.yahoo.com/rw

Web rings are one of the fastest and most exciting ways to navigate the World Wide Web. In each of its tens of thousands of rings, member Web sites have banded together to form their sites into linked circles. Their purpose is to allow more visitors to reach them quickly and easily.

22

Webcasting

Webcasting is defined by Netlingo *(http://www.netlingo.com)* as: "Using the Internet, and the World Wide Web in particular, to broadcast information. Unlike typical surfing, which relies on a pull method of transferring Web pages, Webcasting uses push technologies."

According to a past study conducted by Arbitron New Media and Northstar Interactive, 70% of the Webcast audience clicks for content information, and while listening to or viewing streaming media, nearly 60% click through for advertising information. The study also states that approximately half of the Webcast audience buy online advertised products and 44% click online ads. The majority of Webcast users tune in from home (63%), followed by at-work users (47%). In this chapter, the topics covered include

- Streaming versus nonstreaming media (also known as rich media)

- Advertising with rich media

- Barriers to acceptance of Webcasting

- Uses of Webcasting

- Prominent Webcasters

Streaming versus Nonstreaming Media

Before we explain the marketing implications of Webcasting or rich media, it is important to explain some of the terms and what the end user requires to view them. Webcasting consists primarily of video and audio. Whatis.com defines rich media as

> *Rich media is an Internet advertising term for a Web page ad that uses advanced technology such as streaming video, downloaded applets (programs) that interact instantly with the user, and ads that change when the user's mouse passes over it. For example:*

- *An ad for a Hollywood movie that includes a streaming video sample of a scene from the movie*

- *A mouse cursor that changes to an image on a particular Web site if the user requests it*

- *A standard-size banner ad that includes an inquiry form about ISDN installation, capturing the user's filled-in personal information and telling the user he or she will be contacted by a company representative—all simply by interacting with an ad on an online publisher's Web page.*

This section talks about streaming and nonstreaming content, with most emphasis placed on streaming because it has the highest promotional potential. What is the difference between streaming and nonstreaming? To put it simply, streaming is presented as it arrives. RealAudio files are an example of streaming media. Meanwhile, nonstreaming requires you to download the entire clip or file before you can listen to it or view it. AVI, MP3, and MOV file formats are nonstreaming file formats.

- *Video.* This category would include both streaming (Real Audio, G2, and Windows Media Player formats) and nonstreaming video formats (such as AVI and MOV files). Streaming video is often sent from pre-prepared files but is usually distributed as a live broadcast feed. Examples of this include news clips, movie clips, and online movie presentations.

- *Audio.* Audio also includes streaming and nonstreaming formats. RealNetworks is by far the current king, with its RealAudio. Another major leading provider of streaming audio is Macromedia, with its Shockwave.

Obviously, streaming video file formats contain an audio element to them as well. After all, a movie clip is much more interesting when there is sound associated with it.

Other popular Webcasting or push technology formats include:

- ASF (Advanced Streaming Format)—Designed to store synchronized multimedia data and deliver the data over a large variety of networks and protocols.

- CDF (Channel Definition Format)—Permits Web developers to push information to users through the use of channels.

Push technologies involve sending information to your target market across the Internet. Internet users install software on their system that receives content from the Webcaster. For example, they might receive the latest sports scores, the current weather conditions in 20 cities around the world, or current headlines. The information is "pushed" to the client's system. This is different than with "pull" marketing in which the client specifically requests content from a Web site by loading it into the browser.

Technically speaking, e-mail is one of the earliest forms of push technology. Internet marketers send e-mail messages to individuals in their target market without permission to do so from each of the recipients. However, we all know that this is spam. Savvy Internet marketers can still use e-mail to push their message to potential clients, but they must have the potential clients' permission beforehand.

Webcasters can utilize push technologies much like Internet marketers do with e-mail marketing campaigns. RealNetworks *(http://www.real.com)* has been involved in the Webcasting field for several years. Their RealPlayer software is a prime example of how to utilize push technology. The basic version of the player can be downloaded for free from the RealNetworks Web site. Observing Figure 22.1, you can see how active channels have been incorporated into the RealPlayer application. Clicking on one of the active channels in the "Channels" menu automatically connects the user to a streaming audio/video pre-

Figure 22.1. RealPlayer receives Internet channels. You can subscribe to new channels or view the channel information of RealNetworks' partners.

sentation from the site of one of RealNetworks' partners. In this way, RealNetworks assists its partners (ESPN, Fox, ZDNet, etc.) to brand themselves through the RealPlayer Webcasting software, and RealNetworks likely receives a healthy sum of money in exchange for this advertising. The RealPlayer software permits you to subscribe to other channels as well. Thus, RealNetworks gives users a free application, but the company profits from RealPlayer by selling advertising space. RealNetworks is the perfect example of how Webcasting can be used to quickly achieve brand recognition and earn additional revenue.

Aside from RealNetworks, the following companies also provide software to allow for the distribution of channels:

- Microsoft Active Channels software (*http://www.microsoft.com*)

- Netscape Communicator's Netcaster (*http://www.netscape.com*)

- Infogate (*http://www.infogate.com*) (see Figure 22.2)

Advertising with Rich Media

Companies can use rich media by purchasing a "commercial" that precedes an online presentation or audio event, or a company can develop and use rich media on its own Web site to provide a greater sense of interactivity, which will result in more repeat traffic. For an example of this, go to Yahoo! Events *(http://www.broadcast.com)*. Yahoo! Events provides current streaming audio and video footage of almost any event you could imagine.

Figure 22.2. Infogate (*http://www.infogate.com*) is a very popular tool that delivers customized content directly to your desktop.

For instance, you can listen to the commentary of an entire NBA basketball game. However, just before the game gets under way, you will be greeted by a 25-second audio advertisement. Why is this good advertising?

- Rich media advertising leaves a deeper impression on customers than does a static banner ad.

- Rich media averages higher recall.

- Higher customer recall of rich media makes it easier to brand a company name or product.

- Rich media has higher click-through rates.

- Rich media is more "likeable."

Higher Recall

@Home *(http://www.home.com)* recently conducted a rich media usage study among consumers who had recently switched from dial-up to high-speed Internet access. Their study revealed the following results:

- 93% of users download more MP3s than they did when using a dial-up connection.

- 90% download more music and videos.

- 89% watch more streaming video.

- 86% listen to more streaming audio.

- 79% transfer a greater number of large files.

- 78% share more photos online.

This means that more and more people are likely to remember your company's streaming media presentation than a static banner ad, as they are more apt to view rich media.

Better Branding

It goes without saying that better customer recall leads to better branding. Creating brand awareness with banner ads is difficult because banner ads are not very interactive. The combination of sight and sound possible with rich media advertising makes it much more effective than a static image or looping animated GIF.

More Click-Throughs

A banner ad incorporating Java or Flash Media will have more than twice the number of click-throughs than will a static banner ad. Static banner ads average less than one click-through per hundred impressions. If you have a banner ad that actively engages your customer, you can achieve higher click-through rates and generate more sales leads.

More Likeable

@Home and Intel concluded that a nonstreaming interactive banner ad offers a 20% potential increase in likeability. People will be more likely to interact with a banner ad that has a game of some sort built into it as opposed to a static image. Therefore, an interactive banner ad has the potential to attract a lot of people who are not usually inclined to click on banner ads of any sort. Likewise, a 30-second spot in a streaming multimedia presentation (e.g., watching the Superbowl online) is going to be more acceptable to a user than is a pop-up banner ad.

The bottom line is that if people like you, they will probably buy from you. Both steaming and nonstreaming broadband media advertising increase your chances of making a positive impression on customers.

More Reasons To Use Rich Media Advertising

Given the high recall rates, the cost per branding impression (i.e., the number of times a customer must view the ad before becoming familiar with your brand) decreases. This increases your ROI (return on investment) because you do not have to invest as much in rich media advertising to get your message across as you would with traditional advertising. For instance, to brand your company's name or product using television advertising could require a substantial financial investment. People change the channel during commercial breaks, so it is harder to reach television viewers.

However, when people intentionally subscribe to an Internet channel, they are viewing and listening to information they are interested in. Plus, it is more of an effort to switch channels on the Net than it is to do so watching television. Therefore, the user's tendency to remain "tuned-in" is higher.

Also, the Internet is a worldwide network. Television, magazines, and other traditional marketing vehicles are more regionalized. Therefore, a rich media advertisement streaming across the Internet has the potential to reach a much larger audience.

The Barriers of Webcasting (Rich Media) Acceptance

With every new medium, there are bound to be barriers to its public acceptance. Webcasting, both streaming and nonstreaming, is no different. There are six primary obstacles that Webcasting must overcome before it becomes a publicly acceptable advertising medium.

Cost

The possibilities are there, but so are the costs, and you must be aware of this. The cost of developing streaming media and nonstreaming media can be quite expensive. Moreover, if you're looking to advertise on a site that applies video and audio content, then you must be made aware that most of the sites that apply this technology are high-budget, high-volume, and high-bandwidth sites and will likely ask for quite a fee to advertise.

You must also consider the potential return on investment. We described earlier how rich media advertising has a higher recall rate than standard Web advertising. Also, rich media is more cost-effective and efficient for branding purposes. Therefore, although the initial expense of producing a rich media advertisement may be quite high, it may quickly be recovered by the interest and sales the ad will generate.

Rich Media Advertising Is Not Accepted by All Sites

Although a lot of sites do not have the resources to offer Webcast advertising opportunities, a lot of major sites do. Content sites such as Launch.com and RollingStone.com place ads in front of some of the videos you can view on their site. These streaming media sites offer tremendous exposure opportunities for companies that advertise with them.

There are also sites such as MP3.com *(http://www.mp3.com)* that offer free Webcast advertising. On MP3.com, unsigned music artists can post MP3 versions of their songs for the world to hear. MP3.com is a high-traffic site as a result of the community of artists they have created, and the artists themselves benefit from the increased exposure.

Given the number of Webcast companies and major companies getting involved with Webcasting, companies that do not utilize it may be left behind.

Bandwidth Constraints

Both streaming and nonstreaming media require that users have high connection speeds in order to experience a Webcast as it is intended. To view streaming content, you will need a plug-in or player of some sort. Popular applications used to view or hear streaming content are

- Windows Media Player

- Quicktime

- RealPlayer

- Macromedia Shockwave Player

It is important to note that the higher the connection speed, the more convenient the use of streaming content will be. If you're still using a 14.4 modem, you're simply not going to get the performance needed to make it worthwhile. This presents an obstacle to people with slower Internet connection rates. Also, some people simply do not wish to download and install the plug-ins necessary to play rich media files. You will not be able to target your Webcasting advertising campaign toward these users.

Irritates User

Does Webcasting annoy users? Sure it does. But this will only be the case for people with low bandwidth or less-robust machines. Also, some people despise advertising in any form, so you probably won't win over any of these individuals either. However, @Home discovered from its rich media study that 90% of its users downloaded more streaming audio and video media since they switched from dial-up to high-speed access. Could @Home boast the same level of advertising acceptance for a television ad? It's very unlikely they could.

Too Complicated

The software to create rich media content exists and, with a little initiative, can be learned by anyone. You first should determine if your target market is likely to be a user of rich media. Here are some software applications you should inspect if you have an interest in creating your own rich media or Webcasting files:

Streaming Media Creation or Encoding Software

- RealSlideshow Plus *(http://www.real.com)*—This product allows you to create your own streaming media slideshow.

- Emblaze *(http://www.emblaze.com)*—Designed to enable delivery of rich media over any IP network, over any platform, and under any bandwidth.

- Liquid Audio *(http://www.liquidaudio.com)*—Offers solutions for encoding your music and serving it in a streaming media format.

- Stream Anywhere *(http://www.sonicfoundry.com)*—The all-in-one solution for preparing audio and video multimedia for distribution over the Web.

- Quick Time 4.1 *(http://www.apple.com/quicktime)*—Create or edit streaming and nonstreaming video and audio files.

Nonstreaming Media Creation or Encoding Software

- Macromedia Director 7 Shockwave Internet Studio and Flash *(http://www.macromedia.com)*—Generate powerful presentations and content for your Web site.

- AudioCatalyst 2.1 and Xing MPEG software *(http://www. xingtech.com)*—Create MP3s and MPEGs from source files.

- Real JukeBox *(http://www.real.com)*—Create MP3 files from CDs.

Learning to create rich media just requires a little bit of initiative and patience.

The Technology Changes Too Often

Webcasting is a relatively new medium. Of course, new standards are being introduced every few months. The key here is to watch what technologies the major Internet sites are using. If you see some of the major players in the Internet starting to use a particular Webcasting technology, you should investigate it. Generally, the learning curve for new technologies is not very steep since they are based on previous technologies.

Uses of Webcasting

Despite the existence of a few barriers to using Webcasting as a promotional vehicle, you should investigate it if you think your target market may include early adapters to technology. Some important uses of providing rich media content to the general public include

- Live continuous broadcasts of radio stations and networks

- Broadcasts of cable networks and television stations

- Coverage of sporting events (both streaming and nonstreaming footage)

- Live music including concerts and club performances (both streaming and nonstreaming footage)

- On-demand shows, corporate events, CDs, audiobooks, video titles, and so on.

As bandwidth increases and more people have access to higher-end technology, Webcasting will become a regular part of our lives and be more accepted as an advertising medium. The transition to Webcasting has already begun, as is evidenced by the large number of prominent players already entrenched in the field.

Today we are seeing that many major corporations are providing live Webcasts of their corporate annual meetings. This is a great idea for a number of different reasons. If there are company shareholders who are unable to attend the annual meeting in person, they are able to observe the meeting remotely via the Internet and Webcasting. Similarly, potential investors can view your annual meeting online and gain valuable insight into your organization, which might result in the individual making an investment in your organization. If potential investors or shareholders miss the live Webcast of the annual meeting, they can visit your site and download the event to watch at their convenience. This is just one example of how Webcasting can add value to your Web site, and ultimately your organization.

We are also seeing an increase in the number of professional training organizations providing online training modules, or "virtual seminars," from their Web sites. The increase in online training popularity is a result of the flexibility and cost efficiency offered by these organizations. In order for your clients to attend your seminars in person, they are inconvenienced with scheduling time to go to the seminar. This inconvenience incorporates travel expenses, the seminar fee, and the opportunity costs of being absent from their office. Virtual seminars enable your clients to usually pay a much smaller fee to view the same seminar from the comfort of their desk. Business professionals are also finding online training useful because it allows them to decide when they will view the seminar, as some of the online training sessions can be viewed at their convenience. Others are "live" and available only at a specific time and date.

More popular online training organizations include

- The Learning Library (*http://www.learninglibrary.com*)

- Learning.net (*http://www.learning.net*)

- Learn2.com (*http://www.learn2.com*)

Many professional speakers are now offering live Webcasts, downloadable training modules, and streaming video clips from their Web sites in an effort to increase their online bookings. For example, meeting planners and organizers who are looking for speakers for their upcoming conference can visit my speaking Web site, SusanSweeney.com (*http://www.susansweeney.com*), to download streaming video clips of samples of my speaking. This enables visitors to gain a feel for my presentation style and the quality of content that I deliver.

Emerging telecommunication technology allows us to bridge phone lines so that multiple users can speak and listen at the same time. Commonly known as a tele-seminar, this feature provides speakers and trainers with the opportunity to share their expertise over the phone line to an unlimited number of listeners. I regularly hold tele-seminars that people can register for on my SusanSweeney.com Web site. When participants register to participate in my tele-seminar, I provide them with an 800 number to call the day of the seminar and a code that admits them to the call. Prior to the program I provide them with a URL where they can access a streaming video version of my presentation that corresponds with the tele-seminar. This type of "virtual seminar" is becoming extremely popular in the professional speaking and training industry.

Prominent Webcasters

Recently, Broadcast.com (*http://www.broadcast.com*) and Yahoo! (*http://www.yahoo.com*) merged. Yahoo!'s Broadcast has Webcast over 36,000 live events including the most recent Super Bowl, the NHL regular season, and the Stanley Cup Playoffs, and even the online premiere of *Casablanca*. Visit *http://advertising.broadcast.com/ad_demos/index.html* to learn more about their advertising opportunities. They offer gateway ads, channel and event sponsorships, multimedia ads, and traditional banner ads. More appropriate to this chapter is the ability to purchase slots and insert Internet-only commercials within Yahoo!'s programming.

Vidnet.com (*http://www.vidnet.com*) places video commercials before allowing you to view a video. When selecting to view Destiny's Child's "Independent Women" video, a streaming video commercial for Intel's Pentium IV processor was prominently displayed first (Figure 22.3).

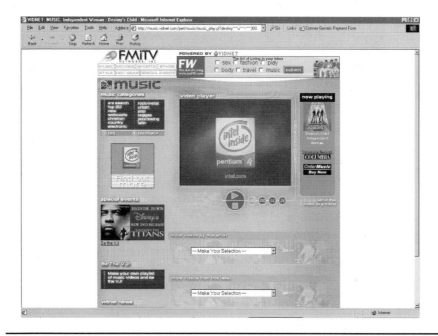

Figure 22.3. Vidnet.com shows us how cross branding can be done with streaming media.

DiscJockey.com (*http://www.discjockey.com*) is another popular site that offers a host of interactive advertising opportunities for multiple demographic segments. Of importance to this chapter is the ability to purchase audio advertisements. Before hearing your selected station, an audio advertisement is played (Figure 22.4). You can contact them through their Web site for more information.

A major use of streaming audio comes in the form of Internet-only radio stations and traditional radio stations that broadcast their signal online. For the radio stations, it's an ideal opportunity to increase market share and increase the number of loyal listeners. Web-Radio.com *(http://www.web-radio.com)* has a large directory of over 2,700 radio stations broadcasting over the Internet. InternetNews.com *(http://www.internetnews.com)* reported in September 1999 that one of every four radio stations with a Web site is Webcasting. At that time, they projected that over 3,000 radio stations would be Webcasting by the beginning of year 2000 (see Figure 22.5).

A radio station will benefit from the broader exposure of Webcasting (worldwide as opposed to regional). These online radio stations pro-

Figure 22.4. Advertise on Web radio stations courtesy of DiscJockey.com.

Figure 22.5. Over 3,000 radio stations now stream their programming across the Internet. The existence of Web-Radio.com is evidence of the growth in this field.

vide an excellent opportunity for businesses to advertise online. Since online radio listeners broaden the potential audience for a radio station, the station could charge advertisers higher rates. This source of revenue is unquestionably attractive, which is why radio stations are scrambling to establish themselves in the Webcasting world.

HotelView's *(http://www.hotelview.com)* Web site is an interactive video library of hotels. Perhaps you own a bed and breakfast near a waterfront location. You can use a streaming or nonstreaming video clip to display this scenery, much like when you receive a videotape from a travel agency demonstrating the beauty of a potential vacation destination (Figure 22.6).

Webcasting is a technological phenomenon that offers Internet companies and traditional companies marketing on the Internet a new way to reach their customers. Many Internet giants have already seized the Webcasting reins and now deliver rich media content and advertising to the world. Perhaps you would be wise to investigate Webcasting and do the same.

Figure 22.6. HotelView.com helps hotels and bed-and-breakfast businesses promote themselves online with streaming video.

Internet Resources for Chapter 22

Broadcast.com
http://www.broadcast.com
Broadcasting over 36,000 live events, Broadcast.com is a streaming media industry giant. It was recently purchased by Yahoo!.

Castanet
http://www.marimba.com/doc/general/current/introducing/introducing.html
Marimba's Castanet is a system for distributing, installing, and updating software and content over intranets and the Internet.

ChannelSEEK
http://channelseek.com
ChannelSEEK is a comprehensive Webcast and streaming media guide for the Web. It even offers streaming MP3 audio from multiple sites. Watch hundreds of movies and listen to music with your computer.

ChannelSeven.com
http://www.channelseven.com
A large resource for Internet development, marketing, and advertising executives. This site contains information on rich media advertising.

International Webcasting Association
http://www.webcasters.org
The IWA serves as the meeting place for companies active or interested in the delivery of multimedia (audio and video) services to consumers or business customers via the Net and other networks.

OII—Webcasting Standards
http://www2.echo.lu/oii/en/webcast.html#RDF
Explanation of Webcasting standards.

OnTheAir.com
http://www.ontheair.com
A reference site listing the best sites that provide links to live radio and television from across the United States and around the world. Over 1,000 stations are available live on your computer.

RealNetworks
http://www.real.com
Innovators in the field of streaming media, RealNetworks has several popular Webcasting software applications, including RealPlayer, RealJukebox, and RealSlideshow.

Scour
http://www.scour.net
Find audio, video, images, and animation at this guide to online multimedia. Search the index for multimedia files or navigate through the category directory.

Streaming Media World
http://www.streamingmediaworld.com
Streaming Media World offers media player reviews, news, tools, tutorials, discussion forums, and cool links devoted to streaming video, audio, MP3, multimedia, and GIF animation.

The Media CHANNEL
http://www.mediachannel.com
A guide to video on the Internet.

VideoDome.Com Networks Inc.
http://www.videodome.com
Offers a variety of Internet OnDemand video solutions to meet your online video needs.

VirtualTuner.com
http://www.virtualtuner.com
Directory of live and on-demand radio links for the Internet.

Web-Radio
http://www.web-radio.com
A comprehensive directory of radio stations (broadcasting) on the Web.

WebReference.com
http://www.webreference.com/multimedia/video.html
A directory of multimedia tools including Windows Media Player, Real, Emblaze, and Macromedia.

23

Grand Opening Tips for Your Web Site Virtual Launch

Just as you would have a book or software launch, you can have a Web site launch. In preparation for the Web site launch, you must develop an appropriate launch strategy. In this chapter, we cover

- Development of your Web site launch strategy

- Web site announcement mailing lists

- Direct e-mail postcards to your customers or prospective clients

Launching and Announcing Your Web Site

A new Web site or your new location in **cyberspace** can be launched in many of the same ways that you would launch a new physical store location. This may involve both online and offline activities. Just as you would prepare a book launch strategy or a new software product launch strategy, you can develop an appropriate launch strategy for your new Web site. Sometimes a launch strategy may be more work than the benefit

> **Cyberspace**
> Virtual location where
> Web sites live.

that will be gained. On the other hand, if you are opening the next Amazon, it is imperative.

Your Web Site Virtual Launch

Let's take a look at a traditional retail store grand opening. For the grand opening, which usually lasts for an evening or a day, there will be invitations to the media, press releases distributed, invited guests, opening ceremonies, advertising, and possibly gift giveaways.

A Web site virtual location launch occurs in cyberspace, and the "grand opening" can last for a day, a week, or a month. Many of the activities you would include in your traditional grand opening can also be included in your Internet grand opening. The effectiveness of your launch can be increased with the following tips:

- Media attention can be generated through the distribution of press releases online and offline. (See Chapter 19 for press release distribution information.)

- Guests can be invited to your online opening through postings in newsgroups, newsletters, "What's New" sites, banner advertising, direct e-mail, and signature files, as well as through offline direct mail and advertising.

- Opening ceremonies can be just as exciting online as offline. They can last for a month rather than a day. The opening must be designed to be of interest to the target market.

- You can feature special guests in chat areas for your grand opening or several special guests over the duration. Again, relate your guests and the topic to be discussed to the needs and wants of your target market.

- You can run contests that require visitors to visit various parts of your site to compete for prizes. Perhaps they have to complete a multiple-choice quiz whose answers are found throughout your site. This way you encourage your guests to visit all those pages you want them to. You can also ask if they would like to be notified via e-mail of the winner. This gives you an opportunity to send them e-mail with their permission.

- You can have audio and video greetings from your site.

- You can have press releases regarding your opening available for download by the media. Make your press release interactive. (See Chapter 19 for details on how to do this.)

- There are many other innovative "grand opening" attention grabbers that can be brainstormed with appropriate marketing and public relations individuals.

- Special free gifts can be provided to the first 20 or 50 visitors to your site. You can also provide prizes to the first 100 to link to your site.

- Do some offline advertising for your new URL (see Chapter 24 for innovative offline opportunities), or take advantage of online advertising via Announcement sites.

Whatever you decide to do, make it memorable, make it appropriate for your target market, and provide reasons for them to return.

Internet Resources for Chapter 23

Best-Web-Sites Announcement List
You can join this mailing list by sending the message "sub BESTWEB your name" to *listserv@vm3090.ege.edu.tr.*

Nerd World What's New
http://www.nerdworld.com/whatsnew.html
The newest links added to Nerd World, and a place to show off your site. Not just for nerds.

Netscape What's New
http://netscape.com/home/whats-new.html
This site selectively publishes information on new sites. To warrant a mention, your site must somehow be unique . . . perhaps using the latest Netscape technologies.

24

Effective Offline Promotion

There are many benefits to cross-promoting your Web site using traditional media and print materials. Your Web site can answer a lot of questions and provide more information than you can print in a magazine or newspaper ad. Your site can be kept up-to-date with the latest information available. People can request additional information or order online. In this chapter, we cover

- Tips for offline promotion of your Web site

- Offline promotion opportunities

Offline Promotion Objectives

Since visitors can be directed from offline promotion to request additional information or order online, you should promote your URL on every piece of promotional material you produce! The more exposure your URL receives, the more likely it is that people will remember it when they go online.

Be creative with your offline promotion campaign. Brainstorm with innovative thinkers to come up with a number of good places to promote your URL; for example, try displaying your URL in your TV and radio commercials, magazine and newspaper ads, and billboards. The more places your URL appears, the more it will get noticed. Some businesses even incorporate their URL into their building and vehicle signage. Answer your telephone "YourCompanyName.com, Good Morning." This is quite effective in letting people know that you want them to visit your Web site and providing them with your URL at the same time. Next time they have a question or want to place an order, they may go directly to the Web site.

Displaying your URL in traditional media encourages people to visit your site for more information about your company. Another benefit is that people usually can order from your Web site. Naturally, your site should be up-to-date, with all of the latest information on products, prices, and sales promotions. If a six-month-old advertisement is seen in a magazine, as long as the URL is displayed in the ad, readers can go to your site and get current information. Your Web site is your most effective advertisement, but it is an advertisement that people have to know about before they can view it.

URL Exposure through Corporate Literature and Material

It is important that your corporate image be consistent in your online and offline promotional campaigns. Businesses should use the same colors, style, fonts, logo, and tag lines on all of their marketing materials. As a rule of thumb, try to place your URL on everything you put your logo on—which means just about every piece of corporate literature. Make sure to include your URL on the following:

- Letterhead

- Business cards

- Corporate brochures

- Envelopes

- Checks

- Fax coversheets

- Report covers

- Flyers

- Advertisements

- Direct-mail pieces

- Newsletters

- Press releases

- Media kits

URL Exposure through Promotional Items

If your company uses promotional items as giveaways at trade shows and events, it is a good idea to incorporate your Web site marketing with these items. Figures 24.1 and 24.2 offer examples of the different promotional products that you can order on the Internet for your business. Promotional items that are used in and around computer workstations are ideal because your URL is visible when people are in a position to actually visit your site. Some examples are

- Mouse pads

- Diskette holders

- Screen cleaning kits

- Software

- Screen savers

- Pens and pencils

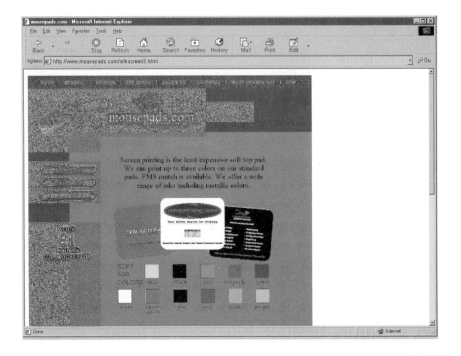

Figure 24.1. Mousepads.com is a site where you can order personalized mouse pads.

- Scratch pads

- Coffee mugs

- Coasters

- Letter openers

- Stress balls

- Calendars

- Sticky notes

Figure 24.2. At epromos.com you can put your business card on a coffee mug.

URL Exposure through Clothing

Articles of clothing are another great promotional item. When people wear an article of clothing with your URL on it, they become a walking billboard for your site. I personally have a jacket that was provided by Webjacket.com (see Figure 24.3), and the quality is great. Your corporate jacket provides exposure for your company and your Web site. If you have a corporate uniform, your URL should be displayed. Put your URL and a catchy phrase or tag line on items such as

- Golf shirts

- T-shirts

- Sweatshirts

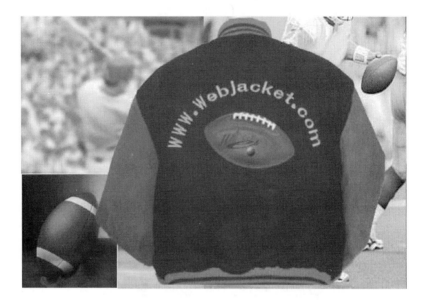

Figure 24.3.   Webjacket.com allows you to customize your corporate jacket with your logo and your URL right on its site.

- Hats

- Aprons

- Jackets

URL Exposure on Novelty Items

Novelty items can be an effective place to print your URL. If your target market is a younger audience, then put your URL on items that will appeal to them, such as

- Frisbees

- Balls

- Beach towels

- Sunglasses

- Keychains

- Magnets

- Chocolate bars

- Bumper stickers

Promotion with a Touch of Creativity

Be creative and come up with catchy slogans that have a connection with the promotional item. For example:

- *Clocks:* "Take some time to visit our Web site at . . ."

- *Rulers:* "For a measurable difference visit us at . . ."

- *Coffee mugs:* "Take a break and visit our Web site at . . ."

- *Tape measures:* "Visit our Web site at *http://www.YourURL.com* and see how our site measures up."

- *Magnifying glasses:* "You don't need one of these to see that our site is the best. Come visit us online at . . ."

- *Watches:* "Isn't it about time you visited us at . . . ?"

- *Bookmarks:* "Take a break from reading and visit our Web site at . . ."

URL Exposure on Your Products

If possible, put your URL on your products themselves. This is an innovative idea that Joe Boxer has implemented. They stitch their URL into the waistband of their underwear.

Internet Resources for Chapter 24

Advertising Concepts
http://www.bumperstickers.com/ad.htm
"Why Use Promotional Products?" This site gives you good promotional ideas and what these promotional products will do for you.

Bizine
http://www.bizine.com/profit.htm
"Increase Your Profits by Coordinating Online and Traditional Offline Marketing," by Bob Leduc.

Digital-Women.com
http://www.digital-women.com/unique.htm
This includes unique ideas for online and offline promotion.

e-Promos.com
http://www.epromos.com
This site has a huge offering of items appropriate to display your logo.

Free Pint
http://www.freepint.co.uk/issues/040399.htm
"12 Offline Ways of Promoting Your URL," by Nikki Pilkington.

Mousepads.com
http://www.mousepads.com
Mousepads.com allows you to choose from many pre-set styles or will develop a custom one just for you. They also allow you to sign up for their e-specials on their site.

PC Mojo
http://pcmojo.com/pcmojo/offline.htm
Information on why you need to promote your site off the Internet.

Promotional Webstickers
http://www.websticker.com/products.htm
Simple ideas to effectively promote your Web site offline.

Webjacket.com
http://www.webjacket.com
Webjacket.com provides a great quality jacket with your corporate logo and Web address. You design your own right on the site. I have one!

25

Web Traffic Analysis

Today, technology not only allows us to generate interactive Web sites for our viewers, it also allows us to learn about our viewers as well. Many Web sites are now using Web traffic analysis software that enables them analyze not only what page of the Web site their visitors came to first, but also where they came from, how long they were there, and what they did while they stayed. In this chapter, you will learn

- What your Web server's log files can tell you

- How analyzing log files with Web traffic analysis software can benefit your Web site

- How to develop a profile of your visitors

- How to optimize your Web site to accommodate your visitors

- How to get the most for your marketing dollar

- How to generate leads for your business

- How analysis software can help you to manage your online advertising business

- How you can get Web traffic analysis software for your Web site

- The popular brands of Web traffic analysis software

Do You Know Who Is Visiting Your Web Site?

Retailers have always spent endless hours trying to analyze the shoppers who visit their stores. They are constantly trying to collect data about their markets so that they can decide what the best forms of advertising are for their target market, what consumers really want in order to make wiser buying decisions, what services are important to them, what product features their target market is looking for, and so on. The same thing is happening today on the Internet. Companies are constantly collecting data on their target market—their needs, wants, preferences, and desires. Most people are unaware that they are even doing this.

Web traffic analysis software is helping companies to focus on their target market like never before. It is helping them to understand the traffic on their Web site and is enabling them to make the necessary changes that are critical to receive the results that they desire from their Web site. "But how do they do it?" you ask.

Using Log Files to Your Advantage

All Web servers log a list of all the requests for individual files that people have requested from a Web site. These files will include the HTML files and their embedded graphic images and any other associated files that get transmitted through the server. These files can be analyzed by Web traffic analysis tools to generate the following data:

- The number of visitors to your home page

- Where the visitors came from in terms of their IP addresses

- How many times each page on your Web site was requested

- What time, day of the week, and season people access your site

- Which browser your visitor is using

- Which keywords or phrases your visitors are using to find your site using a search engine

- Which advertisements are viewed the most on your Web site

- Detailed information on visitors and demographics

This may not sound like very important information; however, there are some very amazing things you can do with this data. Like any good experiment, you must collect the data first, complete the experiment, and then make the recommendations.

Analyzing Log Files with Web Traffic Analysis Software

By analyzing the data from your log files, you can generate results that could significantly increase the popularity and success of your Web site. By tracking the visitors on your Web site in terms of where they spend their time, how they came to your site, and if they do what you want them to do, you can fine-tune your Web site to fit the specific needs of your target market.

Developing a Profile of Your Visitors

By analyzing the log files, you can find out a lot about your audience. You can see how the majority of your audience came to your site and what they like to do while they are there—meaning whether they request information or not, if they download products, or if they are interested in free giveaways. You can use this information to find out if your site needs to be changed to accommodate the needs of your visitors. For example, if you find that a lot of your visitors are spending a lot of time on your What's New page, maybe it would be in your best interest to start a monthly mail list to inform your audience of the happenings of your Web site.

The log files can tell you when your audience is entering your site. For example, if the log files indicate that your traffic is mostly at night, you could predict that most people visit your site from home. Since most homes do not have high-speed access, you may want to check your graphic sizes to make sure that it is not taking too long for your site to load. If your analysis tells you that not many people visit your site on Saturday, you may want to select this day as your maintenance day. You don't want to make changes to your site on days when you receive high traffic because it is very displeasing if your visitors receive HTTP 404 errors because your site is temporarily down.

You can also see your visitor's IP address, which the software will translate into his or her geographical location; some of the software is even capable of narrowing the data down to the city (see Figure 25.1). From a marketing perspective, this can benefit you in planning your marketing efforts in other media. If you are planning a television campaign for your business, you may want to start in a city that frequently visits your site, thus increasing the chance of a successful campaign.

It is very common for Web traffic analysis software to indicate which browser your visitors are using when visiting your Web site (see Figure 25.2). Although you want to have a Web site that is designed to be

Figure 25.1. WebTrends can tell you what cities are bringing you the most online traffic.

compatible with both older and newer browsers, this data can be used to your advantage. Older browsers that cannot read Java scripting properly and that do not have the proper plug-ins for a Flash introduction may still be in use by your viewers. However, if a majority of your viewers are using the latest browsers, you could incorporate more of the latest technology into your site. Remember that you should always offer a "skip flash" option on your site and the latest Java plug-ins for people with older browsers.

Which Pages Are Popular and Which Pages Are Not?

When you look at the log files and see where your audience is spending most of their time on your site, you can also tell where they are not. You can then use this information to determine what the popular pages on your site incorporate that the less popular ones do not. Perhaps the popular pages are similar to the less popular, but are visited by a specific source (i.e., search engines, newsgroups). Maybe there is a content

Figure 25.2. This Web Trends report lets you know which versions of each browser your visitors are using.

problem on the less popular pages, or maybe they take longer to load than the other pages and visitors do not want to wait for them to load. Whatever the case may be, you can use this information and attempt to fix those problems that would keep visitors from spending time on all the pages of your site.

Find Out How Each Visitor Found Your Site

By finding out how each visitor came to your site, you can boost your traffic tremendously. You can determine which of your banner ads is producing the best results (see Figure 25.3). You can use this information to help you with the selection of banners you use and also the allocation of your online advertising budget. You can determine how many visitors found your site through the search engines (see Figure 25.4). You can even determine which keyword led to the most visitors through the search

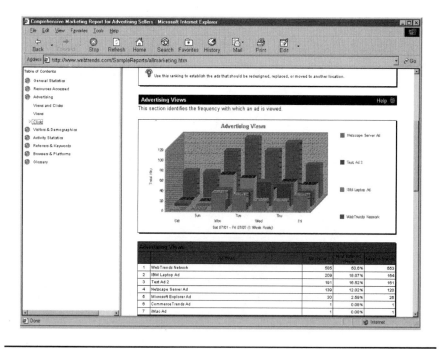

Figure 25.3. This Web Trends report identifies the frequency with which a banner ad is viewed.

engines (see Figure 25.5). If most of your traffic is coming from the Excite search engine (*http://www.excite.com*), you could consider purchasing a banner advertisement on that page. The same theory goes if your traffic is coming from a newsgroup, meta-indexes, and so on.

If you have a number of doorway pages, it would be good to know which ones are drawing the most attention. If the statistics reveal that four out of ten doorway pages are sending most of the traffic to your site, you should analyze the other six doorways to see if you can make them more effective. Maybe the keyword prominence is too low and they are not as effective as you thought when you designed them. If so, you should tweak these pages, then resubmit them to their corresponding search engines.

You can also find out where your visitors go when they leave your Web site. You want your viewers to stay at your site as long as possible. If you notice that the majority of your viewers are not traveling through your entire site and are not viewing important information that you want them to see, you may want to manipulate the layout of your Web site to decrease

Figure 25.4. This Web Trends report illustrates the first time visitor sessions initiated by searches from each search engine.

Figure 25.5. This Web Trends report identifies the specific keywords that led the most visitors to the site through the search engines.

the "flight effect." If you notice that your top exit page is your home page, you may want to try a whole new approach because people seem to be turned off from searching through your site from the beginning.

Single-access pages are pages on your Web site that are accessed through a link or search engine and then are immediately exited. If a high percentage of your Web site traffic is a result of these pages, it is very important that you convey a strong message while you have the visitors' attention. If you have pages like this, you should reevaluate what is on those pages and try to come up with content that will entice your visitor to search through the rest of your site.

Some of the more advanced software can tell you which keywords and phrases your visitors used to find your site using a search engine. This is extremely valuable information because you can use these keywords to increase your popularity in the search engines. By knowing the most popular keywords your visitors are using to visit your site, you can make sure you use them in your meta-tags, Alt tags, and page titles, and in the text of your page for higher placement in the search engines. Also, by seeing which search engines are being used more by your visitors, you may choose to purchase a banner ad or keywords for that engine to achieve maximum visibility to your visitors.

Another benefit of observing who is viewing your site is that you can see when spiders and crawlers from search engines have crawled to your page. This means that your site most likely will be indexed on their corresponding search engine. This is good to know, not only because it reassures you that you are going to be indexed, but also because by knowing this, you will not resubmit your site to the search engine and risk spamming.

Identifying Your Target Market

After you have collected data from your log files and used the Web traffic analysis software to determine which demographic groups are actually visiting your site, you then must determine whether these are the groups that you want to target. If not, you must then determine how you are going to reach your target market. For example, you may find that you should change your online advertising campaign. Or perhaps you should reevaluate your Internet marketing strategy, taking into consideration the new data that you have collected.

Find Out What Forms of Online Promotion Work for Your Site

When you first launch your Web site, you are going to aggressively implement your Internet marketing strategy by experimenting with all of the different forms of online marketing. However, when you analyze who is actually visiting your site and you find out where the majority of your traffic is coming from, you can then determine where to focus the majority of your marketing efforts. You may find that a link on a Web site is resulting in a high amount of traffic to your site; therefore, you may want to consider purchasing a banner advertisement on that site. The same goes for all of the other forms of Internet marketing. If after a short period of time your analysis software tells you that you are receiving low traffic (if any) from a banner ad that you had purchased, you may want to pull it off that site and designate your investment to another site on the Internet. This is a good way to make sure you get the most for your investments in online marketing.

Managing Your Online Business

If you are involved in selling online advertising on your site, Web traffic analysis software can save you a lot of work. When you place your client's banner advertisement on your site, the analysis software can not only track how many people have viewed that specific banner, but also how many people have clicked through. This makes billing your clients very easy, for all you have to do is read the reports generated by your software. If your clients pay per click-through, you simply look up the figure and charge them the appropriate fee. The same goes for paying based on CPM.

How Do You Get Web Traffic Analysis Software for Your Site?

You can purchase Web traffic analysis software if you wish, but for it to work it must be installed on the server where you host your Web site. If you host your own Web site, you will definitely have to purchase your own software; however, if you are paying an ISP to host your Web site, the host should already be able to provide some sort of analysis software. Most people don't take advantage of the tremendous marketing opportunities available by analyzing their traffic; therefore, they do not ask their ISP about the software. It should be available to you, for you are paying for their services. If it is not, simply ask them to purchase the Web traffic analysis software of your choice, for they would much rather have you as a client than say no. In some cases they may charge you an additional fee for this service.

Popular Web Traffic Analysis Software

If you do decide to purchase your own Web traffic analysis software, there are many different brands, which do many different things. Following are some of the more popular brands of Web traffic analysis software:

WebTrends Enterprise Suite
http://www.webtrends.com
The WebTrends Enterprise Suite is one of the most comprehensive Web site analysis software packages available. It provides you with reports

on everything from the number of views your banner ads receive on another Web page to which keyword was used when a visitor found your site using a search engine. You can easily target specific hits and user sessions that include file types and names, entry pages, time and day, user addresses, or any other medium that may have pointed a visitor to your page. WebTrends develops detailed advertising reports, which tell you how often banners on your Web site are viewed and how often people click-through. This assists you in selling and billing space to your clients. This is an all-in-one piece of Web traffic analysis software that does more than answer the question of who is actually visiting your site.

net.Analysis by net.Genesis

http://netgen.com

net.Genesis offers one of the best log analyzing systems. This is one of the first and one of the best for medium to large sites. Great for intranet access and analysis by non-tech-savvy users. Good integration with IBM Net.Commerce.

NetTracker eBusiness Edition

www.sane.com

NetTracker uses an Oracle database engine, which is great for most companies because they don't need a database administrator to use it. The Business Edition can handle really large log files with the speed and agility of an Oracle8 database. The Business Edition also lets you access your data for additional analysis using standard reporting tools such as Crystal Reports and products from Cognos, Information Builders, and more. This product contains 79 standardized summaries, plus you can create and save your own. NetTracker generates usage reports for multiple Web sites, proxy servers, firewalls, and FTP sites.

Internet Resources for Chapter 25

FREE WEB TRAFFIC ANALYSIS SERVICES

AccessWatch

www.accesswatch.com

AccessWatch is open-source shareware. AccessWatch generates browser statistics, referrer, page views, and other Web site traffic statistics.

eXTReMe Tracker

http://www.extreme-dm.com/tracking/

The eXTReMe Tracker is a completely free service that offers comprehensive real-time reporting with no limit on the amount of traffic that you receive on your Web site. It is capable of tracking your visitors' geographic location, their domain, e-mail address, the browser they are using, and much more.

HitBox

http://www.get.hitbox.com

HitBox is designed for ad-supported, personal, or e-commerce sites. It's capable of developing user profiles, tracking which sites refer visitors to your site, and how much traffic you receive on a daily, monthly, and annual basis. HitBox can also track how your visitors navigate around your Web site, which can help you in customizing your Web site to your viewers' needs.

TheCounter.com

http://www.thecounter.com

The Counter provides free tracking services to its members. By placing a small image on your Web site, you will get information such as when your visitors came, from where, and by using what browser. If you are just experimenting with Web traffic analysis, you can't go wrong with The Counter.com

The Hitometer

http://www.hitometer.com

The free Hitometer service offers an extensive choice of counters, and reporting of URL statistics, such as how many visitors visit your site per day, month, and year. You can receive your reports online or have them sent to your e-mail.

SuperStats.com

http://www.superstats.com

SuperStats.com is a free service that allows you to retrieve real-time statistics for your Web site 24 hours a day, 7 days a week. Find out who's visiting your site, how they found it, and when they were there.

About the Author

Susan Sweeney, C.A.

Renowned industry expert and consultant Susan Sweeney, C.A., tailors lively keynote speeches, full- and half-day seminars, and workshops for companies, industries, and associations interested in improving their Internet presence and increasing their Web site traffic and sales. See Susan's speaking Web site at *www.susansweeney.com*.

Susan is the founder and president of **Connex Network Inc.** (*www.connexnetwork.com*), an international Internet marketing and consulting firm. Susan holds both the Chartered Accountant and Certified General Accountant designations. She is an experienced Internet marketing professional with a background in computers, marketing, and the Internet. Susan is the author of several books on Internet marketing and e-business: *101 Ways to Promote Your Web Site, Internet Marketing for Your Tourism Business, Going for Gold, 101 Internet Businesses You Can Start from Home,* and *The e-Business Formula for Success*. She is a member of the Canadian Association of Professional Speakers, the National Speakers Association, and the International Federation for Professional Speakers.

Connex Network is a marketing firm that provides Internet and international marketing consulting and training services to industry and government. Their clients range in size from single-person start-up operations to multimillion-dollar international firms. Their primary services include Internet marketing workshops, Internet marketing strategies, Web site report cards, Internet marketing consulting, market research, and competitive analysis. During their workshops and training sessions, they ensure that their clients have a complete understanding of the principles involved with developing a strong online presence. The team of Internet marketing analysts at Connex are highly trained in the area of Internet marketing, and all stay up-to-date with the latest technological advancements and industry trends in the online marketing world. Every person on the team has extensive practical hands-on experience and the necessary skills to use proven tips, tools, and techniques to generate high volumes of traffic to your site.

As a result of technological change and global competitiveness, a strong Internet presence is essential. Susan instructs individuals with her enthusiastic personality combined with her vast hands-on international marketing experience, which keeps her listeners informed and captivated. Let Susan help you increase your traffic and make your business prosper!

Susan Sweeney, C.A.
Connex Network Inc.
75 Brentwood Drive
Bedford, Nova Scotia, Canada B4A 3S2
Phone: 902/468-2578; Fax: 902/468-0380
www.connexnetwork.com
www.susansweeney.com
susan@connexnetwork.com

Appendix A: Terminology

404—File Not Found.   The message returned from a Web server when a requested document cannot be found.

Animated GIF.   Special image-editing applications can meld several GIF images into a single image, much like slides in a slide show. Each of the images is displayed briefly in turn to create the illusion of motion (similar to cartoon flipbooks).

ASCII Text File (American Standard Code for Information Interchange).   The worldwide standard format for text files in computers and on the Internet. The code represents all the uppercase and lowercase letters, numbers, punctuation, etc. There are 128 standard ASCII codes in which a 7-digit binary number, 0000000 through 1111111, represents each character.

ASP.   Application Service Provider.

Autoresponder.   A program that automatically responds to incoming e-mail. It is like an electronic fax-back system for e-mail.

Backbone.   Large transmission lines that carry data being transferred from smaller lines. These lines or paths connect local or regional networks together for long-distance communication. The connection points are known as network nodes or telecommunication data-switching exchanges (DSEs).

Backend systems.   Software systems—usually inventory, accounts receivable, customer relationship management, and others—that are internal to a company that are sometimes integrated or that interface with a Web site.

Banner ad.   A graphical advertisement on a Web site that links to a particular promotion when the user clicks on it. Banner ads are used to increase product awareness and company and brand identity, and can be a source of (advertising) revenue to the site that hosts the banner ad.

BBS (bulletin board system).   A computer that can be reached by computer modem dialing (or by Telnet) for the purpose of sharing or exchanging messages or other files. Some BBSs are devoted to specific interests; others offer a more general service. The definitive BBS List says that there are over 40,000 BBSs worldwide.

BCC (blind carbon copy). E-mail addresses included in the BCC field of an e-mail message will be hidden from all recipients of the e-mail.

Benchmark. A point of reference by which something can be measured or compared. In surveying, a "bench mark" (two words) is a post or other permanent mark used as the basis for measuring the elevation of other topographical points.

Branding. Creating public awareness of a company, product, or service so that the company, product, or service is quickly and immediately identified and associated.

Browser. The software used to view the various kinds of Internet resources or sites.

Bulk e-mail. A group of identical messages e-mailed to a large number of addresses at once. This is a technique commonly employed by spammers, and it results in many very unpersonalized e-mail messages.

Cache. A place to store something more or less temporarily. Web pages you request are stored in your browser's cache (pronounced "cash") directory on your hard disk. When you return to a page you've recently looked at, the browser can get most of the information from the cache rather than from the original server. A cache saves you time and saves the network the burden of some additional traffic. You can usually vary the size of your cache, depending on your particular browser.

CGI (common gateway interface). Guidelines that define how a Web server communicates with another piece of software on the same machine, and how the other piece of software, the CGI program, talks to the Web server. Any piece of software can be a CGI program if it handles input and output according to the CGI standard.

CGI-bin. The most common name for the directory on a Web server that holds a CGI program. Most programs located in the CGI-bin directory are text files—scripts that are executed by binaries located elsewhere on the same machine.

Chat. Real-time conversation between one or more individuals across a network. IRC and ICQ are common forums for such discussions often held in topic-driven "chat rooms."

Clickstreams. The paths a user takes as he or she navigates a Web page or cyberspace in general. Advertisers and online media providers have developed software that can track users' clickstreams.

Click-through. A hit generated from a banner advertisement when a user clicks on the banner ad.

Click-through rate. The percentage of banner ad views that resulted in a user's clicking on it (a click-through).

Cookie. On the Internet, a cookie refers to a piece of information sent by a Web server to a Web browser. The browser software is expected to save the cookie and send the information back to the server whenever an additional request is made. Cookies may contain information such as user preferences, registration or login information, online shopping cart info, etc.

Cost per click. The rate charged to an advertiser each time a user clicks on the advertiser's banner ad. This is one method site owners can use to collect advertising revenue from banner ads.

CPM (cost per thousand page views). Banner ad rates are typically measured in cost-per-thousand (page views), which is shorthand for the cost of delivering a marketing message to 1,000 people.

CPTM (cost per thousand targeted ad views). This implies that the audience you have targeted is of a particular demographic group (see demographics).

Crawlers. Crawlers quietly comb through Web sites and index the information they find.

CRM system (customer relationship management system).

Cybermall. A collection of online storefronts better known as an Internet shopping mall.

Cybernaut. A person who uses the Internet.

Cyberspace. Used to describe all areas of information resources available through computer networks and the Internet. William Gibson originated the term in his novel, *Neuromancer.*

Database marketing. Actively maintaining and updating a database of clients and potential clients (data warehousing), mining the data for specific demographic information (data mining) and focusing your advertising campaign on the target market. For instance, once you determine the people in your database that fit a particular demographic, you can then send a targeted e-mail marketing message to these people.

Data mining. Obtaining specific information from a data warehouse by running queries. Marketers can determine how many people in a database file fit a certain demographic group and then market to that particular group of individuals.

Data warehouse. A place for storing, retrieving, and managing large amounts of any type of data. Data warehouse software often allows you to conduct fast searches, as well as advanced filtering. Planners and researchers can use this database freely without worrying about slowing down day-to-day operations of the production database.

Demographics. Specific data about the size and characteristics of a population or audience that can be used for marketing purposes.

Domain name. The unique name that identifies an Internet site. A domain name always has two or more parts, separated by dots. The part on the left is the most specific, and the part on the right is the most general. A given machine may have more than one domain name, but a given domain name points to only one machine. For example, the domain names: *connexnetwork.com* and *yahoo.com* can both refer to the same machine.

Download. The transferring of data from one computer to another across the Internet.

DTD (document type declaration). Specifies the organization that issued the language specification and the exact version of the specification. This information is typically found at the beginning of an HTML document or other programming documents. In XML, a DTD specifies the meaning of every tag and tag attribute contained within a set of XML pages.

E-business. Electronic business is the conduct of business on the Internet—not only buying and selling, but also servicing customers and collaborating with business partners.

E-commerce. The process of buying and selling goods and services on the Internet.

Effective frequency. The optimum regularity with which you execute an e-mail marketing campaign.

E-mail (electronic mail). Mail messages, usually text, sent from one person to another via computer. Messages can also be sent automatically to a large number of addresses on a mailing list.

Emoticons. Symbols made from punctuation marks and letters that look like facial expressions. Commonly used in e-mail and in Internet chat rooms to convey expressions and to give additional meaning to written text.

Exposure. How broadly known you or your product is from Internet exposure.

Extranet. A new buzzword that refers to an intranet that is partially accessible to authorized outsiders. Whereas an intranet resides behind a firewall and is accessible only to people who are members of the same company or organization, an extranet provides various levels of accessibility to outsiders. You can access an extranet only if you have a valid username and password, and your identity determines which parts of the extranet you can view.

Ezine, e-zine (electronic magazine). Term used to describe an electronic magazine, including those of print magazines such as *National Geographic* and *Newsweek* that have electronic editions. Thus, E-Zine Database includes both electronic-only magazines and electronic-edition magazines.

FAQs (frequently asked questions). Documents that list and answer the most common questions on a particular subject or problem area. There are hundreds of FAQs on subjects as diverse as car repair and franchise advice.

Firewall. A set of related programs located at a network gateway server to protect the resources of a private network from users of other networks.

Flame, flaming. Usually involves the use of harsh language directed toward a group or individual for sending unwanted messages (marketing) on a newsgroup or mail list.

Forums. Another name for a newsgroup in which people are formed together in a group to chat and discuss.

FTP (file transfer protocol). The common method of moving files between two computers through the Internet medium. FTP is a method for logging onto another computer or Internet site for the purpose of retrieving or sending files.

Hit. A single request from a Web browser for a single item from a Web server; thus, in order for a Web browser to display a page that contains three graphics, four "hits" would occur at the server—one for the HTML page, and one for each of the three graphics. Hits are often used as a rough measure of visits on a server.

Home page, homepage. The main Web page for a business, organization, or person—or simply the main page of a collection of Web pages.

Host. Any computer on a network that can hold files available to other computers on the network. It is quite common to have one host machine provide several services to other machines, such as WWW and Usenet.

HTML (hypertext markup language, HTM). The coding language used to create documents for use on the World Wide Web. These documents have a file extension of *html* or *htm*. HTML code looks a lot like old-fashioned typesetting code, where you surround a block of text with codes that indicate how it should appear. HTML or HTM files are meant to be viewed using a World Wide Web client program, such as Netscape or Internet Explorer.

HTTP (hypertext transport protocol). The most important protocol used in the World Wide Web for moving hypertext files across the Internet. Requires an HTTP client program on one end and an HTTP server program on the other end.

Hypertext. Clickable text that links to another document; that is, words or phrases in one document that can be clicked on by a reader, causing another document to be retrieved and displayed.

Image map. A single graphic that has multiple hot links to different pages or resources.

Impression. Sometimes used as a synonym for "view," as in "ad view." Online publishers offer, and their customers buy, advertising measured in terms of ad views or impressions.

Interstitial ad. Meaning "in between"—an advertisement that appears in a separate browser window while you wait for a Web page to load. Interstitials are more likely to contain large graphics, streaming presentations, and applets than conventional banner ads, and some studies have found that more users click on interstitials than on banner ads. Some users, however, have complained that interstitials slow access to destination pages.

Intranet. A private network inside a company or organization that uses the same kinds of software found on the public Internet, but that is only for internal use and cannot be viewed outside the network.

IP (Internet protocol), IP address. Basically, the set of rules for one network communicating with any other (or occasionally, for broadcast messages, all other networks). Each network must know its own address on the Internet and that of any other networks with which it communicates. To be part of the Internet, an organization needs an Internet network number, which it can request from the Network Information Center (NIC). This unique network number is included in any packet sent out of the network onto the Internet.

ISDN (integrated services digital network). A faster way to move more data over existing regular phone lines. Rapidly becoming available around the world, it is priced comparably to standard analog phone circuits. It can provide speeds of roughly 128,000 bits per second over the regular phone lines.

ISP (Internet service provider). A provider that allows access to the Internet. Usually there is a cost to the consumer, although there are still some free community networks.

Java. Programming language that is specifically designed for writing programs. It can safely be downloaded to your computer through the Internet and immediately run without fear of viruses or other harm to your computer. Using small Java programs, called "applets," Web pages can include functions such as animations, calculators, and other fancy tricks that cannot be done by normal HTML.

LAN (local area network). A network limited to the local area, usually the same building or floor of a company.

List server software. An application installed on a publicly accessible server that manages messages sent to and from a mailing list. This software is required if you intend to administer your own publicly accessible mailing list.

Login. The account name used to gain access to a computer system; not a password. Also can mean the act of entering onto a computer system.

Lurking. Reading Usenet newsgroups, consumer online service forums, or Internet mailing lists without posting anything, just reading. A lurker is a person who observes what everyone else is doing within that group.

Mailbot. Software programs that automatically respond to all incoming e-mail. A mailbot, or autoresponder, replies to them by sending the author a file or message.

Mailing list manager. A software program that collects and distributes e-mail messages to a mailing list (see list server software).

Mail list, mailing list. A system that allows people to send e-mail to one address, whereupon their message is copied and sent to all other subscribers to the list. This method allows people with different kinds of e-mail to participate in discussions together.

Meta-indexes. A list of Internet resources pertaining to a specific subject category, intended as a resource to those who have an interest in a specific topic. A meta-index is simply a collection of URLs for related Internet resources, all arranged on a Web page by their titles.

Net. The shorthand term for "Internet."

Netiquette. Internet etiquette.

Netizen. From the term "citizen," referring to a citizen of the Internet, or someone who uses networked resources.

Netpreneur. An online entrepreneur.

Netscape. A Web browser and the name of a company. The Netscape browser was based on the Mosaic program developed at the National Center for Supercomputing Applications (NCSA).

Newbie. A newcomer to the Internet.

Newsgroups. Name given to discussion groups on Usenet.

Opt-in mail list. People are given the choice to take part in a system that allows e-mail to be sent to one address, whereupon the message is copied and sent to all other subscribers to the list. This method allows people with different kinds of e-mail to participate in discussions together.

Page view. The number of times a page is viewed.

Password. A code used to gain access to a locked system known only to one person or a specific group of individuals. Good passwords contain letters and nonletters and are not simple combinations such as *john12*.

Permission marketing. Marketing to individuals via the Internet with their permission as a result of the individual's either opting in to a mail list or giving permission by other means to receive e-mail and other information.

Portal. A new term, generally synonymous with "gateway," for a World Wide Web site that is or proposes to be a major starting site for users when they get connected to the Web or that users tend to visit as an anchor site.

Posting. A message entered into a network communications system, such as a newsgroup submission.

Privacy policy. A policy for protecting the privacy of individually identifiable information. When an organization is engaged in online activities or electronic commerce, it has the responsibility to implement and post a privacy policy.

Registration. You submit personal information to become part of a mail list or newsgroup, in order to receive other information in return.

ROI (return on investment). The amount of profit you obtain from your original investment.

Secure server. A network-accessible (i.e., the Internet) computer that uses SSL (secure socket layers) for encryption to allow for private online transactions. The encryption protects an online shopper's credit card and personal information from being compromised while conducting an e-commerce transaction.

Search engine. The most popular way to find resources on the Internet. There are numerous search engines, each with its own unique style and capabilities.

Server. A computer that stores information and makes these files available to other users on a network or the Internet.

Signature. A block of information used at the end of every message or online document sent by a particular user.

Site. A unique location on the Internet to post your information and get noticed.

SKU (stock keeping unit).

Snail mail. A slang term for the regular postal service.

Spam, spamming. An inappropriate attempt to use a mailing list, Usenet, or other networked communications facility as if it was a broadcast medium by sending the same message to a large number of people who didn't ask for it.

Spider. An automated program that indexes documents, titles, or a portion of each document acquired by traversing the Web.

SQL (structured query language). A specialized programming language for sending queries to databases.

Storefront. A set location on the Web that stores and displays a collection of information about you and your business.

Streaming media. The simultaneous transfer and display of the sound and images on the World Wide Web.

Subject. The line in an e-mail message stating the topic of the mail.

Subscribe. Submitting information to an e-zine or mail list in order to receive information.

Superstitial. Non-banner rich media ads that can be any size on the screen and can be authored in most any creative format. Preloaded using a patent-pending "polite" delivery system that eliminates the latency problems often experienced with streaming online advertising solutions, superstitials play only on a user-initiated break in surfing, such as a mouse click.

Telnet.   A program that allows people to log on to other computers or bulletin board systems on the Internet and run software remotely from their location.

Thread.   A sequence of responses to an initial message posting. This enables you to follow or join an individual discussion in a newsgroup from among the many that may be there.

Thumbnail.   A term used by graphic designers and photographers for a small image representation of a larger image, usually intended to make it easier and faster to look at or manage a group of larger images. For example, software that lets you manage a number of images often provides a miniaturized version of each image so that you don't have to remember the file name of each image. Web sites with many pictures, such as online stores with visual catalogs, often provide thumbnail images instead of larger images to make the page download faster. This allows the user to control which images are seen in full size.

Unsolicited e-mail.   E-mail (usually ads) sent to people without their consent.

Upload.   The transfer of a file from your computer to a server online.

URL (uniform resource locator).   The standard way to give an address of any resource on the Internet that is part of the World Wide Web (WWW). The most common way to use a URL is to enter into a WWW browser program, such as Internet Explorer, Netscape, or Lynx, and type the address in the location bar.

Usenet.   A system of discussion groups. Comments are passed among hundreds of thousands of machines, with over 10,000 discussion areas, called newsgroups.

User session.   A person with a unique address that enters or re-enters a Web site each day (or some other specified period). A user session is sometimes determined by counting only those users who haven't re-entered the site within the past 20 minutes or a similar period. User session figures are sometimes used to indicate the number of visitors per day.

Vaporlink.   A link within a site on the Internet is supposed to lead to more information (hypertext). A vaporlink is one that has become nonexistent and does not lead anywhere—a dead link.

Viral marketing.   Word-of-mouth or friend-to-friend e-mail marketing.

Virtual community.   A community of people sharing common interests, ideas, and feelings over the Internet or other collaborative networks.

Virus, viruses.   A program (or programs) that, when executed, contaminates a user's hard drive—often with unwanted results (erases files, sends unauthorized e-mail from your machine, contaminates other documents, etc.).

Visitor.   People who have accessed or visited your site.

Web.   The shorthand version of World Wide Web.

WWW (World Wide Web).   The whole constellation of resources that can be accessed using Gopher, FTP, HTTP, Telnet, Usenet, WAIS, and some other tools. Also referred to as the universe of hypertext servers (HTTP servers), which are the servers that allow graphics, text, sound files, etc., to be mixed together.

Appendix B: Implementation and Maintenance Schedule

To accomplish the best results from your Internet marketing strategy, you should develop an implementation and maintenance schedule.

Schedule

Every implementation and maintenance schedule will be different since every company's Internet marketing strategy will be different. Table E.1 shows a sample schedule. We have provided brief explanations in the following paragraphs to help further clarify the items included in this sample.

Search Engine Submissions

You should divide your list of directory and search engine submissions into four groups. Weekly, you should take one group, go to each of the directories and search engines in that group, and search for your company by name and also by several keywords. If you appear in the first 10 to 20 search rankings and are happy with the description, you don't have to do anything with that search engine or directory.

However, if you do not appear or are not satisfied with the description, you should resubmit all your pages to that directory or search engine. The search engines and directories purge their databases from time to time to ensure that all entries are current. The next week, go through the same process with the next group. This way you check every directory and search engine at least monthly to ensure that you are still there and easily accessible.

Name	Weekly	Biweekly	Monthly	Bimonthly	Quarterly	Yearly
Domain name						✓
Search engine submissions			✓			
Press releases				✓		
Banner advertising			✓			
Update/rename titles			✓			
Cool sites			✓			
Check competitors					✓	
Cybermalls					✓	
Newsletter			✓			
Newsgroups	✓					
Mailing list postings		✓				
Guest book	✓					
Signature files			✓			
Mailing lists						
Links		✓				
What's new	✓					
Calendar of events	✓					
Employment opportunities	✓					
Offline promotion					✓	
Tune-ups					✓	
Web browser testing			✓			

Figure B.1. Implementation and maintenance schedule.

Press Releases

Press releases should be scheduled at least bimonthly. If you have a major announcement, the press releases may be more frequent.

Banner Advertising

Check banner advertising locations of your ads every month. Determine the effectiveness of these ads and look for new sites for more exposure. Check prices and traffic flow of these new sites to determine how relevant they may be in increasing the traffic to your site. Adjust your banner advertising strategy accordingly.

Title Pages

Update and retitle your pages monthly unless you add a new section that requires more frequent updates (for example, Tip of the Week). Giving your pages new titles and updating your site are useful for two main reasons. First, spiders, crawlers, and bots are continuously visiting sites to see if there have been changes. (They update their information accordingly.) Second, many of your site visitors use software that lets them know when their bookmarked sites have been updated. They will revisit your site only when they know there have been changes.

Cool Sites

Submit to Cool Sites, Site of the Day, or Top 5%. To better your chances of becoming one, you should check on how often to apply, usually monthly.

Check Competitors

You should regularly review your competitors' sites.

Cybermalls

Cybermalls continually change, as does everything, so do a quick check to find new malls or changes to the ones that interest you.

Newsletter

A newsletter should be scheduled monthly so you are getting your name and information in front of current and potential clients on a regular basis.

Newsgroups

Newsgroups that you participate in should be visited every couple of days, and you should try to post messages. The more often you post, particularly providing answers to queries or assistance, the more recognized and valued you are (and is your expertise). Make sure you attach your sig. file for maximum marketing effect.

Mailing Lists

New mailing lists appear daily. Review (and update if appropriate) those that you participate in on a monthly basis.

Guest Book

Your guest book should be checked and monitored so you can see who is visiting and what they have to say. Weekly, you should copy the new contact list to the appropriate databases (e-mail lists, newsletter, etc.).

Signature Files

Keep your sig. files current. Review and change them on a regular basis with new information or achievements.

Links

The more reciprocal links you can get, the better off you are. You should constantly be looking for additional, appropriate sites from which to be linked. As a minimum, you should schedule time biweekly to actively seek appropriate link sites.

What's New

Your What's New page should be updated regularly, weekly if possible.

Calendar of Events

If you choose to have a calendar of events on your site, ensure that it is kept current, updated at least weekly.

Employment Opportunities

This section should also be monitored and updated weekly, deleting positions that have been filled and adding new positions as they become available.

Offline Promotion

Make sure that your offline marketing materials and your online materials are consistent (message, logos, corporate colors, etc.). Also ensure that, where appropriate, you include your URL in your offline promotion materials. This should be checked at least quarterly.

Tune-Ups

Tune-ups should be done quarterly unless changes are made to the site. One location to check is Web Site Garage at *http://www.websitegarage.com*. Here you can check spelling, browser compatibility, HTML design, link popularity, loading time, and much more.

Web Browser Testing

Test your site with the major Web browsers. This should be done whenever there is a new release of Netscape or Internet Explorer. You should check monthly to determine if there have been new releases.

Appendix C: Search Engines

The Most Popular Search Engines

The algorithms the major search engines use to determine your site's ranking and the information reference to index your site changes quite often, so what may hold true today may not hold true tomorrow. I recommend visiting the respective search engines before you submit and review any material available regarding site submissions. Many search engines have information on their submission pages, help pages, and sometimes on a submission tips page. You can also check out various sites on the Internet that offer submission tips and tricks for the major search engines, some of which are included within Chapters 6 and 7 of this book. Two of my favorites are Search Engine Watch (*http:// www.searchenginewatch.com*) and Search Engine World (*http:// www.searchengineworld.com*).

AltaVista
Site address: *http://www.altavista.com*
Submission address: *http://www.altavista.com/cgi-bin/query?pg=addurl*, or click on "Add a URL" from AltaVista's homepage.
AltaVista went live in December 1995. In August 1999, CMGI, Inc. acquired 83% of AltaVista's outstanding stock from Compaq. As well, Shopping.com and Zip2 became wholly owned subsidiaries. AltaVista consists of multiple platforms: AltaVista Search, AltaVista Live, AltaVista's Shopping.com, and AltaVista Local Portal Services.
Number of pages (millions): 550
Meta-tag support: Yes
Index body text: Yes
Frames support: Yes
Image maps: Yes
Alt text: Yes
Link popularity affects position: Yes
Keywords in title important: Yes
Higher rankings for reviewed sites: No
Description: Meta-tag or first text on page
Time to index submissions: 24–48 hours

Type: Spider—Scooter
Tips: AltaVista likes keywords that are located near the top of your page, so use descriptive keywords where possible. Keywords used in the title of your page also seem to influence page rankings.

Excite
Site address: *http://www.excite.com*
Submission address: *http://www.excite.com/info/add_url,* or click on "Add URL" from Excite's homepage.
Has been around since 1995. Excite bought out WebCrawler in 1996. These acquisitions are still independently operated.
Number of pages (millions): 250
Meta-tag support: Just meta description
Index body text: No
Frames support: Yes
Image maps: No
Alt text: No
Link popularity affects position: Yes
Keywords in title important: Yes
Higher rankings for reviewed sites: No
Description: The few most dominant sentences on your page
Time to index submissions: 2–3 weeks
Type: Spider—Architext
Tips: Make the first 100 characters of your page as descriptive as possible. Excite will try to make the description from the text at the start of your page, but will keep going until it is satisfied that it has enough descriptive sentences. Your sentences must be complete for Excite to use them in forming your description. This does not necessarily mean that uncompleted sentences at the beginning of your page will not be used; Excite would just rather use complete sentences.

Google
Site address: *http://www.google.com*
Submission address: *http://www.google.com/addurl.html,* or click on "Add your URL" from Google's About page.
Google was founded in 1998 by Larry Page and Sergey Brin and has quickly become a very popular search tool on the Web.
Number of pages (millions): 1,347
Meta-tag support: No
Index body text: Yes

Frames support: Yes
Image maps: No
Alt text: No
Link popularity affects position: Yes
Keywords in title important: Yes
Higher rankings for reviewed sites: No
Description: First text found on page, including hypertext links
Type: Spider—Googlebot
Tips: Keywords in your domain name and link popularity will really help you out with Google. To increase your link popularity, get other sites to link to you; perhaps you should consider reciprocal links to other sites.

HotBot
Site address: *http://www.hotbot.com*
Submission address: *http://hotbot.lycos.com/addurl.asp,* or click on "Add URL" from HotBot's homepage.
HotBot was launched in 1996. HotBot uses Inktomi's search engine technology.
Number of pages (millions): 110
Meta-tag support: Yes
Index body text: Yes
Frames support: No
Image maps: No
Alt text: No
Link popularity affects position: Yes
Keywords in title important: Yes
Higher rankings for reviewed sites: No
Description: Meta-tag; if none, uses approximately the first 240 to 250 characters in the body of your page
Time to index submissions: 48 hours
Type: HotBot is a part of the Lycos Network.
Tips: If you do a search and feel that your site is not positioned correctly in the search results, then you can let the people at HotBot know. Send all the relevant information to bugs@hotbot.com.

Lycos
Site address: *http://www.lycos.com*
Submission address: *http://www.lycos.com/addasite.html,* or by clicking on "Add Your Site to Lycos" from their homepage.
Lycos is a well-recognized spider that went online in 1994.

Number of pages (millions): 50
Meta-tag support: No
Index body text: Yes
Frames support: Limited support
Image maps: No
Alt text: Yes
Link popularity affects position: No
Keywords in title important: Yes
Higher rankings for reviewed sites: No
Description: A snippet of the page that has been determined to represent it
Time to index submissions: 2 weeks
Type: T-Rex
Tips: Don't have an image map at the beginning of your page because Lycos will be unable to interpret it.

NorthernLight
Site address: http://www.northernlight.com
Submission address: http://www.northernlight.com/docs/regurl_help.html,
or click on "Register URL" from NorthernLight's homepage.
NorthernLight started in September 1995. Their Web results are combined with information from premium material, giving you access to books, magazines, databases, and newswires.
Number of pages (millions): 350
Meta-tag support: No
Index body text: Yes
Frames support: Yes
Image maps: Yes
Alt text: No
Link popularity affects position: No
Keywords in title important: Yes
Higher rankings for reviewed sites: No
Description: Approximately the first 25 words of the page body
Time to index submissions: 2–4 weeks
Type: Spider—Gulliver
Tips: Submit only ONE of your pages to NorthernLight; let its spider find the remaining pages on your site.

WebCrawler
Site address: http://www.webcrawler.com

Submission address: *http://www.webcrawler.com/info/add_url/,* or click on "Add your URL" from their homepage.

WebCrawler has been around since 1994 and has since been purchased twice. It is now owned by Excite but is still operated independently.

Number of pages (millions): 2

Meta-tag support: Yes

Index body text: Yes

Frames support: No

Image maps: Yes

Alt text: No

Link popularity affects position: Yes

Keywords in title important: Yes

Higher rankings for reviewed sites: Yes

Description: Meta-tag; if none, looks at first textual information body of page

Time to index submissions: 8 weeks

Type: Uses Excite's Spider

Tips: Use of keywords in your page titles, in descriptions meta-tag, in keywords meta-tag, and in content near the top of your page all influence your ranking with WebCrawler.

Yahoo!

Site address: *http://www.yahoo.com*

Submission address: To submit to Yahoo, you must visit the site, find an appropriate category that relates to your page, and then click on "Suggest a Site."

Established in 1994, Yahoo! is a well-recognized directory. It is the largest of its kind and is the most popular with Internet users. Yahoo! is a directory, but it does not read pages on the net like the other search engines discussed here. To have your site added to Yahoo!, you must fill out a submission form on the site. You must register your site in a category, and your site is checked by employees to verify that it matches the category you have chosen. If your site is commercial in any way, you must register it in a subcategory of Business and Economy.

Number of pages (millions): Approximately 2

Time to index submissions: 4–12 weeks

Tips: Yahoo! gives higher rankings to sites that are reviewed. When submitting pages, submit your base URL (e.g., *http://www.yourdomain.com*), as this stands a greater chance of being indexed by Yahoo!. Take your time to find the most appropriate subcategories for your site, and be sure to fill out the submission form completely and accurately. Yahoo! is very picky about who is added to the directory.

OTHER SEARCH ENGINES AND DIRECTORIES

555-1212.com
Site address: *http://www.555-1212.com*
Submission address: *http://www.infospace.com/info.go555/submit.htm*
In addition to looking up telephone area codes, you can shop online, find businesses near you, get your friends' telephone numbers and e-mail addresses, browse classified ads, and much more.

AOL.com Search
Site address: *http://search.aol.com*
Submission address: *http://search.aol.com/add.adp*
This is AOL's search engine. It once ran off the Excite engine, but now it uses the DMOZ.org directory. If you submit to DMOZ.org, Netfind will also list your site.

Ask Jeeves!
Site address: *http://www.askjeeves.com*
Submission address: N/A
Ask Jeeves! accepts fully worded questions and crawls through search directories, engines, and meta-directories until an answer is found. You cannot submit a site directly to Ask Jeeves!.

The Biz
Site address: *http://www.thebiz.co.uk*
Submission address: *http://www.thebiz.co.uk/default.asp?page=submit &listby=all*
The Business Information Zone has been developed for users seeking UK-relevant business information, products, and services on the Internet, whether users are in the UK or overseas.

BizWeb
Site address: *http://www.bizweb.com*
Submission address: *http://www.bizweb.com/InfoForm/*
BizWeb is a Web business guide to 43,165 companies listed in 194 categories.

Cyber411
Site address: *http://www.cyber411.com*
Submission address: N/A
Cyber411 obtains its search results from multiple search engines. You cannot submit a site to it directly.

Direct Hit
Site address: *http://www.directhit.com*
Submission address: *http://www.directhit.com/util/addurl.html*
Direct Hit is a relatively new search engine that bases its search criteria on page popularity.

DMOZ Open Directory Project
Site address: *http://www.dmoz.org*
Submission address: *http://www.dmoz.org/add.html*
DMOZ is a directory in which actual humans review your site's content to determine whether or not it meets their standards. Many major search engines including AOL Netfind and AltaVista incorporate the DMOZ directory listings into their own search results.

Dogpile
Site address: *http://www.dogpile.com*
Submission address: N/A
Dogpile obtains its search results from multiple search engines. You cannot submit a site to it directly.

GoTo.com
Site address: *http://www.goto.com*
Submission address: *http://www.goto.com/d/about/advertisers/*
GoTo is the one of the fastest, easiest, most relevant search engines on the Web, as well as the small advertiser's best friend. You select the search terms that are relevant to your site. Then you determine how much you are willing to pay on a per-click basis for each of those search terms. The higher your "bid," the higher in the search results your site appears. It's targeted, cost-per-click advertising and you set the cost per click.

ICQ iT!
Site address: *http://www.icqit.com*

Submission address: *http://search.icq.com/default.asp?act.addurl=addurl*
Submit your site to one of the largest chat networks on the Internet.

Internet Promotions MegaList
Site address: *http://www.2020tech.com*
Submission address: *http://www.2020tech.com/submit.html*
20/20 Technologies is a one-stop Internet advertising solution. Their services include Web page design, Internet research, and Internet promotions. The submission URL lists dozens of useful search engine submission resources.

Keyword.com
Site address: *http://www.keyword.com*
Submission address: Visit the site and enter a keyword.
This is a free service that allows you to "reserve" a keyword and have searches for a keyword directed immediately to your site. Only one keyword can be reserved per site. Your Internet keyword will remain active as long it is entered a minimum of six times every 60 days.

Linkcentre Directory
Site address: *http://linkcentre.com*
Submission address: *http://linkcentre.com/addurl.html*
Search the Linkcentre Directory or add your Web page immediately for greater exposure on the Internet.

LinkMaster
Site address: *http://www.linkmaster.com*
Submission address: *http://www.linkmaster.com/register.html*

LookSmart
Site address: *http://www.looksmart.com*
Submission address: *http://www.looksmart.com/aboutus/partners/subsite2.html*
LookSmart is a large, selective Internet search directory. Many engines, including MSN Search, currently use it to determine their own search results.

Manufacturers Information Net
Site address: *http://mfginfo.com*
Submission address: *http://mfginfo.com/htm/infoform.htm*

This site provides a complete source of information for industry and services related to manufacturing. Use the search engine to locate information on manufacturers, suppliers, professional services, and many more resources on and off this Web site.

MasterSite
Site address: *http://mastersite.com*
Submission address: *http://mastersite.com/addurl.htm*

McKinley's Internet Directory
Site address: *http://www.mckinley.com*
Submission address: *http://magellan.excite.com/info/add_url/*
Magellan's technology offers a unique way to search the Web: by concept. Like most search engines, they've programmed this search engine to look for documents containing the exact words you entered into the query box. But Magellan goes further and looks for ideas closely linked to the words in your query. This feature broadens your search.

Metacrawler
Site address: *http://www.metacrawler.com*
Submission address: N/A
Metacrawler obtains its search results from multiple search engines. You cannot submit a site to it directly.

MSN Search
Site address: *http://search.msn.com*
Submission address: *http://search.msn.com/addurl.asp*
This is Microsoft's entry into the search engine fray. You can submit one URL per day to their engine.

NationalDirectory
Site address: *http://www.nationaldirectory.com*
Submission address: *http://www.nationaldirectory.com/addurl.html*
Claims to be the "least spammed" search directory on the World Wide Web.

Nerd World
Site address: *http://www.nerdworld.com*
Submission address: *http://www.nerdworld.com/nwadd.html*
Nerd World's most prominent feature is its search engine and subject index.

Netscape Search
Site address: *http://search.netscape.com*
Submission address: *http://home.netscape.com/netcenter/smallbusiness/ onlineessentials/addsite.html*
Netscape, maker of one of the world's best-known browsers, also has its own search/portal site.

SavvySearch
Site address: *http://www.savvysearch.com*
Submission address: N/A
SavvySearch obtains its search results from multiple search engines. You cannot submit a site to it directly.

What-U-Seek
Site address: *http://whatuseek.com*
Submission address: *http://www.whatuseek.com/addurl-tableset.shtml*

Index

<!—Comments Tag, repeat description here?—!>, 99

<H1/H1> (header) tags, 94, 102

<META-NAME="description" CONTENT=."..">, 98

<META-NAME="keywords"CONTENT=."..">, 98

<META-NAME="robots" CONTENT=."..">, 98

<NOFRAMES> tags, 87–88, 94, 115

@Home, 375, 376, 379

@LinkPad, 265

10 Secrets of the Web Masters, 65

24/7 Media, 304–305

100 Hot Web Sites, 276

100 Top Contest Sites, 52

101 Internet Businesses You Can Start from Home (Sweeney), 411

123 Promote, 150, 172

"404—File not Found" error, 29

555-1212.com, 434

800.com, 80–81

A

AAA Internet Promotions, 137

Aaron's Emoticons, 173

About.com, 62

acceptance
    of e-mail, 152
    of signature files, 148
    of Webcasting (rich media), 378

Access Market Square, 321

AccessWatch, 409

Achoo Healthcare Online, 261, 262

Active Channels (Microsoft), 374

activity analysis of Web site, 401–402

Adbility, 306

Add-Me, 125

AddMySite.com, 139

AdRelevance, 278, 284

Ad Resource, 293, 306

advanced search options, 258, 259, 260

Advanced Streaming Format (ASF), 372

Advertising Age Magazine, 306

Advertising Concepts, 398

advertising networks, 295–296

advertising online, 278–307. *See also* affiliate programs; banner advertising; cybermalls; e-zines (online publications); mailing (discussion) lists; media relations; meta-indexes; newsgroups; objectives definition; offline promotion; private mailing lists; Web casting (rich media); Web rings; Web site design; Web traffic analysis
    advantages of, 279–280
    advertising networks, 295–296
    billing and Web traffic analysis, 408
    call to action, 284, 289, 301
    changing ease of, 280
    classified ads, 300–301
    click-throughs, 282, 292–293, 294, 295
    commercial links, 302
    cost-effectiveness of, 152, 153, 279, 325, 352, 360, 365
    cost per thousand impressions (CPM), 283, 292, 293
    development ease of, 280, 284, 286, 289
    enticement with classified ads, 300–301
    exposure maximization from, 279–280
    friendliness of classified ads, 301
    headlines of classified ads, 300
    hits, 282
    implementation and maintenance schedule, 424–428
    impressions, 283, 292
    information quantity delivered from, 279
    IP numbers (geotargeting), 283–284
    keywords, 283
    mailing list sponsorship, 302–303
    objectives, 2–3, 280–282
    offline advertising and, 303
    page views, 283
    publicity versus, 325–326

101 Ways to Promote
Your Web Site,
Third Edition
by Susan Sweeney, C.A.
488 pages
$29.95
ISBN: 1-885068-45-X

Marketing
With E-Mail,
Second Edition
by Shannon Kinnard
352 pages
$29.95
ISBN: 1-885068-51-4

Business-to-Business
Internet Marketing,
Third Edition
by Barry Silverstein
528 pages
$29.95
ISBN: 1-885068-50-6

Marketing on
the Internet,
Fifth Edition
by Jan Zimmerman
512 pages
$34.95
ISBN: 1-885068-49-2

Internet Marketing
for Information
Technology
Companies
by Barry Silverstein
464 pages
$39.95
ISBN: 1-885068-46-8

Internet Marketing
for Your Tourism
Business
by Susan Sweeney, C.A.
592 pages
$39.95
ISBN: 1-885068-47-6

Building Intranets
with Lotus Notes &
Domino 5.0,
Third Edition
by Steve Krantz
320 pages
$39.95
ISBN: 1-885068-41-7

Internet Marketing for
Less Than $500/Year
by Marcia Yudkin
334 pages
$29.95
ISBN: 1-885068-52-2

To purchase a Maximum Press book, visit your local bookstore
or call 1-800-989-6733 (US) or 1-850-934-4583 (International)
online ordering available at *www.maxpress.com*